A Tale of Three Cities

A Tale of Three Cities

Or the Glocalization of City Management

BARBARA CZARNIAWSKA

OXFORD

UNIVERSITY PRESS

Great Clarendon Street, Oxford OX2 6DP

Oxford University Press is a department of the University of Oxford.
It furthers the University's objective of excellence in research, scholarship,
and education by publishing worldwide in

Oxford New York

Auckland Bangkok Buenos Aires Cape Town Chennai
Dar es Salaam Delhi Hong Kong Istanbul Karachi Kolkata
Kuala Lumpur Madrid Melbourne Mexico City Mumbai Nairobi
São Paulo Shanghai Taipei Tokyo Toronto

Oxford is a registered trade mark of Oxford University Press
in the UK and in certain other countries

Published in the United States
by Oxford University Press Inc., New York

British Library Cataloguing in Publication Data

Data available

Library of Congress Cataloging in Publication Data

Data available

ISBN 0–19–925270–X (hbk.)

ISBN 0–19–925271–8 (pbk.)

10 9 8 7 6 5 4 3 21

Typeset by Newgen Imaging Systems (P) Ltd., Chennai, India
Printed in Great Britain
on acid-free paper by
Biddles Ltd., Guildford and King's Lynn

To the memory of Inga Hellberg, 1943–2002

CONTENTS

ACKNOWLEDGMENTS

This book is based on the results of fieldwork conducted by the author and her collaborators within a research program, called *Managing the big city: a twenty-first-century challenge to technology and administration.* The idea was conceived in 1993, during a stay at the Bellaggio Rockefeller Foundation. It has been brought to fruition thanks to a financial contribution from the Daimler-Benz Foundation and significant sponsorship from the Bank of Sweden's Tercentenary Foundation. The program was initially hosted by the Department of Business Administration at Lund University and, since 1996, has been hosted by the Gothenburg Research Institute at the School of Economics and Commercial Law, Göteborg University. I am profoundly grateful to all these foundations and to my employers.

The program encompassed several studies that have been documented in various publications quoted in this book. I wish to thank my collaborators: Petra Adolfsson, Hervé Corvellec, Peter Dobers, Carmelo Mazza, Tatiana Pipan, and Lena Porsander. Special thanks go to my research assistants: Jessica Enevold, Lise-Lotte Olausson, and Anders Ottosson. Many thanks are due to our colleagues, who helped us – and criticized us: Fabrizio Batistelli, Ania Biedzinska, Nils Brunsson, Francesco Cerase, Miroslaw Duchowski, Bernward Joerges, Sten Jönsson, Gideon Kunda, Monika Kostera, John W. Meyer, Thomas Polesie, Richard Rottenburg, Kerstin Sahlin-Andersson, and Rolf Solli. I am eternally grateful to Nina Lee Colwill for making this book readable. I also thank all our interlocutors in the three cities. Their names cannot be listed, because we promised them anonymity; but they are the ghostwriters of this book.

1

Studying Management in a Glocalized City

The city, as one finds it in history, is the point of maximum concentration for the power and culture of a community. It is the place where the diffused rays of many separate beams of life fall into focus, with gains in both social effectiveness and significance. The city is the form and symbol of an integrated social relationship: it is the seat of the temple, the market, the hall of justice, the academy of learning. Here in the city the goods of civilization are multiplied and manifolded; here is where human experience is transformed into viable signs, symbols, patterns of conduct, systems of order. Here is where the issues of civilization are focused; here, too, ritual passes on occasion into the active drama of a fully differentiated and self-conscious society.[1]

Lewis Mumford's point of view has been widely shared in the social sciences and humanities, in technology and art. The city is an exciting place and an exciting object of study. Organization scholars have, however, been somewhat reluctant to share this interest in the contemporary metropolis. Yet, overcoming this reluctance offers a unique opportunity for furthering organizational insights. This is what Rosabeth Kanter said in the late 1970s in her justification of the need to study big corporations:

[The] corporation is the quintessential contemporary people-producer. It employs a large population of the labor force, and its practices often serve as models for the organization of other systems.[2]

Writing in the early 2000s, I feel fully justified in replacing the noun 'corporation' with 'big city', since the big city does host a growing proportion of the population everywhere, and its practices do serve as models for the organization of other places. The big city is a societal laboratory.[3] Big cities have traditionally been the birthplaces of invention and innovation, but are also sites permitting intense imitation. After all, even when a new organizational form appears in a small town or in a large corporation, it will be quickly adopted and tested in big cities.

---

[1] Lewis Mumford, 1938/1995: 21.   [2] Kanter, 1977: 3.   [3] Solli and Czarniawska, 2001.

The laboratory is an apt metaphor for the big city, for in our civilization the city is the site for most attempts at renewing the social order. Thus, one can readily apply Karin Knorr Cetina's definition of a laboratory to a big city: 'an "enhanced" environment that "improves upon" natural orders in relation to social orders'.[4]

Yet there are also differences between the big cities and laboratories that are worthy of the attention of organizational scholars. Knorr Cetina, a *connaisseuse* of laboratories, has outlined five of their characteristics. First, laboratories need not deal with things *as they are*; they have a mandate to reduce or transform. This observation applies equally to the big city. Second, as Knorr Cetina notes, a laboratory need not deal with things *where they are*; they can be moved from place to place. This is only partially true for big cities, as not everything is movable (remember infrastructure!); however, more things are movable than we tend to believe. Third, laboratories need not deal with events *as they happen*, as big cities must. In addition, as the big city is not an exact replica of the laboratory, one cannot expect clearcut results from all the experiments conducted there. All reforms and changes produce unexpected consequences: some are negative and some positive. And finally, although laboratory work changes the laboratory only in extreme situations (like when a Bunsen burner explodes), every change in the city changes the city itself.

Thus, the big city is an interesting subject of study for an organization scholar – because it is so much like the laboratory and because it is so different.

CITIES AS WORK-WORLDS

. . . histories naturally deal more with the people whose unique works are still with us . . . than with those who mostly reproduced whatever, under the circumstances, was common sense.[5]

Although Ulf Hannerz probably did not have city managers in mind when he wrote this passage, his words apply to them literally. City management has never commanded sufficient attention in either urban or management studies. For the Chicago sociologists, the city was its inhabitants; for economists, the city is an arena of economic activity; for political scientists, the city is its governance; for urban planners and architects, the city is a stage to be built and rebuilt. Often comparing cities to theaters, urban studies set great visionaries and rulers on the stage, citizens and tourists in the audience. But who pulls the ropes when the curtain rises? There are but a few studies that concentrate on the invisible stage-workers, on those who make the city run or else grind to a halt. Even studies of its halting tend to focus on technical areas: water and sewer specialists, traffic specialists, or racial integration specialists. The Big City program has focused on the people who stand between plans and their implementation, between

---

[4] Knorr Cetina, 1999: 26.   [5] Hannerz, 1992: 174.

citizens and politicians, but also between politicians and technicians – that is, on managers. Seldom glorified and often abused by those they seek to serve, city managers rarely attract the attention of scholars.

What do managers do when they manage? There are many possible ways of describing such a process, none of them necessarily truer than the others. But my observations in big cities and in other places have brought the following three features to my attention:

- *Muddling through*.[6] The study of practice shows convincingly that organizing is not about reaching goals or implementing plans. Rather, it is about coping with daily problems. It is about managing, as the double meaning of the word neatly suggests. Muddling through does not preclude the activity of planning and constructing visions; it is merely that the two activities are rather loosely coupled.
- *Framing and reframing*.[7] As in film and photography, what is framed and what is left outside the frame is a strong determinant of meaning in a picture of the world. With time, an habitual framing develops, which may, in the end, stop providing the picture of the world needed for successful action – thus the modern need for constant reframing.
- *Anchoring* always converges with a change of frame. Any new idea, especially an idea that results from reframing, is pretested on those actors who are potentially involved, ideally to secure their cooperation, but at least to minimize their resistance.

At this point it is important to specify that the focus of the studies reported in this book is not on managers, but on management.[8] Muddling through, reframing, and anchoring might be individual pursuits, but individual pursuits do not constitute city management. Management consists of many collective and interconnected actions, which can be conceptualized as an *action net*.[9] Such

---

[6] Lindblom, 1979.   [7] Goffman, 1974.

[8] Note also the difference between 'city management' and 'city administration'. Although most dictionaries inform us that 'management' and 'administration' are synonyms, the linguistic practice of recent decades has attributed 'management' to the private sector and 'administration' to the public sector. The neologism 'public management' was intended to attract attention to the fact that the public sector in Western countries is committed to following the models of private industry (Power, 1997; Olson et al., 1998). Consequently, city administration was increasingly equated with city planning. But since the fall of planned economies, even city planners believe that they must withdraw and regroup. (See the special issue of *Planning Theory*, 1991, 5/6.) The use of the expression 'city management' in the present context denotes neither approval nor disapproval of the recent changes in discourse and practices. Rather it highlights the differences among city planning, city politics, and city management – the running of the city – each of which is connected to the other two in complex and non-obvious ways. It is also understood in a much wider sense than 'City Manager-reform', which was introduced in the USA in 1908 (Chapin, 1928) and continues to trickle down to Europe.

[9] The idea that a starting-point in social science research might be *action* (rather than an actor or an object) can be traced to a great many disparate sources: the seventeenth-century 'linguist' Francis Lodwick (Eco, 1994: 129; 1995: 260ff.), Gabriel Tarde's (1904/1969: 139) idea of 'groups of

collective actions are not performed within the boundaries of a specific 'organiza-tion', either. An action net of this sort engages many and varied organizations – municipal, state, private, voluntary – as well as loosely and temporarily organized groups of people. The task of a researcher who undertakes an exploration in this field is to follow the creation and re-creation of connections among such actions, rather than contacts among people, however difficult it is to make the distinction.

The two main fieldwork techniques on which this book is based are observa-tion (especially shadowing) and the interview (complemented and enriched by document analysis, particularly press analysis). The choice of these techniques has a bearing upon the form of this book, which strives to preserve voices from the field in the form of a collage. It contains excerpts from interviews and field-notes (set with rules above and below), newspapers and official documents (set with rules left and right), and the opinions of my fellow researchers (set without rules). And finally, my running commentary provides an interpretative frame for the whole.[10]

This approach was designed to avoid the fallacy of seeing the big city as one formal organization. By following events rather than attempting to impose a structure a priori, we intended to come close to the multi-organizational realities of the big city. City management is conceptualized, therefore, as a particularly complex and disorderly action net, a seamless web of interorganizational net-works, wherein city authorities constitute just one point of entry and by no means provide a map of the entire terrain.

Thus conceived, this study of city management encompasses three European cities: Warsaw, Stockholm, and Rome.[11] Although the study embodies compar-isons, they are comparisons neither of abstract concepts, nor of units extracted from their context. As Saskia Sassen has said, there is a large difference between

studying a set of cities from a classical comparative approach and from a global approach. The issue of comparability in the latter is not standardizing in order to compare. It is, rather, tracking a given system or dynamic . . . and its distinct incarnations in different countries.[12]

The approach applied here corresponds to the precepts of 'constant comparative analysis', so aptly described by Glaser and Strauss in their grounded theory approach.[13] This means that the units of comparison were the result rather than the starting-point of the comparison. At the outset of each study, the leading politicians and officials in each city were invited to list the major problems and

actions', the 'actantial model' of Algirdas Greimas (Greimas and Courtés, 1982), Paul Ricoeur's (1981) parallel between action and text, John Law's (1994) 'sociology of verbs', and, above all, Karl Weick's (1979) idea of *organizing*. I have written more about the notion of action nets in Czarniawska, 1997, 2000.

[10] The interviews and observations (the result of shadowing, and therefore distinguished from the field diary) are numbered for the convenience of the author.

[11] According to the original design, run on geopolitical lines, we aimed to study five cities. However, Berlin and Brussels have been excluded for access and financial reasons.

[12] Sassen, 2001: 348.   [13] Glaser and Strauss, 1967.

projects in which their city was engaging. In Warsaw, these issues included the metro construction, improvement of waterworks, city reform (centralization), and city finances. In Stockholm, the focus was on city reform (decentralization), computerization, the environment, and the Cultural Capital project. In Rome, the attention of city politicians and officials had been captured by traffic, privatization, and the Third Jubilee of Christianity. These projects were chosen for a detailed study, and their similarities and differences are reported here. The comparison was constant, but what was compared was created in the process. This stance is the result of an attempt to explore organizing processes in their local context, and of following the connections between such contexts.

An attempt of this sort creates a picture of an action net situated among many other action nets operating in the same terrain, dispersed all over the world, yet connected by the same activity – the managing of big cities. In this sense, such action nets may be said to constitute an *organization field*, as Paul DiMaggio defined it.[14] This field, like other organization fields, is said to be witnessing the all-pervasive phenomenon of globalization. Put simply, the number of connections between actions and the speed with which the actions are connected, disconnected, and reconnected seems to be growing, eliminating the geographical limits of organization fields.

A question may be arising in the mind of the reader: Do these three European cities provide good examples of the workings of globalization? The usual focus of globalization studies in and of big cities is the 'world cities': New York, Los Angeles, Tokyo, Hong Kong, São Paulo, Mexico City, Sydney, London, Paris.[15] But if the scope of globalization is the world, surely it is just as important to study it in less obvious places.

As I mentioned at the outset, this research program, focusing as it did on big city *management*, was intended to fill a gap in urban studies by addressing a neglected aspect of city life. This book is also intended to fill, or rather fit into, yet another gap: that of macro-descriptions of globalization and the everyday experience of globalization. Typically, depictions of globalization take a determinist or a voluntarist angle. According to the determinists, globalization follows the laws of nature, or laws similar to those of nature, and nothing can be done about it. According to the voluntarist approach, globalization is decided at World Trade Organization meetings, for example, and a different decision could always have been taken. Attractive in their simplicity, these pictures are of little help in understanding city management. In this book, globalization is seen as a combination of

- forces beyond people's intentions (for instance, sedimented institutions),
- purposeful action performed by people and machines (including its unexpected consequences),
- random events, and
- collective sensemaking.

---

[14] DiMaggio, 1983.   [15] I am borrowing the list from Edward Soja (1995).

Sensemaking is the weakest and the strongest of these forces.[16] Although it cannot reverse the chain of events and its material consequences, it has the upper hand as it classifies and reclassifies the other three. All four must be observed together and in interplay, as they develop and change over time.

Where is an appropriate place to watch such an interplay? There are many, but my observation point could be called *work-worlds*. This concept is inspired by Benita Luckmann, who categorized the life-world of modern people into segments or sub-universes. One of the 'small life-worlds of modern man'[17] was the world of work.[18] Accepting Luckmann's thesis requires a deviation from the common viewpoint that workplaces are ruled by the rigid arm of the 'system', and stand in opposition to the 'life-world'.[19] Providing a description that precedes and corroborates that of Arlie Hochschild,[20] she showed two interesting traits of such small life-worlds. First, they are surprisingly similar to traditional communities. Second, the main difference between 'the modern person' and her traditional equivalent is that there are several such worlds in modernity, requiring and permitting a frequent gear-shifting. It would, therefore, be both possible and interesting to trace the different routes of globalization in the different small worlds of the same person. In this context, however, I searched for traces of globalization in one type of a small world – the work-world. And although it is obvious that cities *host* workplaces, it is less often acknowledged that cities *are* workplaces for many people – cities as work-worlds, in other words.

GLOBALIZATION IN OUR TIMES

... civilization is in a fair way to become oceanic, that is to say, world-wide; and the critical period of growth being now past, the grand harvest season is about to begin.[21]

Globalization is often understood as a process that contributes to the compression of the world. This is a variation on the well-known definition by Roland Robertson, who primarily stresses the results of globalization: compression of the world and its accompanying 'intensification of consciousness of the world as a whole'.[22] I prefer to leave the evaluation of the results to sociologists and historians, as my experience in the study of organizing taught me that any collective action produces many unintended consequences – consequences that are frequently the opposite of those intended.

---

[16] For the concept of sensemaking, see Weick, 1995.
[17] Benita Luckmann, 1978. It is worth noticing that although she speaks of 'modern man', all her examples concern women.
[18] The other two are family and the ecological community. The latter should now be extended to include virtual communities.
[19] 'System' and 'life-world' are Husserl's terms, much used by Alfred Schütz and his disciples.
[20] Hochschild, 1997.   [21] Gabriel Tarde, 1899/1974: 114.   [22] Robertson, 1992: 8.

The notions of 'intentionality' and 'purpose' are treated in what follows as commonly used sensemaking devices rather than as ontological attributes of an action. Therefore, I shall speak about globalization simply as *translocalization*:[23] the phenomenon consisting of local practices, ideas, customs, and technologies that are spreading to localities beyond their origins – spreading, in fact, all over the globe.

Understood in this way, globalization has a long history with many threads. It encompasses *colonialization*, in the sense not only of conquering new lands, but also of conquering new markets, new domains. It encompasses the voluntary *imitation* of non-local practices, technologies, and customs. Colonization and imitation have been known for millennia, indeed, as long as civilization itself. But there is another less ancient aspect of globalization: *modernization*. It consists of imposing or voluntarily adapting new ways of being in the name of formal rationality and technological progress.[24]

Reluctant to evaluate the results, one can instead pay attention to the characteristics of the process itself. The first question, then, is: How does it happen? Or, as it has been formulated in another context: *How* do ideas, forms, and practices travel?[25] On horseback? Aboard ship? Through radio waves? By plane? On the worldwide web? Because all these questions can be answered in the positive, a more general mechanism must be postulated. Traditionally, it has been suggested that the spreading of ideas, objects, practices, customs, and even institutions takes place by diffusion. This physicalist metaphor, however, was embedded in many a physical and chemical connotation that proved to be of doubtful utility in a social context, and has recently been replaced by the notion of *translation*.[26]

The concept of translation better describes the emergence and construction of various types of connection around the globe because it is polysemous: usually associated with language, it also means the transformation and transference, not only of utterances, but of anything. It attracts attention to the fact that a thing moved from one place to another, and thus from one time to another, cannot emerge unchanged: to set something in a new place is to construct it anew. Thus, translation is a concept that immediately evokes symbolic associations, while at the same time being stubbornly material: only a thing can be moved from one place to another and from one time to another. Ideas must materialize; symbols must be inscribed. A practice not stabilized into an institution cannot last; it is bound to be ephemeral. A practice or an institution cannot travel; it must be simplified and abstracted into an idea, and thereby converted into words or images. Neither can words and images travel until they have materialized, and until they are embodied or objectified. Only bodies or things can move in time and space.[27]

---

[23] Czarniawska and Joerges, 1996.   [24] John W. Meyer, 1999.
[25] Czarniawska and Joerges, 1996.   [26] Latour, 1986; Czarniawska and Sevón, 1996.
[27] Czarniawska and Joerges, 1996.

There is nothing unusual in this way of conceptualizing the travel of ideas. The chain of translations depicted here makes perfect sense in pragmatic terms. If this conceptualization sounds like a functionalist one, however, that is exactly as it should sound. Throughout the book I will be quoting functionalist readings of organizational practice. This approach should not be mistaken for an adherence to structural functionalism, however. I am not arguing that structures emerge from functional needs. Quite the contrary. Structures are sediments of past functionalist interpretations, which are always hopelessly behind present interpretations unless reinterpreted in a novel way. Buildings and other public structures are the best example because they result from current functionalist theories, but even as these structures are being built, the theory marches on. Sometimes they are left with purely aesthetic functions, as monuments of the past. More often the users assign them new functions, to the dismay of the architects. At worst, such structures become mere monuments to a bygone functionalist thinking – like *La Défense* in Paris, that was built to accommodate a demand for office space, which never materialized.

The functionalism that underpins this text expresses itself in an assumption that *functionality is a powerful sensemaking device*. This is indeed how I understand Malinowski's functionalist reading of Trobrianders' customs: as an expression of the amazing faculty of an anthropologist to interpret practically anything in functionalist terms. And this is not the last time in this text that the analogy between what anthropologists do and what is done by the people they describe comes to mind.

It is also important to consider that functionality as a sensemaking device relies heavily upon satisfying rather than optimizing logic – the logic that says, 'Who cares if this is the best way. It works!' Functionality as a sensemaking device has a strong aesthetic value, and not only for engineers. There is a beauty in smoothly working machines and in smoothly run meetings.

At the same time, I fully realize that functionality is not the only sensemaking device, not even in the context of management (nor of engineering for that matter). There are times and spaces – and contemporary organization theory is one such space – where antifunctionalism achieves the upper hand. I do not intend to delve further into a history of art and architecture, which is full of perplexing examples such as the baroque sofas that look non-functional but are not, and modernist armchairs, which look functional but are not. Suffice it to say that functionality is one of the most important sensemaking devices in the field of organizational practice, competing with – and often losing to – the symbolism of power. And functionality is a crucial marker of the two cultural contexts I best understand: in Sweden, functionality is taken for granted; in Poland, functionality is a romantic dream. This reality is reflected in management practices in Stockholm and Warsaw. Rome, on the other hand, reflects yet another type of cultural context, which is a contested terrain for functionality claims.

The functionalist reading of the ways in which ideas travel is not the only possible reading, however. The process of translating practices into institutions by giving them a normative justification can be seen as rational, and therefore modern, even if it requires the extension of modernity back to at least the Roman Empire. Yet, the translation of ideas into objects has a much longer and wider tradition. In his review of anthropological studies of mimesis and early globalization, Michael Taussig points to the importance of 'reification-and-fetishization' – of catching the spirit of something by making an object that will embody its spirit. As Taussig explains, 'the making and existence of the artifact that portrays something gives one power over that which is portrayed'.[28]

In this book, I will continue to draw analogies between studies of supposedly modern, rational behavior and anthropological studies of allegedly 'primitive' societies. This is not to reveal 'the common human nature', but to further illustrate the thesis, widely accepted by now, that globalization has been known and practiced for millennia, and that certain forms of it are repeated and recycled. This is to claim *resurgence*[29] rather then continuity or rupture, for ruptures occur daily. It is a view that has little to do with a determinist interpretation of history. Rather, it has much in common with a belief in the simultaneous existence of two phenomena: habits and the movement of ideas across time and place. On the one hand, there are habits 'where unconscious strata of culture are built into social routines as bodily disposition'[30] (and, one must add, into things and machines[31]). On the other hand, there is the continuous travel of ideas across time and place, aided by the same bodies and machines. Embodiment permits both stability and movement. This view can be summarized by the title of one of Bruno Latour's books, *We Have Never Been Modern*,[32] or by a quote from Michael Taussig, who, inspired by Benjamin, speaks of

the surfacing of 'the primitive' within modernity as a direct result of modernity, especially of its everyday-life rhythms of montage and shock alongside the revelation of the optical unconscious that is made possible by mimetic machinery such as the camera and the movies.[33]

Were he speaking of city management, Taussig would have mentioned photocopiers, faxes, and of course computers, which neatly incorporated cameras and movies. By the same token, the more dominant role of functionality in some contexts does not mean that Stockholm is managed in a modern way and that Rome is not. Functionality is a contestant in sensemaking in Rome, much as the symbolism of power is ever present in Stockholm's modernist moves. There is also a moral dimension in sensemaking that has big city management as its topic, but even this dimension is part of the globalization processes and is redefined accordingly.

---

[28] Taussig, 1993: 13. See also Latour, 1996, for a further analogy between modern science and magic in his theory of 'factishes'. If this analogy seems to be far-fetched, I appeal to the reader to recall the feeling of having captured something after preparing a satisfactory set of overheads for a presentation or after writing an article. Taussig compares two such captures: the anthropologist's capturing of the Chocó Indians' culture by writing about them in a report and the Chocó's capturing of the spirits of the Westerners by making a figurine of their boat and crew.

[29] Taussig (1993) borrows the term from Walter Benjamin.   [30] Ibid.: 25.

[31] Joerges and Czarniawska, 1998.   [32] Latour, 1993.   [33] Taussig, 1993: 20.

All these considerations reveal another limitation of this way of portraying the travel of ideas as chains of translation. Its spatial dimension is insufficient, connecting only two points in time–space, and thus missing the thrust of globalization that happens exactly when *more* than two times or places are connected. From a spatial and dynamic perspective, this process can be depicted as a spiral rather than a linear road in any specific direction.[34] But even so, the question remains: What is special about globalization in our times? Although it is difficult to judge whether a spiral is good or bad, it is always possible to ask if the spiral is becoming bigger or smaller, if it is moving faster or slower.

The most likely answer seems to be: bigger and faster. It took 90 years for the 'City Manager plan' to travel from the USA to Italy,[35] but only 10 years for New Public Management to travel from the USA to the UK to Australia and New Zealand and back to Europe.[36] Incessant translations multiply and increase in volume and speed, covering more and more of the globe, though by no means all of it. But these travels bring about, simultaneously and connectedly, two opposing tendencies: homogenization and heterogenization.

EVERYTHING BECOMES MORE ALIKE . . .

Many cities were world cities before the 1960s, but since then . . . the globalization of the city has itself become increasingly globalized. Every contemporary city is to some significant degree also a world city in much the same sense as it is postmodern.[37]

The work of homogenizing forces is often described by the metaphor of *isomorphism*.[38] The new institutionalists, Paul DiMaggio and Walter Powell, distinguished three types of isomorphism: *coercive*, *mimetic*, and *normative*. This classification is an answer to another important question: *Why* do ideas travel?

In 1994, the European Union (EU) issued a directive according to which the appropriate form for contracting suppliers of services and products within the public sector was to be public tender. All external contracts above a certain level of expenditure were to be announced publicly (not only within a given country, but throughout the EU), and the contractor was to be selected by certain transparent procedures. The EU members have now been legally coerced into choosing this form of contracting, as we shall see in Chapter 4.

A mimetic isomorphism, in the case of organizations, seems to be a simple case of imitation resulting from spatial or ideological proximity. DiMaggio and Powell used the notion of organization fields in a way similar to the notions of a

---

[34] See the figure in Czarniawska and Joerges, 1996: 46.   [35] Chapin, 1928; Panozzo, 2001.
[36] Power, 1997; Olson et al., 1998.   [37] Soja, 1995: 131.
[38] Powell and DiMaggio, 1991. It is worth noting that 'isomorphism' is a Greek word for the Latin 'conformism'. The latter concept, however, has its own career in sociology and social psychology, with a decisively negative ring.

branch in industry or a sector in public administration: organizations that are considered to be in the same industry, whether private or public. Such organizations monitor, and often imitate, each other, even in the absence of official regulations or professional norms. DiMaggio and Powell added that mimetic isomorphism is a sign of uncertainty. Considering that uncertainty is a human condition, this explanation is not quite satisfactory. I believe that the phenomenon of *mimesis* deserves greater attention, and will return to it in Chapters 3–5. The interest in imitation found its most clear expression in the works of Gabriel Tarde, whose insights into this matter are still unparalleled.[39]

Norms, especially professional norms, are another factor behind translocalization, or the travel of ideas. Big city management comprises many professions and specialties; they in turn are organized into such bodies as associations and unions, and have their own professional organizations to spread and propagate 'best practice', innovations, and inventions. The reader will find examples of such normative influence in every chapter of this book, although I tend to see it primarily as a means of directing imitation into one route or another. Norms as such are subject to mimesis and are influenced by *fashions*.

But there seem to be even more ways by which organizing processes become homogeneous. In a study of the 'greening' of well-known Swedish companies, Birgitta Schwartz discovered yet another type of imitation of organizational forms, which she named *automorphism* – an isomorphism of a structure with itself.[40] Rather than imitate other companies in their organization field, these giants, proud of their history, imitated their own successful solutions. This mechanism seems also to be present in big cities, as best illustrated in Chapter 5.

Gudbjörg Erlingsdottir, on the other hand, pointed out that a growing similarity is not always limited to form. It happens that organizations imitate practices, a phenomenon that she called *isopraxism*, or the equivalence of practices.[41] Isopraxism, examples of which can be found in Chapter 6, is most likely to emerge through mimesis in action nets that are physically close to one another rather than in thought-worlds[42] such as organization fields. Practices also spread with people: a person who moves from one field to another is likely to bring along habitual ways of organizing. It is unlikely, however, that practices will spread with the help of abstract ideas only, although such is the wish of most reformers.

But globalization consists of both homogenizing and heterogenizing moves. When ideas, forms, customs, or practices travel from one place to another, they have to be 'disembedded', as Giddens called it, from their original context, and

---

[39] I want to thank Bruno Latour for prompting me to retrieve Tarde from my previous life as a social psychologist. Much as I am fascinated by Tarde's poetic language and convinced by his idea – developed by Latour – that the key to the understanding of macro-events lies in the study of micro-events, I do not espouse the romanticism of his political visions. Yet, it is always easy to be wise a hundred years in retrospect.

[40] Schwartz, 1997; *Oxford English Dictionary*, 1993: 153.

[41] Erlingsdottir, 1999. The use of Greek terms is prompted by the need to relate to the notion of isomorphism.   [42] Expression coined by Mary Douglas, 1986.

're-embedded' in whatever locality they 'take root' again.[43] The result, which can be called a 'local translation', is, of course, never identical to the original. Thus, diversity increases with each translation, and isomorphism is accompanied by and inadvertently produces its opposite: *allomorphism*, or difference of forms.

...WHILE DIFFERENCES MULTIPLY

Even as the world becomes more integrated globally, it continues to differentiate locally – the second in some measure stimulated by the first.[44]

This combination of homogenizing and heterogenizing forces attracted the attention of Japanese marketers as early as the 1980s, when, according to Robertson, they coined the expression *dochakuka*. The word, in Robertson's translation, means 'global localization' or 'telescoping *global* and *local* to make a blend'.[45]

There exists a useful analogy that might help to explain the concept and the phenomenon of *glocalization*. During recent years, the detective story reader has witnessed the enormous success of several European writers who became famous quite independently of one another, first in their home countries and then internationally: Colin Dexter in England, Manuel Vázquez Montalbán in Spain, Henning Mankell in Sweden, and Andrea Camilleri in Italy. These authors have created immensely attractive heroes who could well be clones. Each one is a man between 40 and 50 who sometimes feels young and sometimes old; who has problematic relationships with women and distinct difficulties in adopting a nuclear family; who believes in the importance of his profession, while feeling the injustice and cruelty of the world that this profession forces him to confront; who is considered by his superiors to be both a genius and a pain in the neck; and who willingly collaborates with colleagues abroad – colleagues who tend to resemble him in their turn. The most obvious common trait, however, is that all four heroes have a local tint – they are all intensely regional. Inspector Morse is from Oxford and could be from no other part of England, even as Pepe Carvalho, who is Catalan, and Wallander, who lives and works in Scania (Southern Sweden), are products of their own localities. Montalbano (Camilleri, the latest arrival, openly admits his connections to Montalbán) is fiercely Sicilian. Thus, there is a paradox: their common trait – their locality – is the main source of their differences. Montalbano talks and thinks in the Sicilian dialect, whereas the Scanian dialect can be detected only in the way the words are pronounced by the reader. The donnish Oxfordian is seen primarily in the contrast between Morse

---

[43] Giddens, 1991; Czarniawska and Joerges, 1996.   [44] Marshall Sahlins, 2001: 170.
[45] Robertson, 1992: 173; 1995: 28–9.

and his sergeant; whereas Carvalho treats his readers to quotes and poems in Catalonian. Carvalho and Montalbano are constantly eating gourmet food; Morse and Wallander, who live on alcohol, coffee, and fast food, occasionally land in the hospital with gastric ulcers. Carvalho and Morse are programmatically male chauvinists to the point of misogyny. (In his later years Morse improved, undoubtedly because of the criticism directed against Dexter by British feminists.) Wallander and Montalbano respect women but are too busy to cultivate emotional bonds with them, however strong the need; instead, they tend to bond with younger male colleagues. Morse and Wallander love the opera; Carvalho and Montalbano love literature, and so on. On the one hand, a schematic, repetitive template; on the other, an incredible richness in differentiating detail: landscapes, food, people, and drinks.

Of course, detective stories have long been globalized. It is the glocalization pattern that is new. Take, for example, Dorothy Sayers' Peter Wimsey or Agatha Christie's Miss Marple. Although they were known all over the world, they were forever frozen in their localities – the British aristocracy, the British village. Even when copied and imitated, they did not become localized in their new locale, for they remained a British export to the Commonwealth and beyond. The opposite example is Nicholas Freeling's Castang and his clones, who could live in any European city, but effectively do not live in any. They are only global; their locality is abstract. In this sense, cities became 'glocalized' much earlier than detective stories. And although the domains are different, the prescriptions and the practices are the same.

The three cities under study were keen on following the 'European ideal' but were equally committed to their local particularities. Neither one nor the other was singular and well defined. There was an entire repertoire of global, European, and local traits from which to choose. And fashion – this mechanism of collective choice – did the choosing. It is now fashionable to privatize, to decentralize, to build a database – but all this in a Swedish, Polish, or Italian way, or even in a way that is typical only to Stockholm, Warsaw, or Rome. The impact of the European models, and also of other models – North American, South American, Asian, and Australian – is enormous, but is always counterbalanced by local tradition. The definition of 'local' is also shifting: sometimes meaning 'of this city in this time', and sometimes enlarged into 'Nordic capitals' (as when Stockholm, Oslo, Copenhagen, and Helsinki organized a common marketing campaign targeting North American and Asian tourists), 'Mediterranean cities' (the common denominator is tourists and high temperatures), or 'central Europe' (as carefully contrasted with 'Eastern Europe').

The phenomenon of glocalization was first described, under a variety of names, by anthropologists, who, after the decades of hostile reactions toward the modernization of the so-called developing countries, have discovered that this apparently homogenizing move creates more differences than similarities (assuming that it would be possible to make such counts). As Marshall Sahlins said during a talk at Lund University in 1995, he could never possibly envisage that there might exist such a variety of creative uses for a simple Coca-Cola can.[46] There is no doubt that the world is becoming more homogenous and more heterogeneous: isomorphism is accompanied by allomorphism, and allopraxism (difference of practices) by isopraxism. As I write these words on October 2, 2001, EuroNews is showing a picture of an Islamic leader in Pakistan leading a protest against the USA. He is riding in a car, on the windows of which are fixed two parking decals that could be found everywhere in the world that he is opposing.

The interpretations of these tendencies – both of their cause and of their result – are as varied as the phenomenon itself. Among the most provocative are the writings of Swedish ethnologist Orvar Löfgren, who studies the creation of national and regional identities. He claims that local differences are constructed according to global prescriptions. A national or regional identity that does not conform to such prescriptions does not count as an identity in the eyes of an international community.[47]

Another claim is that heterogeneity results from the resistance to homogenizing forces, or, in the words of Taussig, 'the resistance of the concrete particular to abstraction'.[48] Robertson speaks of 'deglobalization' – 'attempts to undo the compression of the world'.[49] As Featherstone and Lash suggest, however, both interpretations are likely to be correct: the local opposes the non-local and the global invites the creation of 'local particularities'.[50] If there were no tourists in France, it would make little sense to proclaim every village 'the world capital' of something or the other. I will add a third interpretation: heterogenization as an error in translation – diversification happens at each attempt to imitate, even at attempts to imitate exactly,[51] for not even a photocopier makes identical copies every time. As George Steiner has justly noted, mistranslations are the main source of language renewal, if not of all creativity.[52]

A picture emerges in which globalization and localization happen simultaneously and intertwine, becoming the cause and the result of one another. In such a picture, globalization might mean the movement of a form, or a practice from one locality to another, or a translation of an embodied practice into a set of abstract concepts; and localization might mean a 'construction of a distinct identity'[53] according to a global prescription, or an opposition to the forces of globalization via a defense of a local tradition.

In management practice as well as in management theory, however, the attention focused on *identity construction* overshadows the simultaneous process of

---

[46] Sahlins, 2001: 'Sentimental Pessimism and Ethnographic Experience or Why Culture is Not a Disappearing Object', September 16, 1995; published in 2001. One should add, however, that the enthusiasm at this growing symmetry must be carefully measured against the symmetry of costs and profits, as Marianne Torgovnick (1990) rightly cautions.

[47] Löfgren, 1993.   [48] Taussig, 1993: 2.   [49] Robertson, 1992: 10.

[50] Featherstone and Lash, 1995.

[51] Eco, 1995. For examples of the ways in which standardization leads to differentiation, see Brunsson and Jacobsson, 2000.   [52] Steiner, 1975/1992.

[53] Featherstone and Lash, 1995: 4.

alterity construction, of constructing oneself as different.[54] Indeed, while 'identity' entered everyday parlance, 'alterity' remained a precious concept limited to the circles of cultural studies. Yet, there is no reason to suppose that the question 'Who am I like?' is more important than the question 'Who am I unlike?' and, even more poignant, 'How am I different?' Identity and alterity form the self; it might be speculated that the focus on the former is a sign of time or place.[55] Identity construction dominates the present discourse, but practice reveals the constant copresence of alterity construction, in persons and in cities.

An image of a city depends, therefore, on both identity and alterity construction, and has many constructors: politicians and officials, tourists and citizens, writers and filmmakers, architects and media people. It is impossible to show the whole of it, even in a fleeting moment, but it is possible to show fragments of its continuous construction. It is also possible to make some simplifications, rendering the picture more comprehensible. Yet, this picture is made even more complex by setting it in motion: these processes do not take their turns in time or place, but happen simultaneously, in connection, possibly, within one and the same organizational practice.

[54] See e.g. Whetten and Godfrey, 1998; and Schultz et al., 2000.

[55] It seems obvious that a political regime is an important contextual matter. The postwar Poland where I grew up was clearly a culture of alterity: there were plenty of 'them' to be different from; 'us' was a suspicious proposition. I was neither a Catholic nor a Communist, and those alterities were critical parts of my image.

2

'The European Capital': The Work of Representation in Identity and Alterity Construction

... if there is a crisis of representation, we should not forget that it is also that which is represented which is in crisis, in transformation, changing. What will be the city of tomorrow?[1]

The theory of crisis in representation has enjoyed a great deal of attention. In practice, however, a crisis of representation in the city means that there are too many representations: neither the sources nor the results have a clear legitimacy. This does not make representation work any less important. Although management is not merely a matter of representation, it strongly depends on the work of representation.

In an attempt to capture the richness of field meanings, three meanings of representation are used here, all simultaneously present and interacting. Thus, representation is seen as *a relationship between an image and its assumed referent* (the correspondence theory of truth is the dominant theory behind managerial practices), as *a political relationship* (standing for or speaking for somebody or something else), and *as grasping the 'nature' of something in a symbolic utterance*. These three meanings highlight the different aspects of representation: whether it is faithful (the model-copy question), whether it is legitimate (the question of the mandate), and whether it is compelling (the question of attraction). Although the espoused norm postulates no disparities among the three, managerial practice finds them constantly at odds: faithful depictions are often found to be unappealing, and attractive simulacra are illegitimate or distorting. These worries are echoed by city theoreticians who are concerned that, in the flurry of texts setting the city as a representation, the boundary between reality and its image has been blurred.[2]

---

[1] Lefebvre, 1996: 212.

[2] For a review of the symbolic approaches to the city and their critics, see Linda McDowell, 1997: 38–41.

But I shall set this worry aside and concentrate on representation work, its sources, mechanisms, and products. One way of summarizing this representation work, as I saw it in the field, is to say that the interlocutors in all three cities described their cities and their own work in relation to 'a modern European capital'. It turned out, however, that although this notion hosted many recognizable topics that are common to the three cities, it also contained dramatically different visions of such a capital, given that the different frame of reference constructed by the city's inhabitants, its managers, and its politicians differed from one city to another. These different frames included different constellations of model cities, but also specific, local stories of developments in the three capitals. Such stories were intended to set the city apart – from all the other cities, and from specific cities. Such targets of identification (models), of negation, and of differentiation (anti-models) shifted in form and in content.

IMAGES OF 'A EUROPEAN CAPITAL' IN WARSAW

A European Capital has a Metro

The increase of motor vehicles in Warsaw has been so dynamic that in 1994 it had already reached the level estimated for the year 2010. On the other hand, the Warsaw roads are in a very poor condition, with their surfaces remaining unrepaired for years. To complicate the picture, bridges and tunnels are rare and often under repair. And so the search for realistic solutions continues.

One question asked during the search concerned the choice of a model to emulate. Should the main transport strategy be aimed at the facilitation of private transportation, as it is in the USA; or should it focus on the development of public transport, as in the majority of European cities? Even if public opinion in the late 1990s was beginning to lean toward the latter solution, under the banner of 'this is a European city', difficulties were still mounting. The performance of public transport units depends considerably on whether the roads are congested with private vehicles, and their number has continued to increase, so that today Warsaw can boast of traffic jams that are as dramatic as those of Rome.

The public buses were inadequate, not only because they were old, but because they were already of an inferior quality when they were purchased. New, high-quality buses were very expensive. The tram situation was similar: there was no money for substantial investments and only homemade improvements and repairs were considered. City workers overhauled the trams in the city plant.

It was the subway, however, that aroused the greatest controversy and the highest hopes. The leading question I was asked was: 'Do you know that there are only two capitals in Europe without a subway – Warsaw and Tirana?' (Tirana, the capital of Albania, was Warsaw's Other, and not only in matters of transportation.)

My pointing out that Copenhagen did not have a subway had no effect.[3] Everyone agreed that a subway would solve many of the problems connected with urban transportation. That is, it would solve them if it were possible to immediately service the neural points of the city with the subway. At present, however, only one subway line is in service.

Opinions about the metro varied from 'It's about time!' and 'Better one than none' to 'Well, you can't bury it now, after all these years' and 'The World Bank was against it'. Comparing Warsaw to Johannesburg, the World Bank had argued for a surface transport system – a position that gained few supporters in Warsaw.

Here, we come to the alterity aspect of the image of 'the European capital'. By definition, it cannot be in any place other than Europe. One continent in which it, most emphatically, must not be located is Africa. Johannesburg was, at that time, an important prop in the alterity construction,[4] and this construction revealed, among many other things, the untamed strength of racial prejudice. Western consultants were accused of trying to 'Africanize' Poland. This accusation had its root in the fact that many of the aid programs had turned away from Africa and toward Eastern Europe.[5] But while Western liberals were despairing of the consequences for African countries, at least some Eastern Europeans were annoyed that their situation could be seen as paralleling that of Africa. Johannesburg may be a more modern city than Warsaw, but, alas, it is on the wrong continent. Tirana may be a symbol of poverty and belatedness, but it is, at least, a European capital, so it is more the opposite than the Other.

Not everyone was equally impressed by the weight of the 'European capital' argument. During my shadowing days at the Metro Construction General Headquarters, I witnessed a visit from one of the new TV stations. After filming the interview, the two young men packed their equipment and chatted with the managing director and his deputy directors in the secretaries' room. The journalists wanted to know why a subway, and not, for example, the environmentally friendly zeppelin was chosen for the city. The 'Warsaw–Tirana' contrast was produced, to no avail. The 'European capital' argument meant nothing to the young journalists; for them it was an image from their parents' past.

A European Capital has Water Treatment Plants

Warsaw has had serious problems with the quality of its water. Its waterworks were built by a British engineer named Lindley in the last quarter of the

---

[3] Quite rightly, as it turned out. Copenhagen built a subway at the end of the 1990s at amazing speed.

[4] Given Poland's uncomfortable closeness to Russia, it has historically been Asia that played the role of 'Significant Other' to Poland. Now Asia is being used for identification purposes, being seen as an example of a swift economic success.

[5] An exhaustive and provocative description of Western aid to Eastern Europe can be found in Janine Wedel's *Collision and Collusion* (2001).

nineteenth century, and it still works admirably. The city takes pride in this glori-
ous monument to early technology, and in fact, some people say that its quality
is superior to the waterworks built in the 1960s and 1970s. Unfortunately, the
water in the Vistula River has changed since Lindley's time.

The poor water quality in Warsaw is partly a result of shallow intakes, dirty
water, and obsolete technology, but primarily due to the fact that Warsaw has
only one water treatment plant, which collects the wastewater from one side of
the river. For this reason, in fact, Warsaw has been classified by the Helsinki
Convention documents and by the Baltic Water Protection Program as their most
difficult case.

Waterworks was exchanging surface intakes on the Vistula for deep-water
intakes, because water from the bottom of the river is much cleaner. At the time
of the study, water from both intakes was mixed in the pipes, and hope for further
improvement lay in treatment technology.

During my tour of one part of the waterworks I was mistaken for a journalist,
and before I visited the plant itself, I was taken to the office, given a glass of tea
(tea is drunk in glasses in Poland) and shown a long record of water quality
'as measured against the background of European norms'. Things were getting
better, or at least the water was.

The wastewater treatment plant was first planned in the 1970s but, like many
plans conceived during that period, it was interrupted, and did not open until
1990. Here is an excerpt from my notes, taken during the tour of the plant:

Our guide ended the tour by saying that two new water treatment
plants in Warsaw, which would take care of the left riverbank,
would greatly improve the quality of water. With 3 purification
plants and 12 infiltration water intakes, Warsaw would have better
water than any other city in Europe! He also used a variation of
Metro's favorite adage: Until recently, Warsaw and Tirana were
Europe's only two capitals without a wastewater treatment plant.

I asked if this was the first wastewater treatment plant in Poland.
The guide looked at me with surprise and said that in Poland, as in
the rest of the world[!], treatment plants were known at the end of
the previous century, when the same mechanical–biological
method was applied. Wastewater would flow down a pile of stones
and the heavy waste would remain there; then it would flow
through the filtering grit, and only then to the river. In past times,
however, there was little to treat, because detergents were not being
discharged into the river. But now, especially on Fridays and
Saturdays, when people are likely to be doing their washing, the
plant has a significant problem with balls of scum that float in the
water. The Danes, he said, complained about problems with plastic
toothpicks and cotton tips. (Warsaw, Observation 3/3)

As for the peculiarly Danish problem, it must be added that until recently there were no plastic toothpicks or cotton tips in Poland. This deficiency has been quickly corrected, however, and in the near future the chemical treatment of wastewater will be necessary, not only because of detergents and small plastic items, but because of an increasing amount of chemical waste. European problems were arriving more quickly than European solutions.

A single-proprietorship city company, financed mainly through credit from a European Investment Bank, was created to build another wastewater treatment plant. Appropriately enough, a European bank helped in the completion of the 'Europeanization' of Warsaw.[6]

A European Capital has a Centrally Managed Infrastructure

During the time of my study, Warsaw underwent a reform of its governance system, which I have described in detail elsewhere.[7] It created one unit called the 'Municipality Centrum,' which, along with ten suburban municipalities, constituted the Capital City of Warsaw. The character of their mutual relationship was the topic of many conflicting interpretations. Some of my interlocutors pointed out that the idea of municipal corporations had been borrowed from Germany, where it was being applied to small towns rather than major cities. A counter argument was that the intention of the reform was to merge Warsaw with the region and, thus, dissolve the city into a metropolitan area. In such an area, as is common in the USA, suburban municipalities might associate themselves either with the city center or with other municipalities outside the city. Warsaw, however, as we know already, lies in Europe, which appears to have a clear-cut solution to those matters:

> The basic issue, when it comes to the management of a city, is municipal engineering and all the matters of infrastructure. All the large cities in Europe are moving not toward decentralization but toward centralization. Even among such crowds of people as in London, matters of infrastructure are on the top. At any rate, they are managed jointly.[8] . . . In a municipal organism like Warsaw's – which, by the way, was built as a centralized system – these matters simply must be centralized. It has to be done in an efficient, homogeneous manner, and it's difficult to talk about some kind of self-government in this matter. (Warsaw, Interview 2: 1)

---

[6] See Chapter 4. [7] Czarniawska, 1998.
[8] On May 8, 1998, the inhabitants of London voted in favor of a central governing authority and an elected mayor.

This is the classic argument that assumes the incompatibility of democracy and efficiency. Such an argument, however, is especially strong when applied to emergency situations, and the next quote reveals that indeed such situations were in the minds of the interlocutors.

> The municipal corporations would be yet another dissipation of control, transferring decision-making to some undefined levels of power without specifying the extent of their authority. . . . I believe that the concentration of power is necessary in moments of danger. It doesn't mean that it has to be a non-democratic, authoritarian government, but it has to be concentrated. (Warsaw, Interview 2: 16)

A tendency to expect a threat and an emergency is typical of 'Mitteleuropa', and atypical of Sweden, where this historically induced sense of threat is unknown. 'Emergency management' also requires rules and procedures, but different perhaps from those of 'normalcy management'. This, among other factors, makes a tendency to imitate contemporary cities less pronounced in Warsaw than in Stockholm, as we shall see below.

These short excerpts are intended to show that the image of an 'ideal city' has a multifaceted role in managerial practice: it motivates and legitimates, focuses discourse, guides action, and serves as an argument. Such an image is a composite of pictures, some of which could probably be traced back to some concrete producers of images, but many of which seem to be produced by the actors evoking them. This composite uses identity ('Warsaw is a European city'), negation ('Warsaw is not an African city'), and alterity ('Warsaw is different from all European cities'), which in turn are collage-like. 'London', 'Berlin', 'big cities', 'the Danes', and 'America' were all used in the composition. Interestingly enough, Stockholm, which invited itself as a model and a helper in matters of water treatment, was kept at a distance by the Warsaw authorities. 'The Danes' were perceived as being 'more humble' and were treated with greater sympathy.[9] 'Tirana' and 'Africa' were used for alterity purposes, and it was clear that knowledge of the 'antimodels' was thin, if not nonexistent.

Even though these composite models were produced locally, it was believed that they operated universally, and that all the other European cities utilized them. But did they?

IMAGES OF A 'EUROPEAN BIG CITY' IN STOCKHOLM

By Warsaw standards, Stockholm fulfills all the requirements of 'the European capital': it has a subway, it has water treatment plants, and its infrastructure is

---

[9] More on these matters can be found in Czarniawska (2000).

centrally managed (in a company form, one might add). But these images were not those present in the minds of Stockholm politicians and managers. For them, the 'big European city of the twenty-first century' had to fulfill quite another set of requirements. Because the big-but-not-capital cities like Milan, Stuttgart, Naples, and Gothenburg rebelled against the hegemony of capitals, the scope of the positive model had to be extended. Stockholm was aware of being a not-so-big big city, and watched the agile moves of her 'younger sisters' with interest.

A European City of the Twenty-First Century Invests in IT

The current urbanist reflection suggests that computerization is a *sine qua non* of city development,[10] not only reflecting the real developments, but also prompting them. City images are also produced by consultants and various 'field-servicing' organizations, such as the Organization for Economic and Community Development (OECD). Opening one of the many OECD conferences on 'The City and New Technologies' in 1992, Michel Delebarre said that information technology (IT) was the only way to increase the efficiency of municipal services, while attracting the computer industry to a big city that had disposed of its heavy and light industry. As a consequence, the city managers began to market their cities within the frame of IT: Osaka represented itself as a *City of Intelligence*, Barcelona as a *City of Telematics*, Amsterdam as a *City of Information*, Manchester as a *Wired City*, and Stockholm as an *Internet Bay*.[11]

Stockholm was stricken by the IT-bug very early. At the time of my study (1996–7), Stockholm put a big amount of money into CityNet, a new optic-fiber net connecting all municipal offices, and created a company called Stokab to construct the 'new city infrastructure'. Stockholm had created a home page early in the history of the Internet, and its politicians believed that computer education was the best way to deal with the unemployment caused by a new immigration wave from the countryside to the city. The IT industries could not but agree. Here is a story, told in various versions by my interlocutors, of how Stockholm was becoming an 'IT capital of the world'. (Observe that Europe is no longer the adequate reference space.):

> It started already with the previous Mayor, and it must be said that even now, as the opposition leader, he cooperates with the present Mayor on certain issues. Even if they are competitors, there is something they have in common, and that is their love for the city. IT was such an issue, and it was presented very well, so that all politicians agreed that Stockholm has to become an IT metropolis. (Stockholm, Interview 16: 2)

[10] Castells, 1989; Hepworth, 1990; Borja and Castells, 1997; Graham and Aurigi, 1997.
[11] Peter Dobers made a specific study of Stockholm's investment in IT (Dobers, 2001; Dobers and Strannegård, 2001).

I do not know how this idea of an optic-fiber net arose, but I believe that it was a pragmatic response to the fact that practically all tele-communication companies operate in the Stockholm market, and it would be unthinkable to allow them all to dig in the ground and lay their own cable. It would paralyze the city. The experiences from London showed clearly what a nightmare it can become, even if they do not have as many competing companies as we do. We just wanted to save our city . . . (Stockholm, Interview 16: 10)

Bill Gates was in Stockholm and was very impressed. I have pictures where he is shaking hands with the Mayor. And now he travels around and tells everybody that if they want to see something excit-ing happening in the world, they should travel to Stockholm. 'Look at them, they don't sit and wait; they do something!' So after Gates' visit to Brazil, the head of Brazil's IT network came to see us. Since then we have visitors continuously: 'What do you do?' they ask. 'How did you solve this problem?' 'What is it that Gates thinks is so good?' (Stockholm, Interview 33: 5)

This story summarizes the entire process of image creation, circulation, and translation into a local practice.[12] A globally floating idea of an Information City is adopted and successfully propagated by local politicians. The political will provides the impetus for concrete action. While the idea is being put into prac-tice, various problems arise, and are solved in a local way, aided by the experi-ences from other places (London becomes an anti-model). Once the practice nears completion and can be presented as an image, it is blessed by the Pope of the IT Church, and it spreads around the world.[13] Pilgrims arrive to witness the developments. Here, we can see both directions of globalization: translating global models for local use and attempting to launch a local model for global use.

The religious metaphors bring to mind the Holy City. Rome appreciated the importance of IT, but considered it to be an internal project; whereas the Vatican set the highest priority on IT.[14] Meanwhile, Warsaw, haunted by financial prob-lems, dreamed of an optic-fiber net, but the politicians considered it to be merely the icing on the cake, and not an investment that is central to the city image.

---

[12] For a complete description of the chain of translations, see Dobers, 2001.

[13] On February 7, 2002, Bill Gates received a honorary doctorate from the Royal Institute of Technology in Stockholm, further cementing the connection between IT and the city.

[14] Ever since Pope Pius XI instituted Radio Vatican in 1931, actually installed by Guglielmo Marconi in person, the Catholic Church has continued to use the radio and television to evangel-ize to the secular world. But it was Pope Wojtyla who made television the main mode of commun-ication with the world. With the arrival of IT, the Catholic Church transformed itself into an 'electronic church,' and it is speculated that, in time, the 'holy web' would remove the need for such structures as confessionals and church offices (Czarniawska, Mazza and Pipan, 2001).

The image of an IT city did not originate in Stockholm, but it was here that it found a natural home. Although there were many competitors, Stockholm won the first prize in the 'Bangemann Challenge,' an EU contest in IT-big-city projects. In 1999, when broadband became a home expression in Sweden, Stockholm was again in the lead. The local ideas have also been sent abroad, thus gaining the approval of 'the center' (USA). Thanks to this move, what was known at home as the 'Stokab-model' has, after traveling abroad, became known as a 'Stockholm-model,' a unique way of constructing an information network for a city.[15]

A European City of the Twenty-First Century is a Spectacle

Cities aren't villages; they aren't machines; they aren't works of art; and they aren't telecommunication stations. They are spaces for face to face contact of amazing variety and richness. They are spectacle – and what is wrong with that?[16]

Stockholm might have taken a cue from Elizabeth Wilson's statement, above. Interestingly enough, the modern city as a spectacle and the modern citizen as a spectator (*flâneur*) are images from the previous *fin-de-siècle*, but they seem to have reached their full expression today.[17] Allan Pred recounted the story of three spectacular spaces on which hangs the history of modern Stockholm: the Stockholm Exhibition of 1897; the Stockholm Exhibition of 1930; and the multi-purpose arena, the Globe, which opened in 1989.[18]

The notion of the city as a spectacle points to the fact that even Stockholm, intent as it is on following the current development in other cities, also follows its own tradition – images and ideas travel not only through places but also through time. I shall return to this topic in Chapter 5; at present, however, I would like to focus for a while on the latest spectacle that Stockholm offered the world in 1998, in its role as the Cultural Capital of Europe.[19]

During the end of the preparations for the cultural year, voices were raised about a lack of vision or a unifying theme that would permit spectators to form a comprehensive picture of the event. The day after the release of the program for 1998 featuring over a thousand projects, one of the evening tabloids commented: 'Headless culture '98: Our reporter looked in vain for vision in the watered-down program offerings' (*Expressen*, 1997: 10–22).

To an observer of managerial action a rather fragmented picture emerged. As a result of inspiring cross-contacts between different genres and artists, the action net became not so much a net as a loose web, incorporating fragments that are only vaguely connected to other projects, or even to the cultural program as a whole. Any possibility of supervising what was actually happening had been minimized.

---

[15] Dobers, 2002, 2003.   [16] Wilson, 1991: 158.   [17] Zeidler-Janiszewska, 1997.
[18] Pred, 1995.
[19] This relation is based on a study by Lena Porsander, 2000; Pipan and Porsander, 2000.

This fragmentation attracted criticism throughout most of 1997. 'What actually is the overall theme for 1998?' a journalist asked one of the authors of the program. 'Something is needed to tie the whole sack together'.

'Yes, [*the content of the Cultural Capital Year*] is like a huge kaleidoscope', said the Information Manager in an interview with Lena Porsander in March 1998. To demonstrate what she meant, she rummaged through the pages of the thick program catalog. Spectators were to witness different scenes taking place in the city. Each scene or fragment represented the Cultural Capital project in its own way. Thus, rather than creating a unified picture, the loosely knit action net produced a view-finder, a kaleidoscope.

Such a product is not without precedent in urban history. A century ago, arcades had become fashionable in big European cities, and one of their common attractions was the Panoramas, or, as Walter Benjamin called them, the *phantasmagorias*. A Panorama was a mechanical device in which visitors could look through a little window at quickly shifting pictures. The pictures gave the spectator the illusion of moving – faster and faster – through the world. In Stockholm a century later, spectators could still peek at phantasmagorias, constructed now by the action net called the Cultural Capital. Common to these events was the feature of being regarded as a kind of viewfinder.

This kaleidoscopic city was in turn supported by other *past-modern*[20] devices: a hybrid organization that incorporated the various traits of public administration offices and private companies as well as a database program that, like the Globe, was to be a heritage for the future city. Similarly, as we shall see later, the organizers of the Jubilee of the Third Millennium of Christianity in Rome sized down their ambitions from grand monuments to a set of emergency procedures.

A European City of the Twenty-First Century is Clean and Green

We are in Stockholm at a big public square, a modest version of our Concorde. In its center solemnly reside two obelisks in a neo-Egyptian style. Is it another product of postmodern architecture? No, it is His Majesty Carl XVI Gustaf who has ordered them to be raised in Anno Domini 1994. What? Did the Swedish king, a humble monarch who usually behaves like an average citizen, suddenly see himself as a Ramses II, Mohamed Ali, or Louis Philippe, deciding to erect those obelisks to revere the sun? What did he believe himself to be – a pharaoh? Not at all. . . .

It is difficult to see at a first glance, but instead of hieroglyphs that usually adorn such monuments, one finally notices strings of neon lights twisting against the stone producing an Egypto-Disney effect. A plaque explains the scientific and mediatic wish of the sovereign: the hieroglyphs (sacred inscriptions) gave way to 'épistémoglyphs' (scientific inscriptions).

---

[20] This expression, coined by Karin Knorr Cetina (1994), offers a comfortable solution to the dilemma of whether things are 'late modern' or 'postmodern'.

The point is to show the people, with help of moving contrasts and vivid colors, the level of two basic elements: air and water (earth and fire are still missing). . . . Each obelisk is the extreme point of a vast network of instruments that show, in real time, the state of pollution in Stockholm.[21]

This was Bruno Latour's reading of photographs produced by Petra Adolfsson in the course of her study of environmental measures in Stockholm,[22] for Stockholm is also marketed as a Clean City with fresh air and pure water.

The difficulty with this enterprise lies in providing the evidence. A modern city cannot rely on the impressions of its tourists or its inhabitants, especially if these impressions are positive only through a negative statement, 'no pollution'. Representation work is necessary. Thus, an impressive apparatus for the measurement of air and water pollution, involving many people and machines, was constructed. In the beginning of the 1990s, the Environment and Health Protection Administration in Stockholm created a special department, the Stockholm Air and Noise, to manage the testing of air pollutant levels and noise in the city.

Unfortunately, for all its work, this representation produces no dramatic results. The neon light indicators rarely darken. While 'dirty cities' (with apologies to Rome and Warsaw, which both sin, at least in the air aspect) can engage in comparisons showing effectively diminishing pollution levels, Stockholm's measurements lie almost constantly beyond the permissible EU norm. Although an enormous amount of exertion goes into demonstrating the cleanliness of the city, it is difficult to use it for either identity or alterity construction. As clean as . . . what other city? Cleaner than . . . any city? That is why politicians spend so little time discussing the instrument readings, leaving them, instead, to children, tourists, and His Majesty. When they need to engage in ideological battles, they do it within the proper discourse of pollution, wherein the present state must be described as a horror, and the clean city as a Utopia prevented only by the opposition.[23]

Water is an easier subject, in that its quality had been effectively marketed during the Stockholm Water Festivals, organized each summer for a number of years, again with the participation of His Majesty. The difficulty here lies in the fact that although counterexamples abound, there are several Cities on the Water and many competitors to the title of Clean Water City (with Rome claiming the historical precedence on the basis of its famous aqueducts). Furthermore, it seems that the state is not willing to cosponsor the Water Festival anymore. So, although Stockholm remains the Clean City, it has difficulty in putting this image to practical use.

There was a stock of city representations in Stockholm as well as in Warsaw, but with a difference. The Warsaw composite model is recognizable but not usable in Stockholm, and its images of the Other need to be used with caution (although in the debate about a general traffic solution it has been said that apart from

---

[21] Latour, 1999*b*: 326 (my translation).   [22] Adolfsson, 1999, 2002.
[23] See the debate about the so-called 'Third Track' in Stockholm: Corvellec, 2001*a,b*.

Stockholm, only Tirana does not have an inner ring road).[24] Gothenburg is usually seen as Stockholm's at-home Other, and Copenhagen, Oslo, and Helsinki the Others abroad, although in terms of competition, not of contrast. This meant that any elements of managerial practice in these cities might be incorporated in both the model and the anti-model – at different times. Thus, Gothenburg was an anti-model in 1985 when Stockholm decided not to introduce a sub-municipal reform, but it became a positive model in 1996 when the decision was reversed.[25] Additionally, Stockholm's managers (with the approval of its politicians) were busy producing an image that could be a model for others. Rome, on the other hand, wished to be placed on a different map entirely.

IMAGES OF THE 'LEADING EUROPEAN CAPITAL' IN ROME

There was a well-deserved grandiosity in the city images present in Rome. While Warsaw was painfully aware of its belatedness and Stockholm of its small size and Nordic location, Rome dreamed of joining the fashion leaders – Paris, Berlin, and London. It shared with Warsaw the belief that rapid modernization was needed, with Stockholm an interest in the newest managerial fashion, and with Athens the pride of a unique past that is incorporated and preserved in the city. All these elements found an expression in the images of the leading European capital that seemed to be guiding both political visions and managerial practices.

A Leading European Capital has a Traffic System

There were some palpable similarities between the traffic issues of Warsaw and Rome. One was the citizens' love of the automobile, which has a parallel only in the USA. This passion results in the congestion of city traffic of which the citizens of Stockholm, with all their complaints about traffic problems, know little. Another similarity is the late arrival of the subway. By the time of the study, however, Rome already had two subway lines, and the subway construction problems were mostly local and related to Rome's historical past (as anyone who saw Fellini's *Roma* can appreciate). The uniquely Roman problem, however, was that the city did not have a traffic *system*. There was no urban transport plan, and neither the tariffs nor the networks were integrated. Rome is truly a *palimpsest city*, as defined by Bauman.[26]

[24] I also found a piece of local prejudice: Stockholm was derisively compared to Korpilombo, a small village in the north of Sweden.   [25] Czarniawska, 1999.

[26] Bauman, 1998: 40. The irony of history is that Rome is not, what in architecture is known as a 'Roman city', designed on a neutral geometric base: the grid (Benevolo, 1993). Worse still, it is uncertain whether there is any urban system in Rome (Ferrarotti, 1995).

> BC: Is there some historical explanation for of this state of affairs?
>
> Interviewed person: You have to go back centuries, to the creation of Municipalities and Dominions, that is, 1300–1500, when the empires disintegrated. From then on the local particularism was of the utmost importance, the so-called villageism, which drags on until today. In the city, and even in the region, there are clearly areas that are economically and culturally homogenous and that could be more rationally planned and managed. This is, alas, excluded by administrative divisions. The regional authorities were supposed to take care of these problems, but they did not. (Rome, Interview 15: 2)

In contemporary times, at least during the previous political regime, this local particularism took a baroque expression: it was claimed that the political parties divided the bus and tram lines among themselves, so that the existence of a given communication link could well depend on where the mother-in-law of a leading politician lived. Or so the Roman wit would have it.[27]

The models to follow were the big European cities like Paris and Rome, with effective public transportation systems. Berlin, especially, was attractive because its double networks of local trains and subway were close to the Roman program 'to activate the iron' – the many unused railway lines that criss-cross the city – and because of Berlin's recent experiences:

> The situation could not remain as it was, and thus the City Management ordered a traffic system project, at a European level, from a consulting company with Berlin. They had an experience in Berlin from work on the integration of the two networks.
>
> They came up with a project of a new network on wheels . . . This is a very ambitious project, which suggests a structure composed of principal lines and then of lines we never dared to introduce – so-called express buses to substitute for a subway by connecting distant points of the city with a minimal number of stops and advanced types of vehicles. We had similar vehicles in the 1950s; they were called accelerated buses, but they could operate then because there were few cars and the streets were passable. Today this possibility is very doubtful; this is why we never suggested it ourselves and there is a general skepticism as to its feasibility. (Rome, Interview 2: 4)

An interesting aspect of the model translation is that the designers rarely seem to be interested in the peculiarities of the local situation. This does not mean, however, that the locals have a monopoly on the right diagnosis. The same

---

[27] A national monopoly on wit is also one of the marks of a 'European capital' – with the exception of Stockholm. In Sweden, the wit resides in Gothenburg.

skeptical respondent was enthusiastic about another project:

> As far as the tram lines are concerned, in a few days [*which turned out to be three months*] we will open a very important new line of rapid trams across Trastevere . . . We think that this is going to be a grand idea, as it will put a stop to the interpenetration of all those bus lines that go towards the center; it will bring us significant earnings; it will shorten the time spent on transportation by the citizens; and it will diminish the air pollution. (Rome, Interview 2: 10)

Tram No. 8, the rapid tram, became the center of journalistic attention in the following months. It had to battle undisciplined drivers and pedestrians, and the number of accidents during its first months of functioning, earned it the nickname of 'The Bad Luck Tram'.[28] Perhaps it was not such a grand idea; however, it still functions.

Additionally, the complicated process of setting the rapid tram in circulation made it obvious that the sediments of the old regimes were residing not only under the ground, as archeological monuments. It was, in many ways, a heroic enterprise to create a traffic system in a big city rather than merely extending or modernizing an existing system.

A Leading European Capital Lives Off its Cultural Capital

. . . Rome . . . has learned the art of growing old by playing on all its parts.[29]

The idea of the city as a spectacle was obvious to the Roman politicians, officials, and citizens. If anything, they were tired of it, as the relief of having lost the Olympics and the general wariness toward the Jubilee of the Third Millennium of Christianity clearly indicated. But with the approach of this last spectacle, forced onto Rome by the Pope, the city was determined to make the best of it. The best had to be more durable than the event itself, and the past had to be turned into the main asset of the present. The Jubilee was to become a marketing opportunity: a unique possibility of spreading the image of Rome around the world. The image was to be the City of Faith, City of Solidarity, City of Culture and Nature, a Modern City (a kaleidoscopic list, if ever there was one).

The image of Rome as a City of Faith, or perhaps The City of Faith, was not, of course, of the managers' doing, but they were forced to embrace it and do their best with it. (During the time of the study the city was under the leftist governance and remains so in 2002.) The City of Solidarity, however, evoked many and

---

[28] The story of the 'Unfortunate Tram No. 8' is told in detail in Czarniawska, 2003.

[29] Michel de Certeau, 1984: 91.

rich associations to be cultivated:

> Rome is a city capable of assimilating all cultures, which in turn leave their mark on the city. The result is an enormous tolerance for diversity.
>
> This was already true of Rome in a time when foreigners in Athens couldn't even become citizens. Whoever comes to Rome – no matter what race or religion – is assimilated into the texture of the city. Some call it indifference. I call it tolerance. The Jews remained here after the destruction of Jerusalem, and in my opinion they were accepted because they were people, not because they were Jews. (Rome, Interview 44: 7)

This image was, of course, severely contested, but a contested image is not the same as an ineffectual image: on the contrary, contestation, like every translation, gives life to an image. It is such contestations and dramatizations that make a representation attractive to public opinion. The problem, rather, was that many elements of the Roman image had already been exploited. As Tatiana Pipan, who studied the entire process very closely, expressed it,

Rome as the city of culture and atmosphere is not a new identity – it has its variations as 'the capital of Italy', 'a museum in the open air', 'the metropolis of Christianity' and so on. It is rather the last image, the image of Rome as a modern city, which is a part of a new identity. According to Roman architects and urbanists, a city which wants to continue to be alive, rather than limit itself to the function of a museum, must continuously measure up to the new, without damaging the old. The antique and the modern must live side by side, but the new must respect the rules sedimented in thousands of years. The Jubilee cannot accomplish all these changes, but it can be one step towards the desired goals.[30]

Rome should, therefore, become a city that offers its tourists all the modern comforts, so they can better enjoy the beauty of the past. Financial constraints rendered most of the construction projects infeasible, but there were many small projects and a great many ideas. And while the City of Rome emphasized the esthetic and financial aspects of the celebration, the Vatican was appalled by what it perceived as blatant commercialism, and tried to steer the Jubilee toward more spiritual dimensions. The city authorities and the Vatican administration often played the role of the Other to one another – an easy task in light of the fact that they cohabit the same geographical space.

The city management group, however, had the economic dimension of the event clearly in focus. This meant, first, that the emphasis was placed on the reception of tourists; but it soon became obvious that it was not tourists as such (a common presence in Rome) but their large numbers at any one time that constituted the managerial challenge. Leaving the management of the spectacle

---

[30] Pipan and Porsander, 2000: 18.

to the Vatican, the Roman authorities concentrated on perfecting their skills in *emergency management.*[31]

Emergency management was confined to the Jubilee, and was not the only managerial novelty in Rome. Another, more pervasive and far-reaching one was the privatization of the public services.

A Leading European Capital has Privatized Many of its Services

Although it is practically impossible to establish the source of popular ideas,[32] the notion of improving urban services by privatization, at least in the last part of the twentieth century, came from London. It reached everybody but, as usual, it was translated locally. Thus, Stockholm not so much privatized as 'company-ized' its major public utilities in the early 1990s. (That is to say, it changed the legal form but not the ownership of its utilities, which are still owned by the city.) Warsaw, on the other hand, experienced only a minor wave in the ocean of privatization accompanying the political transformation of the country. Rome took privatization to be a turning point in its management style.

The first case in point was to be the privatization of the *Centrale di Latte*, the city-owned dairy monopoly. At the close of the nineteenth century and, because of the Depression, well into the 1930s, many cities owned the production or distribution of such organizations as bakeries and dairies that were considered to cater to the basic needs of its citizens. The Centrale di Latte was probably seen as the easiest privatization target because it was such an obvious anachronism. The process turned out to be far from easy. The citizens were not in favor of the privatization, and union protests and street demonstrations followed. The subsequent privatization of ACEA, the conglomerate of the water, sewer, city illumination, and many other services, proceeded slowly and cautiously.

Carmelo Mazza claims that Rome used the Centrale di Latte as a learning case for further privatization.[33] The outcome of this learning is still controversial in practice, as the following examples of privatization in Rome and in Italy have amply demonstrated – but in one aspect: it has undoubtedly contributed to the legitimization of the privatization discourse in Rome.

Why, one might ask, did this discourse need to be legitimized? One answer is that its legitimization permitted the city managers to follow a global trend with the acceptance of its local audience. Another, more pragmatic and 'managerialistic' reason is that privatization opened new vistas and possibilities for the utilities in question. Far from throwing itself into competition with local suppliers of water and electricity,[34] ACEA moved 'abroad': to Apulia, in order to manage its

---

[31] Pipan, 2001.   [32] All ideas are here all the time, claimed Merton (1985).

[33] For a more detailed description of the process, see Mazza (1999, 2001).

[34] To the contrary, one of ACEA's first moves was an oligopolistic agreement with ENEL, its main competitor in the energy market in Rome.

waterworks, to Tunis, in order to illuminate a mosque, but also to the telecommunication industry, and therefore to the 'new economy'.

As if in anticipation of comments like mine, the CEO of ACEA announced its
new place in the city of Rome thus:

> *Il Messaggero*, April 24, 1998
> ACEA: a Roman company that will become ever more dedicated to
> urban projects addressing the needs of the most deprived of the
> city's inhabitants; a company whose 'Romanness' explains its *lead-
> ership* in the area of monument illumination, but also a company
> orientated toward the highest qualitative *standards*, and therefore
> toward the global service market, the technical innovation and the
> complex management systems . . .
> We have no ambition to 'colonize' other territories, but we aspire
> to, and are prompt to enter, all kinds of collaboration that augment
> our *know-how*.[35]

To paraphrase a dictum from another place and time, it seems that what is good
for ACEA is good for Rome.[36]

The privatization of public utilities in Rome can thus be seen as following a
fashion in the world of public management, and as a signal of change in the
managerial paradigm. Every change has, however, its unintended consequences.
The complexities of privatization revealed that the public–private division was
neither as old nor as solid as it has usually been represented. It announced the
possibility that, if no new attractive dichotomies were found, the hybrid forms
and the fluid borders would become a norm rather than an exception. There is no
reason to suppose that privatization will dramatically improve the quality of
urban services, just as there was no reason to suppose that the earlier municipalization would achieve that end.[37] The modernist hope of dramatically successful
solutions is, however, still alive and well in all European cities.

IDENTITY AND ALTERITY

Two important products of the globalization of a city are its identity and its alterity. These terms have recently enjoyed a renewed attention, but they appear in
two versions, which can be situated on two extremes of the exclusion–inclusion

---

[35] This is my translation. Words that are italicized here were written in English and italicized in
the original. The seepage of English terms into the Italian public discourse is further discussed in
Chapter 3.

[36] Attributed to Per Gyllenhammar, the famous CEO of Volvo: 'What is good for Volvo, is good
for Sweden.'

[37] Senior employees at ACEA still remembered the municipalization of the company, which
was conducted under the same premises as the present privatization.

dimension.[38] One version is typical for cultural studies and is strongly influenced by Michel Foucault, who claimed that 'the forceful exclusion and exorcism of what is the Other is an act of identity formation'.[39] The other end of the dimension is represented by post-Hegelians, who see the interplay between identity and alterity as a dialectical move, resulting in 'increasing expansion and incorporation, assimilating or at least harmonizing all otherness in terms of expanding identity'.[40] Michael Taussig, whose work on mimesis I am using here, follows Benjamin in the belief that mimesis is yielding into the Other.[41] Thus, in the discourse of and on identity, alterity is either *attributed* ('they are different and therefore not us') or *incorporated* ('they are actually very much like us'). The third possibility, the *affirmation of difference* ('we are different'), is omitted. And yet, as Gabriel Tarde so forcefully said,

To exist is to differ; difference, in one sense, is the substantial side of things, what they have most in common and what makes them most different. One has to start from this difference and abstain from trying to explain it, especially by starting with identity, as so many persons wrongly do, because identity is a minimum, and hence a type of difference, and a very rare type at that, in the same way as rest is a type of movement and the circle a type of ellipse.[42]

The two first views – exclusion and inclusion – are grounded in the anthropological studies of relations between Westerners and their Others. Although this aspect makes for a useful analogy in studies of globalization, it is also important to see these differences in the context of big cities. Big cities apply the moves of exclusion and inclusion toward other cities, but these moves never achieve permanence, either in an expanded, harmonious identity, or in a permanent relegation. The interplay of identity and alterity is continuous; new cities become objects of desire and old objects of desire serve as negative examples; the Other is not passive, but is involved in symmetrical work at all times. Also, an important aspect in identity–alterity play that I want to illustrate is of little interest to either of the schools mentioned above, as they focus on the 'construction of the Other'. I am speaking here of creating a distance and a difference as a way of *self-*description. Interestingly enough, when Castells defines identity, he quotes Calhoun as saying: 'We know of no people without names, no languages or cultures in which some manner of *distinctions* between self and other, we and they, are not made . . . (my italics).[43] In the beginning there was a distinction.

This process of calling attention to distinctions has sometimes been called a negativity (what we are not), or a game of internal difference, in contrast to 'true

---

[38] This dimension in urban studies refers to the treatment of immigrants; it is not, however, the context that I evoke here.

[39] Corbey and Leerssen, 1991: xii. The anthology edited by these two scholars, *Alterity, Identity, Image. Selves and Others in Society and Scholarship*, is an excellent example of this school of thought.   [40] Ibid: xi.

[41] Taussig, 1993.

[42] Gabriel Tarde, 'Les monades et les sciences sociales', 1893, as quoted and translated by Bruno Latour, 2001.   [43] Castells, 1997: 6.

alterity,' that of the Other.[44] In terms of Gilles Deleuze's anti-Hegelian project, influenced by Tarde, it could be said that negativity is the last point on the identity continuum constituted by The Same, The Similar, The Analogous and The Opposed, and needs to be distinguished from the 'affirmation of difference'.[45] For the Foucauldians, negativity is uninteresting in the face of the 'true', irremediable alterity, which, however, cannot concern oneself. For the post-Hegelians it is but further proof of the incorporation, of a harmonizing removal of differences in the process of identity formation. While Deleuze is criticizing philosophy's unreflective subordination of difference to identity in order to focus on difference as such, I would like to show examples of intentional subordination of difference to identity and also affirmations of difference, in the city management discourse.

In the examples above, the Other was poorly constructed: cities were constructing their own difference for which the Other was but a foil. The representation work consisted of a constant mix of identification, negation, and differentiation. While the Other might be constructed in this process, it was often no more than a prop that was amorphous and shifting in adaptation to the creation of the City. I am not evoking here the Freudian and Tardean idea of 'the Other within', but trying to shed light on the construction of 'we are different', of one's own alterity.

While the simultaneous presence of exclusion–inclusion movements have been acknowledged before, the simultaneous construction of the identity and alterity of such collective images as the 'city' and the 'city management' requires attention. The need to distinguish between the two is justified by the different places they occupy in different attempts at construction of an image. Thus, if a text or a living discourse focuses on the cultural alterity of immigrants living in Sweden, the creation of 'Swedishness' thus obtained is implicit; it is a by-product of the construction of the Other. The text *attributes* difference. The opposite can be said of a text or a discourse aimed at discerning the 'Swedish identity'. The images of the Other are secondary to its main aim, they are its by-products. The text *affirms* difference. While the attribution of difference has received much attention in recent social science writings, the affirmation of difference has not. What they have in common is an interest in others that conceals an interest in oneself, but they differ in the ways they proceed.

Another distinction is that between opposition (as a degree of sameness) and alterity (as an affirmation of difference): Stockholm is different from Oslo in a different way than it is different from Korpilombo. Even more distinctly, Warsaw and Rome are 'unique'. They differ from any other city; no image of the Other is necessary. Thus, instead of the exclusion–inclusion dimension, which describes operations performed on the Other, we can have two dimensions describing operations on a Self: an identity scale as sketched by Deleuze (same–similar–analogous–opposite) and an alterity dimension that extends from the unique (different from anything) through various degrees of difference to 'minimal difference' – to identity. Therefore, it is not the alterity of the Other but the alterity of the Self.

---

[44] Zahavi, 1999: 196.   [45] Deleuze, 1968/1997: 265.

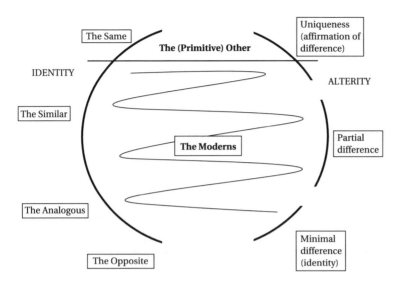

Fig. 2.1. The identity–alterity interplay

Let me illustrate my reasoning with Fig. 2.1, where identity and alterity are two dimensions (the alterity dimension is non-continuous).

Although The Same can be seen as an ideal on the identity continuum, it is not so. It is only The Primitive who returns to The Same, and therefore does not progress.[46] The Savage Other imitates and The Moderns emulate. One can thus portray the identity–alterity dimensions as a circle, the larger part of which the Moderns have reserved for themselves. The Primitive Others are supposed to remain at the extremes: they repeat themselves, and they are unlike anybody else. The Moderns are free to engage in the identity–alterity interplay in many diverse fashions.

My examples tell a different story, however. The whole field is open to everybody, even if fashion might prefer some modes and some kinds of interplay; The Primitive Other is but an invention to be used in the interplay.

Why does an already complex picture require an additional dimension? As this is not a philosophical project but a social science project, I would like to suggest that the subordination of identity to alterity or vice versa is a local and historical phenomenon. One can venture that the cities under study, and most of the social sciences, subordinate alterity to identity, at least partially due to the Americanization of the media. But this was not always and not everywhere the case. Tarde, speaking at the turn of the previous century, was perhaps aware that alterity would one day vanish, as one of the victims of globalization. But because globalization is always met with resistance, the alterity moves have never vanished completely.

---

[46] de Certeau, 1975/1988.

Bringing them to light can therefore aid in the interpretation of phenomena that are puzzling in terms of identity only, as they were puzzling to me in my studies of the three cities. This is why I traced the representation work: because it left marks in inscriptions, texts, pictures, artifacts, and action patterns that are the objects and content of city management.

THE PARADOXES OF REPRESENTATION WORK

Localization: Constructing Identity and Alterity

The interplay of identity and alterity work was visible in every example above. One could claim that such an interplay was explicitly demanded. As Orvar Löfgren pointed out, contemporary norms prescribing how identities – national, regional, local – should be built, include a somewhat paradoxical requirement that it should be built around the image of uniqueness.[47]

Thus, Rome is comparable to Athens because it is a cultural capital, but Athens is a city with many problems and no solutions.[48] London is the model of privatized municipal services, but its citizens do not enjoy the ancient cultural heritage of Rome. Berlin has a model traffic system with the railway at its center, but German cities are over-organized, and the charm of Rome lies partly in its anarchy. Two Italian cities were often mentioned for two opposite reasons: Milan for its reputation as a well-organized city, and Naples for being an old Mediterranean city (thus useful for identification), which, until recently, was the epitome of disorder (thus useful for differentiation). The recent improvements in Naples' management were dismissed, for they made the alterity work more difficult. In this way, the images of other cities become fragmented, however, and appropriate and still recognizable fragments are used to construct the images of both an ideal and a horror city, to provide a contrast.

It was not always cities that supplied images: in the case of preparations for the Jubilee and for the Cultural Capital year, the reference points were great events. The Olympic Games in Atlanta were considered a negative example in Rome. Stockholm chose to follow the example of Glasgow and Copenhagen, but not of Antwerp. In most cases, however, the alterity construction was subordinated to the identity construction; in Deleuze's terms, the negative examples form the Opposite, which is the extreme end of the identity continuum, but remain within it. The cities (or actions within the management net) differ, but on the same dimension.

An interesting example of the identity and alterity work is to be found in a frequent comparison between Rome and Barcelona. Barcelona was a model to

---

[47] Löfgren, 1993.
[48] Rome, albeit ancient Rome, seems to be the model for Moscow (Boym, 2001; Groys, 2001).

imitate – not as a city, but as a case of transformation: from a pre-modern to a late modern city. The managers in Rome did not want their city to become another Barcelona, but they wanted the same managerial success that their counterparts in Barcelona enjoyed. Guje Sevón called this phenomenon, after René Girard, the *imitation of desire*.[49] The ambiguity of such an imitation resulting from the simultaneity of the identity and alterity work is well exemplified in the following quotes:

> ... everybody is talking about the [architectonic] reconstruction of Barcelona. The city was practically transformed by Mayor Maragall, but one needs to remember that he was given a powerful mandate and precise instructions: this was to be de-centered city, developed in a synergy with economic actors, etc. Having this, you can really transform a city, you can truly start a radical renewal. Whether this is a replicable model I wouldn't know ... I am sure it has a strong local value, but that the experiences from Barcelona, or for that matter Paris, can be transported to Rome, is a doubtful proposition. (Rome, Interview 4: 12–13)

> Tomorrow I am going to Barcelona to see how they work over there. I have an enormous respect for the Spaniards, who at present reveal a truly innovative capacity, practically unlimited, in the positive sense of the word. In my view, we Italians have a tendency to keep to ourselves. Take an example: in Spain they follow the fashion, but reflect upon it. They take great care to cultivate relations between the public administration and the private industry; whereas we sell out everything we can because 'the public administration is horrible'. (Rome, Interview 10: 5–6)

Thus, two managers in Rome would like to transform the city management as it was done in Barcelona, but do not believe – for opposite reasons – that it can go the same way. In Deleuzian terms, they located themselves on another point of the identity continuum – that of 'The Analogous'.

But alterity was not only an aid in identity construction. In the case of Stockholm, there was also an affirmation of difference: Stockholm is the only truly Nordic and truly big city; Stockholm combines, in unique ways, the continental and Scandinavian traditions; Stockholm is the only capital situated both at the sea and on a lake; Stockholm is different ... But in romantic terms, Stockholm is also the Venice of the North. In terms of management, Amsterdam, as another city on water, was Stockholm's counterpart. The identity construction used The Similar and The Opposite (in the case of London it was the wrongly built CityNet) positions on the identity dimension.

---

[49] Sevón, 1996. It is Gabriel Tarde who suggested that there are two kinds of imitation: imitation of belief and imitation of desire.

The 'uniqueness of Warsaw' was a topic to which the interviewees often returned. Warsaw is different from all other cities in Poland, because it is a capital; because after the war it was dealt with by a special Decree; because in 1990 it was exempted from the Local Government Law. Warsaw is different from any western European capital because it has a different history; it is different from any eastern European capital because it has a different geopolitical position. Warsaw, in short, is different, and the affirmation of its difference dominated the city image. The identity moves were usually located on the Opposite point and consisted of politically incorrect negations such as 'not in Africa' and 'unlike Tirana'. The Warsaw management had identity problems: a city unlike any other cannot legitimatize its actions by following the examples of others. An image built only on alterity is an unclear image. The 'decisive difference' – the one that supposedly determines the result of any market competition – must allow placement on a common dimension. It can be: Similar, Analogous, Opposite, but on the same scale.

The city councilors and managers in all the three capitals seemed to share at least one idea – the notion that there is a universally (where Europe stands for the universe) shared model of how a big or a capital European city ought to be run. An examination of such models shows, however, that although there were some common traits, many of the elements were different. There is no doubt that these models are developed through communication between different times and localities. The images and ideas travel from place to place, from time to time, incessantly. When they take root, however, they are translated into a local version. The resulting differences are in themselves expressions for the specificity of a time or place and the peculiarities of travel.

There was, however, a common repertoire, and although local actors did not use all of its elements, they were both the users and producers of such a repertoire. All the elements constituting the model of the modern city in Warsaw would have been recognized in Stockholm, but as belonging to the past. The Warsaw model was, in fact, constructed from old images of successful European cities. Warsaw has recently restored its ties to western Europe, and at the beginning of this new phase of communication, it has simply activated images that arrived from the West the last time around – in the 1930s.

Neither the transmission nor the construction of identity and alterity is an activity that ever stops. The elements of the image of a big European city of the twenty-first century as perceived in Stockholm – the information network as the new infrastructure, spectacle production, and the green city – were not unheard of in Warsaw, but they still occupied the margin. Warsaw's specificity will render these elements somewhat difficult to incorporate; perhaps a time lag will exist for some time, which in itself might produce new standards and new images. There is nothing that Stockholm could teach about spectacles to Rome, but there is quite a lot about the IT nets. Such an exchange could take place, however, only with contact. Alas, Stockholm, not being one of the leading European capitals, is a white spot on Rome's map of the world.

Globalization: What Models Were on Display?

Although all cities produce their own representations and do their best to propagate them, the fate of such images differs and is only marginally influenced by
the quality of the image or the intensity of the popularizing efforts. The images
must be produced and circulated, but a belief in a possibility of their 'arriving
intact' to a target can only lead to frustration. As we can see, what creates differences among people and organizations are not the images that are sent but those
that are in use, and use denotes a constant (re)construction – truly a work of
re-presentation. Such images in use are always composites of the various images
in circulation, with some elements that are invented – or at least untraceable to a
concrete source. Although it is frustrating to image producers, they must accept
that there is an enormous gap between the production and use, between projec-
tion and reciprocation: a gap in time and space filled with acts of translation.
Stockholm, for example, wishes to be a model of water management and invests
in its image of a City on Water. When I mentioned this to my interlocutors in ACEA,
not only did they fail to recognize the image, they were practically offended by the
idea that anybody could show Rome how to manage its water. They had been
managing it successfully for a thousand years, and were, in fact, planning to men-
tor Tunis. My interlocutors in Warsaw, on the other hand, knew about Stockholm's
ambitions, but were more interested in the Danish and German cities.

Also, a city might acquire an image without any intentional activity because it has
been primarily constructed by others. Warsaw and Rome have traffic problems, and
look to Berlin for solutions. It is not Berlin, but the followers of Berlin who have constructed it as a model. Image construction means more than the active attitude of a
receiver, for receivers do the representation work themselves. They are quite capable of inventing the messages that senders might graciously admit or deny. But this
invention and construction does not happen randomly and in a void.

A historical contingency might have a decisive hand in globalizing a local practice. At the time of this study, the hallmark of city management in Warsaw and
Rome was emergency management, which seemed to be an automorphic sediment, anachronistic in the present times. After September 11, 2001, emergency
management might become the major preoccupation of big cities. I am not
saying that Rome or Warsaw will become leading models for it, but most certainly
a practice that seemed ephemeral or on its way to be eradicated will return to the
center of attention of city managers.

The organization of the Jubilee in Rome was an interesting case. On the surface, this was an event that seemed to be typically local, and not even organized
predominantly by the city managers. Nevertheless, there have been many
attempts to make it translocal (and also transchronic). The Jubilee exemplifies
the variety of uses to which an image can be put.[50] Obviously, it had an important

---

[50] For other examples of using events for the organizing and marketing of a city, see
Kociatkiewicz and Kostera (2001) and Mazza (2001).

function internally: the city authorities wished to convince the inhabitants to adopt a positive attitude toward the event. At the same time, this positive image could be used in a straightforward marketing of the city. The image, however different from those produced by the other cities, shares a common trait with the other two: whether by design or by default, it is kaleidoscopic, mobile, polysemic. Such a fragmentation and the collage-like character of the construction of models, anti-models, and city images appears to be a true sign of the representation work of present times.

I have, thus, sketched the contours of an organization field – that of the big city management, to which all three cities belong. Concrete experiences in the field become abstracted and thus universalized, circulated as images, then picked up, interpreted, and translated into local versions. The field has its own collection of past and present images, its repertoire of models – assembly parts for representation work – and its fashion leaders.

In Chapter 3, the focus will shift to the differences between the ways in which similar kinds of events are symbolically elaborated and thus produced.

3

Traffic and Transport, or the Difficulties of Reframing

In the contemporary world, other mass media also serve the function of town crier, but particularly in today's Italy, newspapers remain the medium with the broadest coverage of community affairs.[1]

Newspapers were, in fact, the city criers in the three cities that I studied. In Sweden, almost every citizen subscribes to at least one daily newspaper. Although the Polish journalistic tradition has often been severely interrupted during the past two centuries, the mass media in Poland, including newspapers, quickly readjusted to the new political situation after 1989, and began to cover community affairs very thoroughly indeed. And true to Robert Putnam's word, Italian journalism flourishes unabatedly, especially in its capital. *Il Messagero* is a Roman daily; and nationwide *La Repubblica* and *Corriere della Sera* have their Roman supplements.

Traffic is certainly among the most popular topics in the three cities I studied, as reflected in the newspaper coverage. Therefore, I decided to re-present traffic management through its media representation. The counterparts of the Roman dailies are at present *Gazeta Stoleczna* and *Zycie Warszawy* in Warsaw, and *Svenska Dagbladet* and *Dagens Nyheter* in Stockholm. The coverage of traffic problems in other newspapers in the respective capitals are also quoted.

One obvious way to keep up with the ideal of a modern city is to modernize its traffic system. In the case of Warsaw, it was a matter of subway construction; whereas Rome, which built its subway in very dramatic circumstances not long ago, was involved in the introduction of the rapid tram. Although the actual traffic developments in these two cities were obviously embedded in the local situation, they shared two similar features: the unavoidable conflagration of practical (technical), political, and symbolic aspects of traffic handling; and the role of the mass media, which took a vivid interest in the negative side of the process. This

---

[1] Putnam, 1993: 92.

approach is contrasted with the relaxed attitude of the Stockholm press, where matters of public transportation do not cause much emotion, even if the issues of traffic, in general, do.

A concept that permits a better insight into these differences is a *frame*:[2] a contextualization of an event or an interaction that suggests a sensible interpretation (sensemaking) by connecting it to a wider context. It is important, however, not to see a frame as something static or 'out there', as an object like a picture frame. Although Goffman sometimes used the term in inconsequent ways, he intended it mainly in the sense used in film and photography. A frame is thus a result, sometimes repetitive but sometimes fleeting, of the process of 'framing'. A certain way of framing can be characteristic of a given photographer or film director, but also of a certain period or place. I use the term, writ large, to speak of framing and reframing a public discourse. Accordingly, the Warsaw story presents a series of reframing acts that took place over a long period; the story of Rome is about a frame that got stuck; and the Stockholm story tells of framing that supports rather than obstructs organizing efforts.

WARSAW: THE METRO IS A CARRIER BETWEEN THE PAST AND THE FUTURE

As explained in Chapter 2, Warsaw was attempting to control its traffic and improve its public transport in many ways, but the subway was, at the time of the study, and still is, the focus of everyone's attention. On April 14, 1995, Warsaw's first subway line, connecting the southern suburb of Ursynow with the Polytechnic (situated near but not quite in the city center) was put into service, on the twelfth anniversary of the day on which its construction had officially begun.[3] The line was 12 km long, and it has been said that the easiest way to summarize the history of the metro's construction was: a billion zloty[4] per kilometer per year.

An Underground, Not-Quite-Existing Fact

One could say that Warsaw's transportation problems in general, and the Metro's problems in particular, could be reduced to a lack of money. Although nobody can deny that, it would be a truly simplistic explanation. The difficulties were not limited to a lack of funds or even to Warsaw's sandy soil. The Metro – with its

---

[2] Goffman, 1974, borrowed the term from Gregory Bateson, 1959.

[3] The first station in the center was opened in 1997, the second in 2000. The construction of the line continues in a northerly direction.

[4] The 1994 budget allocated $423 million for the metro construction. When sums of money were mentioned for rhetorical effect by the interlocutors, they were expressed in Polish zloty. The effect is purely rhetorical because the Polish currency fluctuated wildly during the period of the metro construction.

double meaning of the actual subway (metro) and the organization involved in its construction (Metro) – was embedded in a solid historical and political context. To understand the 1994 situation of both the subway and its constructors, it is necessary to go back in time, maybe not as far as 1927, when the work on the project began and was interrupted by the depression, or to 1939, when the trial drilling was interrupted by the Second World War, but certainly to the beginning of the postwar period. A survey of the press during 1949–81 proved to be an interesting journey into the past.

> *Express Wieczorny*, April 16, 1949
> With a subway running under the Vistula, we will soon travel from Wola to Praga.[5] The year 1955 will be one of great conquests, and completion of the subway will certainly not count among the least important achievements of the 6-Year Plan.

The year 1955 was not a year of great conquests. No subway appeared, but an explanation did emerge:

> *Stolica*, August 5, 1956
> **Metro – the key to the situation?**
> There was a time when a title like the one above would be accepted without question or comment. If one spoke of Warsaw's transportation problems, the subway was first on the list.
>   The subway was supposed to be the spine of the Warsaw transportation system and quite soon at that – in 1956. . . .
> **'There isn't . . . and there won't be?!'**
> The disappearance has been sudden but total. The metro suddenly does not exist anymore, even as a philological concept. The word cannot appear in print under any circumstances. A senseless 'suppression' of a very public matter had to produce very definite results. The first result concerns the urbanists who noticed that there is no metro and have drawn constructive conclusions. Tearfully, but the decision had to be made; a tram line has to be built along the south–north axis, with roads being turned up and parks in Independence Avenue being partially destroyed. An annoying but necessary decision.
>   The second result is the public opinion of Warsaw, with its typical sarcasm: 'There isn't any . . . and there won't be any'. . . Let's dig through a jungle of gossip, a natural consequence of stamping a seal over a matter that concerns everybody. How did this happen? Why, all of a sudden and for no apparent reason, was the metro pushed into the realm of the 'unmentionable'?
>   Let's go back about twenty years, when the idea of an underground train had already appeared here and there and was being considered, at least theoretically. I remember a conversation with the then-Director of the Geology Institute, Prof. Morozewicz. If I am not mistaken, the professor described the issue as following: . . .

---

[5] A northern and a southern district of Warsaw.

Here, the author of the article explicates the so-called quicksand theory according to which there is nothing but a mixture of sand and water underneath the city, forcing the construction of a more expensive 'deep subway'. After Piotr Jaroszewicz's retirement from the post of Prime Minister, he claimed in his memoirs that the quicksand had been a cover-up for the fact that a deep subway had been demanded by the Soviet Union, so that it could function as a bomb shelter and a means of underground army transport in case of war. This is why the first line was to have run beneath the Vistula, from the East to the West, and not, as discussed in the years before and after the under-river plan, from the South to the North. The metro, like many other investments of the 6-Year Plan, was deleted from the priority list during the Korean War, which had required unanticipated armament expenditures.

The article quoted above ended with the conclusion that there was no cause for shame; there was nothing to hide. There was simply too little money, and the work had to be delayed. It was delayed for the day when costs were reduced through new, inexpensive technologies, but never halted. There is no need to add that this pious wish remained a wish: everything cost, as might be expected, more than planned.

For many years the press was silent on the metro-related issues. In 1980 there was only one article, but then, in 1981, Metro Headquarters collected 63 press clippings, plus one satirical design. The clippings focused on two issues: that Warsaw was one of the few cities with a population exceeding one million that did not have a subway system, and that the subway protects people from bad weather conditions. (The notorious malfunctioning of the surface transport system made the long waits at bus stops one of the biggest complaints of passengers.) A review of the titles of these articles is the simplest way to re-tell the 1981 debate. It is recommended that the headings be read as one story; that is, the extreme right column should be read downwards.

Date	Newspaper	Headings
10/01	*Express Wieczorny*	Metro – Warsaw's necessity.
27/01	*Nasza Trybuna*	The price of delay in metro construction.
26/02	*Zycie Warszawy*	Ultimatum ('no matter what the costs, we are doomed to the metro').
2/03	*Slowo Powszechne*	Begin subway construction now!
3/03	*Trybuna Mazowiecka*	We have to wait for the metro. By tram to the new Warsaw districts.
20–22/03	*Sztandar Mlodych*	Metro free of myths (Turnpikes Construction Headquarters Director: 'It isn't impossible to start subway construction now').
27/03	*Zycie Warszawy*	By metro – without pollution.
2/04	*Express Wieczorny*	Quicksand isn't an obstacle for the construction – especially

Date	Newspaper	Headings
		as there is none (an interview with a Professor from Warsaw Polytechnics).
21/04	*Zycie Warszawy*	It will start in 1984 at the latest! Waiting for the decision about the Metro.
4/05	*Trybuna Ludu*	Metro – the expensive delay.
7/05	*Slowo Powszechne*	The Warsaw metro question – is 25 billion zl a lot or a little?
10/05	*Stolica*	Subway in Warsaw.
17/05	*Stolica*	In whose hands lies the future of the capital?
20/05	*Trybuna Mazowiecka*	The irreversible metro construction.
25/05	*Trybuna Mazowiecka, Zycie Warszawy, Trybuna Ludu, Kurier Polski*	City executives received by Prime Minister W. Jaruzelski: 'Only a subway can effectively relieve the capital's transportation problems' 'The entrance to the metro leads through the Prime Minister's cabinet'.
26/05	*Kurier Polski* *Zycie Warszawy*	Can we afford this? Billions lost without the metro. What have we got? Before the subway construction.
27/05	*Zycie Warszawy*	Are we really ready for subway construction?
28/05	*Express Wieczorny*	In a month, the government decides about the fate of the metro.
24/06	*Kurier Polski*	The subway goes fast – on the draftsmen's desks. Waiting for the government's decision.
10–11/07	*Kurier Polski* *Express Wieczorny*	The metro is waiting for the green light. Socialist renewal is a necessary condition for getting out of the crisis . . . one important task is the construction of the metro.
27/07	*Slowo Powszechne*	The metro is making a career.
30/07	*Zycie Warszawy*	How will people commute to work if there is nothing to take them there? . . . Will the city transport survive the winter?
	Express Wieczorny	Alarm for municipal transportation.
5/08	*Slowo Powszechne*	Expanding paralysis of the city's nervous system. . . . Without the subway we can't even dream about decent travel through the city.
12/08	*Slowo Powszechne*	Will we remain without transportation? . . . Even talks about metro stopped.
	Trybuna Mazowiecka	The situation in the municipal transport system is getting worse . . . the assumption that transportation in the new parts of the city will be based on the subway was erroneous, too.
28/10	*Slowo Powszechne*	Municipal transportation the day before total collapse . . . Not a step forward without the metro

This was how the metro, accompanied by journalistic drums, was altered in status from a taboo to a top-ten press issue. In May, 1981, the frequency of press coverage increased, culminating in the disclosure of the project's patron, Mr. Jaruzelski. Shortly thereafter, a brief legitimizing prelude was played; three articles in a row began with a question, suggesting that the matter was being discussed from every side. It was at this point that someone coined the unfortunate phrase that came to define the construction of the metro as 'an important task in the continuation of the socialist renewal'. With a few exceptions, the tone of the articles was invariably positive, albeit sometimes apprehensive. The quicksand issue appeared and disappeared, just like the quicksand. Toward the end of August a different element entered the campaign – the bleak picture of the state of municipal transportation without the metro. It is difficult to imagine why, during peak vacation periods, the negative aspects of Warsaw's transportation were being so acutely felt – unless one interprets the response as a preparation for what was about to happen. In October, 1981, the Mayor of Warsaw and the Minister of Territory Administration and Environmental Protection requested that the Prime Minister make a decision about the metro. But on December 13, the day martial law was imposed in Poland, the metro, like many other matters, vanished as a top-ten press issue.

On January 25, 1982, Wojciech Jaruzelski delivered a speech in parliament where he said, in a rhetoric typical of the times:

> *Zycie Warszawy*, 26 January, 1982
> Working hard, we shall create the foundations of a better life. . . .
> More than half of society lives in cities. The level of the municipal structures, and especially the level of the municipal transportation, is low. Commuting to work is very tiresome and shortens people's leisure time. Steps are being taken to arrest deterioration of municipal transportation and then to improve it. Thanks to multilateral help from the Soviet Union, announced personally by comrade Brezhnew, the metro construction in Warsaw, among other things, will begin next year.

On May 14, 1982, the government presidium made the decision to begin preparatory work for the construction of the first line. On June 7, 1982, an agreement was signed between the governments of the USSR and the Polish People's Republic concerning 'the economic and technical cooperation for the construction of the first subway line in Warsaw'. But the population of Warsaw concluded that the metro was Jaruzelski's attempt to redeem martial law – and decided to take a dislike to it.

This short trip through four decades of the Warsaw Metro illustrates the ease with which the public discourse was reframed, when there was no requirement of anything but a political anchoring of a new frame. The press flicked through the frames, as in a kaleidoscope. In 1994 such an easy reframing was no longer possible. What is worse, the previous frames did not vanish with clicking. They were all simultaneously in place, and this was the reframing situation that the

Metro Headquarters – an organization I was visiting – had to face. The relations between Metro and the media were intense and not without problems; and the past played an important role.

> Director: Our norm here is to contact the press at least three times a week. We decided that we will not give up these contacts even though right now it's a difficult period. Although we're extremely busy with other stuff, we don't underestimate the press.
>
> BC: You don't have a press spokesperson?
>
> D: We used to have one. But it was during the times when contacts with the media were different, when TV used to show grain being beautifully harvested by combines in the sunny fields and cement plants and ironworks exceeding their production limits. Information in those days was about success: how many pales had been driven into the ground, how much cement was used. Now nobody is interested in things like that, just watch any American TV program: catastrophes, floods, saving people from fire, you see it several times a day. Successful results are talked about in different circumstances, as a part of technical programs that sum up results or something like that. (Warsaw, Observation 4/1)

The spectacular breakdowns and incidents were not the only aspect that the media emphasized in their coverage of the metro, but they were the main feature. After all, the spectacular is a basic principle underlying contemporary reporting, and we shall see more of it later. Metro was forced to learn that lesson at its own expense.

The Metro's public image was a key to understanding both the problems and the achievements in this particular action net. An important element of this image was the underground character of the metro.

Under and Above Ground

> The metro is a 12 km long object, and if we took it all 10 m above the ground, you would see what an enormous building it is. All this is hidden underground, and nobody realizes what is down there. That's why so many legends were created – about misappropriation, abuses, errors, deviations, Soviet influences, secret dictatorships, all those kinds of things. (Warsaw, Interview 1: 13)

It would seem that there is only hard reality underground: soil, machines, concrete, tunnels. But even 'nature', coming in contact with humans, becomes socialized and moves into the sphere of 'culture', acquiring symbolic and political characteristics.

Underground there was geology, technology, and ecology; above the ground there were property laws, construction laws, organization, ecology, and politics.

The point is not only that, as my interlocutor says above, fantasy replaces information. The issue of quicksand was brought into the action net, and mobilized or silenced according to the situation. It was presented one way in the political context and in a different way in the context of professional expertise. The quicksand was, however, a capricious and troublesome ally on the professional stage, for it was never certain where or even whether it existed. Perhaps that is why it was a perfectly suitable ally in the political and organizational contexts.

Metaphorically speaking, the color of the metro was important. The Metro Headquarters was often perceived as 'red' (that is, 'Communist'), whereas it would have liked to be perceived as 'green'. Metro realized that it had been conceived in a period that was not famous for responsiveness to environmental concerns, but it believed that it had, on its own, developed an extremely high degree of ecological sensitivity. Metro's pride lay in its ecological consciousness.

The metro as a threat to the environment has a history longer than 70 years. The metropolis was invariably considered to be hostile to nature. In her review of the sociological and urbanist literature and of belles-lettres writings on big cities, Rosalind Williams has demonstrated how the underground structures (*infra*structure, a structure that is below, underneath, or down), became a symbol of the unnatural that was equated with a big-city life style. At the beginning of the nineteenth century the sewage network was such a structure; at the beginning of the twentieth century, it was the metro.[6] The metro, short for 'metropolitan train', is the symbol of a modern city; small wonder it is treated with hostility by the promoters of both pre and postmodernism. The metro debate also takes place in the symbolic sphere: must Poland and Warsaw first catch up with modern times, or can they bypass the process and land directly in the new epoch?

Such disputes took place frequently in the media. The media also conveyed an image of the metro that was frequently set in a 'red' frame, which exasperated Metro. Alas, the metro cars were still imported from Russia.

The following fragment of an interview held in my presence by a journalist from the *Gazeta Wyborcza* is interesting, not only for the constantly returning issue of the metro's 'redness' but also because of the contrast between the interlocutors who represent two different generations:

> Journalist: Our newspaper is very different, it's very young and very American. That's the future of the press. Not like before. It doesn't surprise me that you didn't have self-government but that you couldn't write, for example, about the metro, right? The censor wouldn't let you. The problems close to life were forbidden.

[6] Williams, 1990.

Director: The force of propaganda is enormous. If you ask, 50 percent of the people asked will tell you that it is impossible to build a metro in Warsaw. It was not until [*the last Communist prime minister*] published his memoirs that people learned the true causes of why the construction of the metro was interrupted. The whole 6-Year Plan was completed except for the metro.

J: Yeah, it was built in Prague, and in Warsaw we had the Culture Palace instead of the metro.

D1: Rubbish. This is not true, this is all wrong! The Culture Palace was not built in the place of anything else. The 3-Year Plan of 1946–49 was completed and exceeded. The Cold War hadn't yet developed. The 6-Year Plan was very limited, but when the Korean War started, heavy industry was redirected entirely to military purposes.

J: That was paranoia; agriculture was completely destroyed . . .

D1: What's that now? What agriculture did they destroy? We might not have had modern agriculture, but we had agriculture. In Lithuania, for example, they would plow down an entire village and build a couple of housing projects in its place. Well, we digressed far from the metro. (Warsaw, Observation 4/4)

Paradoxically, the young journalist in this epoch of thought liberalization saw only one correct version of contemporary history, a solid black picture in which everything was wrong; while the older director tried to maintain a more diversified, checkered vision. The director also pointed out the specific logic of all institutional orders, which, apart from openly controlling and censoring the repertoire of permissible actions, almost automatically removes some prospects and retains others. For the sake of comparison, one could say that it would be as difficult at present to found a newspaper based on the Soviet tradition as it was then to plan a metro based on Parisian tradition.

Time, however, seemed to be working in favor of the metro. Even though no one was certain that it would ever become 'greener', its 'red' frame seemed to be fading month by month, especially as it emerged from the underground of legends and suppositions into the surface of everyday operations. It will certainly take a long time (measured not in months or years but in lines and stops) before the metro acquires the Varsovian color, whatever that will be.

During my stay at Metro, I was asked to comment on their problems and to suggest ways to solve them.[7] In my opinion, the most important was Metro's public image, which was negative in the past, but with the opportunity to recover when the subway began operation. But the frame of an 'image' that I used was not deemed appropriate for Polish management practice. It seemed too frivolous, even though, as my examples show, humor and self-irony were integral elements of the organizing process that I observed. Had I mentioned

[7] This comedy of errors is related in detail in Czarniawska, 2001.

'representation work', the directors would be appalled. They were there to inform, not to represent.

The Metro managers were actively involved in reframing and in representation work, but they didn't want to talk about it. Truth and reality were supposed to speak for themselves, with no need for re-presentations, metaphors, or frames. They were not alone in this belief, nor were they in the most difficult situation imaginable. To change one frame for another is difficult, but to discard a frame that is taken for granted seems impossible.

ROME: A WAR LANDSCAPE

In 1998, at the time of my study, Roman authorities were involved in a heroic effort to improve the traffic conditions by introducing a rapid tram track leading to the historical center, restructuring public transportation enterprises, reform-ing parking rules, deregulating the taxi market, and other measures. I followed the press coverage of traffic issues in Rome through 1998 and until the beginning of 1999, to see if 1998 was in any way exceptional. It was not. The leading story in the first part of the year was the story of the rapid tram: Unfortunate Tram No. 8. The second half of the year hosted, as the journalists used to say, a soap opera called a 'bus and taxi war'.[8] The same technique of reading – extreme right column downwards – is recommended.

Date	Newspaper	Headings
13/09	*La Repubblica*	From tomorrow an increase – of buses and of traffic police. The Autonomous Unions proclaim their first strike. **Everybody to school. Of traffic.**
14/09	*La Repubblica*	The anti-chaos plan and the road works connected with the Jubilee put to a harsh test. '**The collapse of traffic is imminent.**' The head of the traffic police sounds the alarm: 300 road works and 500 000 more pupils.
15/09	*La Repubblica*	The city jammed on the first school day. Romans can thank the Jubilee, striking buses and the upset unions. **Thank you for the chaos.** The Mayor angry, the traffic police defensive. '**The strikers can talk themselves to the Romans.**' Lines and road works, a day to forget. '**Even scooters in a mega-jam.**'
16/09	*Il Messaggero*	**Our daily hell. The city a hostage to coaches.** A new traffic jam: this time the epicenter is St. Peter's, invaded by 350

---

[8] Here, I am quoting the 'soap opera' metaphor from the Roman media. I have used it myself to highlight the similarity between TV series and developments in public administration (Czarniawska, 1997). One can say that art imitates life, but also that collective life imitates the forms learned from popular art. Private companies model their conduct on action series; while soap operas are the genre of the public sector. Each installment solves some problems and cre-ates many others, and the series survive their actors.

Date	Newspaper	Headings
		'bisons'. **War bulletin:** Two traffic officers attacked by a ferocious driver. One person faints because of smog.
17/09	*La Repubblica*	The Pope's audience on Wednesday: 4 hours of chaos: Task force: 350 persons against 500 tourist buses. **Coaches away!** Traffic police and technicians: 'Stay away from St. Peter's.' A suggestion for the Jubilee: hotel-trains for tourists on the stations. Buses and metro on strike.
18/09	*La Repubblica*	The Autonomous Unions announce a strike for the 1st and 2nd of October. The agenda behind clearly political. **Buses and metro, a trial of strength.** 'Throw Di Carlo[9] out – otherwise we will stop the city for two days.'
19/09	*La Repubblica*	Public transport at a turning point: Campidoglio[10] needs to make up its mind by the 15th of November. **ATAC and ATAC 2, last battle.** Di Carlo: we are ready to privatize tourist and suburb lines.
20/09	*Il Messagero*	Councilor Tocci and Director Di Carlo want to reward those who buy annual Metrebus cards. **ATAC, a revolution of fees.**
23/09	*Il Messagero*	The long silent Vice-Mayor in charge of the traffic speaks about the future: 'It is up to the Olive[11] to connect the Capital to the Country.' **Tocci: Rome must fight against union cartels.** There is a plan for coaches. ATAC tries to block the strikes.
26/09	*La Repubblica*	The street of Dolce Vita for the traffic for the festival of Roman song. No information, no alternative routes. **Via Veneto closed, the center of the city jammed.** Aleanza Nazionale [*an opposition party*] against ATAC: 'Consulting fees for nabobs.'
27/09	*La Repubblica*	A hot week for Roman transport: tomorrow a debate on ATAC in Campidoglio, Thursday and Friday strikes. **Re-bus.** 'Murderous routes, thousands called sick.' 'Victimized passengers, it is time to raise your voices.'
29/09	*Il Messagero*	Modernization of many bus stops to begin at the end of October. The disadvantages will be countered by buses going all the route. **After 22.00, everybody on foot: Metro Line A will close down. Reason: works on the new line.** The majority divided on the issue of transports, but at last the Communists sign a common agreement.
	La Repubblica	**Strike metro-bus.** Fighting to avoid the strike, the two left parties insult each other in the square. The iron hand of the Union. **ATAC, a wall against a wall. Municipality:** 'It is up to us to decide.'

[9] Di Carlo was then the CEO of the municipal company responsible for transport, called ATAC/COTRAL.   [10] City Hall in Rome.

[11] The Olive was, at that time, the ruling center-left coalition.

Date	Newspaper	Headings
30/09	*Il Messagero*	**There will be a strike, the city risks a chaos.** No more talks with the Union, tomorrow and the day after because come to a halt. More expensive tickets: by 2.000 lire. **Collision on the rails: Tram No. 8 blocked.** At viale Trastevere trams stopped at the traffic hour. ATAC: we shall demand the damage compensation.
2/10	*La Repubblica*	**Bad air.** Benzene alarm: the municipality must do something. **ATAC, the number of people calling in sick has doubled.** Buses and metro practically punctual: 682 drivers came to work.
	Il Messagero	**Striking fever.** Boom of sick personnel, ATAC, K.O. '**We have no time to pee on new routes.**' The committee Rome the Capital: 200 billion on its way, to be spent on the new line. **Metro C, the Council does 'pressing' on the Government.**
3/10	*La Repubblica*	The second day of the call-up, the second day of epidemics among the drivers of ATAC. Traffic in crisis. **The strike of the sick.** 747 drivers at home, 2100 routes cancelled. Mario Di Carlo, the CEO of ATAC-COTRAL, says he is 'horrified by this murderous joke'. '**Unions, enough of call-ups, now we shall see who is stronger.**'
4/10	*La Repubblica*	**Di Carlo, the war of the buses.** Public managers and citizen-customers. ATAC, yesterday a record of sick drivers. A new agreement signed in line with the understanding from July. **ATAC, a new pact with the employees.**
7/10	*La Repubblica*	ATAC prepared to redesign its network according to the plan of Berlin consultants. Everything will change in two years.[12] **Buses. The revolution.** Express lines, streets for special traffic, more routes. Beginning in January. Tocci: in this way I will stop the cars and the benzene. '**The flop of Tram No. 8 will never be repeated.**' Smog puts 800 people in hospitals every year. **Those who drive poison you, too.**
8/10	*Il Messaggero*	Collapse of public transport. Suing for 1200 billion, but only the company's lawyers will gain. **More legal suits than collections. Buses overwhelmed.** The CEO Di Carlo: 'The situation is very grave. The employees turned the company into a self-help enterprise.' **Paralysis ahead: even taxis are on strike.** The unions accept a referendum on the agreement, but Passion Week lies ahead. **Traffic helped by intelligent lights.**
9/10	*Il Messaggero*	**The Grand Turtle Award goes to buses.** Public transport slows down, Rome on last place in Italy: 13.8 km/hr. **Everybody stop: traffic police in demonstration, taxis and ATAC on strike.**
10/10	*La Repubblica*	Buses and taxis on strike, 8 days that can block Rome. **The ultimate of Black October.** 'The traffic kills us, and you call us

---

[12] It is practically superfluous to add that it has not.

Date	Newspaper	Headings
		rebels.' One group prepared to go on strike against Tocci's plan: **'Free tariffs and working hours? This is not New York.'** Rutelli: 'I will not close the center to two wheels.' **Coaches no, scooters yes.** Tourist buses away from St. Peter's, some deviations for hotels.
11/10	*La Repubblica*	On the eve of the union's uproar Municipality risks all and calls the users in. **What game does ATAC play?** 80 000 commuters against the announced strikes.
	Il Messaggero	**Di Carlo: 'Drivers, you are welcome to ATAC.'** The response of the CEO to the confirmation of the union strike: 'Go and manage the public transportation yourselves.' **Certain hell: tomorrow buses on strike.**
13/10	*La Repubblica*	Today and tomorrow the [Drivers'] Union stops public transport. It's taxis' turn on Thursday. **Immobile buses, everybody for themselves!** Yesterday on the Ring 10 km long line.
14/10	*Il Messaggero*	**Everybody stop.** Yesterday a traffic jam, today an encore and pilgrims arriving in two days. At St. Peter's, 400 bisons on march. **Wild cheers for a driver who decided to drive.** Passengers against strikers: 'Why do you want to humiliate us?'
	La Repubblica	**'Shame on you, you've blocked the city.'** The fury of Romans against the drivers: 'Watch out that we do not boycott you . . .'
15/10	*Il Messaggero*	**The morning awakes angry.** Strike, and therefore everybody in line, passionately. 30 km long line at dawn. Other cities cheer: 'Keep on ATAC; do not give up.' **And yet we move, knowing the art of how to make the best of the worst.** The government departments have more people at work than usual, few absences in banks and hospitals. The shop owners cry bitter tears.
	La Repubblica	**'We might be ill-behaved and privileged, but we have a right to strike.'** The leader of the taxis against the Traffic Councilor. A truly iron hand. And the Romans? Let's hope they will manage . . . **A holy war for free taxis.**
16/10	*Il Sole-24 Ore*	The Council accepts the bill that deregulates tariffs and working hours. **Roman taxis in competition.** But the war explodes immediately after and the agreement is frozen. Hot front even for buses and metro.
	La Repubblica	Paralysis in center and battles in Campidoglio. The taxi drivers withdraw and apologize: 'We will pay for the damages.' **Taxis, throwing bottles and insults. Tocci stops, strikes suspended.** Today a trial of a new procedure with 400 coaches from Poland. **Motor-coaches away from St. Peter's.** Revolution for pilgrims, they have to stop at Olympic Stadium and at Villa Farnesina.
17/10	*La Repubblica*	**Rutelli insists: 'Free taxis'.** Tocci: the bill goes ahead. Taxi drivers: we will be back to the streets. **The anti-coach plan has**

Date	Newspaper	Headings
	Il Messaggero	**failed: the beasts defy the prohibition**. In spite of the promises, also this time the buses with pilgrims arrived at St. Peter's. **Public transport flunked**. The citizens condemn both the strikes and the quality of services. **June '99**: Scooters, your black cloud will become illegal.
20/10	*Il Messaggero*	**Fake stripes**. A parking meter? There is one, but invisible. **Thursday, new taxi strike. Friday, perhaps a new march on Rome**. The inhabitants protest against the invasion of coaches: 'We asked an audience with the Pope.'
21/10	*Il Messaggero*	The protest: 'We are ready for anything.' Tomorrow an attempt to mediate. **The taxis prepare for a march on Rome.**
22/10	*Il Messaggero*	**They demand money: arrests among traffic police**. Corruption and fraud, many uniforms tainted. **CEO Di Carlo: 'Taxi drivers? I don't give a damn...'** A joking duel: 'You will stop the rapid Tram No. 8 with your cars? Careful, the 8 has powerful buffers.'
23/10	*La Repubblica*	The unions announce two more strikes (12 and 13 November). **Hard-headed ATAC: hunger strike.**
24/10	*La Repubblica*	No problems for a protest demonstration of 6000 cars that will part for their job places at the same time. **The taxi drivers all in the streets, while their leader negotiates**. Last suggestions on Monday but the strike goes on. **Traffic, a No-Front.** An opposition against Tocci's plan stabilizes.
25/10	*La Repubblica*	The Court takes a hard line: open an investigation into the fights at Campidoglio. **300 charged taxi drivers risk losing their license**. Tomorrow the Council will discuss the deregulation bill. Augello: 'Tocci is like Pol Pot.' **Free taxis, the Right constructs the barricades.**
26/10	*La Repubblica*	**Taxi, strike with your family**. Taxi drivers immobile for 24 hours. 'Charged? We will demonstrate with our wives and children.' **Catch at Metro A: 351 'free riders' caught**. At Piazza di Spagna, every minute revealed more than two 'irregular' passengers, including a nun. **An electronic card to enter a vehicle**. It will have the data of its possessor in memory.
27/10	*Il Messaggero*	**Taxi, strike until Thursday**. The bill returns to the Council's table in two days, in the meantime the drivers go on foot. **A puddle of spilt diesel jams the circulation at Piazza Venezia.** ATAC-COTRAL campaign against the graffiti painters: an experiment in 5 subway stations. **'You smear? We clean in 48 hrs.'** In two days a torchlight procession against benzene. See you at Fori Imperiali.
28/10	*La Repubblica*	**In Rome, even wild taxis are against deregulation**. Six strikes in two weeks. **Taxi therapy**. 'Dialogue yes, vandals no.' Rutelli prepared to talk.

Date	Newspaper	Headings
29/10	*La Repubblica*	Fini[*an opposition politician*]**encourages taxi drivers: 'We will beat the Mayor yet.' Taxi, two other strikes**. But the Minister is on the side of the Mayor.
	Il Messaggero	**Taxi, an endless strike**. Taxi drivers stop on the 2nd and the 5th of November. But Treu [*the Minister*] will follow Rutelli's line. **And the polluted people will take to the streets.**
30/10	*La Repubblica*	**The No-Front**. Taxi drivers, tram drivers and traffic police demonstrate. **New strike on Monday, after a blockade. Tocci speaks, the Polo** [*an opposition party*] **joins the taxi drivers**. Central Station, Airport, Piazza Venezia: another day out of hell for travelers, tourists, and Romans. **'This city is a mishap . . .'** After the criticisms of *New York Times*, the Municipality shows its data: 'Horrible parents'. **'One in five children uses a scooter.'**
31/10	*La Repubblica*	A counterattack from Campidoglio: 'The No-Front does not exist. I have Romans on my side and in two weeks all will be done. **'Charming Mayor no more'**. Rutelli: 'Fini? He is in crisis and he's found himself a place to rest'. Tocci exits (alive) from the lions' den – ATAC. Taxi drivers change their minds: no strike on the 2nd. **'I am going to win this battle.'** Rutelli the day after: 'I am going ahead no matter that some make noise.'
1/11	*La Repubblica*	**'Dear Rutelli, we are going to win.' The Front of No challenges the Mayor**. Carlo Bologna (taxi drivers): 'We are ready to die in this battle.' Bruno Perroni (trams): 'Our answer? Strike.' Mauro Cordova (traffic police): 'He wants a war? We are ready.'
3/11	*La Repubblica*	The reform approved in Campidoglio: never-ending comments from Polo, torches in the square. **Taxi drivers, the first divisions**. Taxi union [1]: strike to the bitter end. Taxi union [2]: let's wait. **To be able to distribute more driving permits Tocci appeals to a 'collective'**: The bill on the taxis does not limit the freedom of the taxi drivers, but offers it to everybody.
4/11	*La Repubblica*	**Taxi, the final iron hand**. The tough unionists: 'If we do not reach an agreement the strikes will recommence.'
5/11	*Il Messaggero*	**Taxi drivers, strike-breakers get a beating**. The 'tough front' punishes those who do not strike: punches, flat tires, and requisition of receipts. **Public cars in service? Tocci negotiates. Bus.** Suppressed routes. **San Lorenzo protests with an 'invisible' Barrera: 'Traffic officers, join the citizens.'** But 54 municipal cars are in traffic 'illegally'.
6/11	*La Repubblica*	Break of negotiations: the accusation of the Vice-Mayor and the response of Fini. **It is a taxi-war**[*Eng. in original*]**, and the strike goes on.**
7/11	*La Repubblica*	**COTRAL, the buses separate from subway and trains.** The 'rough' taxi drivers threaten the Vice-Mayor. **'Tocci, get yourself bodyguards.'** The debut of the African taxi-driver.

Date	Newspaper	Headings
		Traffic plan according to the Greens: 'On Sundays, in the center only the buses and service cars.'
8/11	*La Repubblica*	**The traffic disease.** Four days without taxis, two without buses and metro. **Rifondazione**[*an opposition party*] **on the streets together with tram drivers.** Two other opposition parties join the 'rebelling' drivers of buses and subway cars. Tocci to taxi drivers 'Come back to the table. **I will explain to you the advantages of a deregulated taxi driver.'**
10/11	*La Repubblica*	**The No-Front divided.** Bus drivers tired of striking. Among taxi drivers, the toughs win. 'To Rome from all the rest of Italy'. **The reforms to be explained to the city. The No-Front seduces the Romans. Survey on traffic: traffic officers, tram and taxi drivers win over the city government.** But some people say: 'Bravo Tocci'.
	Il Sole-24 Ore	**Taxi and buses, Rutelli holds a hard line.** The head of traffic police prevents the blocking of buses, but the unions promise a stop next week.
	Il Messaggero	**Strike emergency.** Blocked airports, motionless taxis in Rome.
11/11	*La Repubblica*	**Black November in transports.** A chain of protests. But in Rome the taxi drivers are divided. '**Stop the strikes.**' The Association of Trade Unions: 'Enough of strikes, this is a dirty battle.' **A march forward to Rome or a step back?** 'Taxi drivers from all over Italy unite.' And then perhaps not. **The 'toughies' threaten.** 'They even refuse to drive the handicapped.' Transport, open way for companies, but subway remains with the municipality.
12/11	*La Repubblica*	The new line will serve half a million commuters. Cost: almost a thousand billion. Start: after the Jubilee. **In 2005, the metro will reach Aniene.** The day of the taxi: 25 000 in procession, the Council votes. Tram SuperEight jammed again. **Fini on the board of a subway: 'Visibly worsened.'** The drivers' union cancels the strikes: 'Rutelli is now committed.' **Buses and subway, the peace breaks out. Taxis, the charge of the inflexibles.** The leader: 'This is a war.' The mayors of other big cities express their solidarity with Rutelli.
13/11	*La Repubblica*	**The taxis sequestrate the cities.** A non-stop night in Campidoglio.
	Il Messaggero	**The taxis come back after their siege at Campidoglio.** The heart of the city blocked by protesters. But as of today the public cars in service again. **'Strike', is the explanation to foreigners. And they pay.** . . . The tourists in the hands of car rentals and black taxis: a fare from the airport to the center can cost as much as $100.
14/11	*La Repubblica*	**Long night.** The taxi drivers fall asleep at dawn and afterwards everybody claims to have won.

Date	Newspaper	Headings
15/11	*La Repubblica*	**Metrebus, the 'clients' start to rebel**. Traffic, an acid critique from the *Independent*.
16/11	*La Repubblica*	**'Bus people, help us.'** Di Carlo: new vehicles and reserved lanes. **On the stage: furious passengers.**
17/11	*La Repubblica*	**Bus obstructed, ATAC claims damages.**
18/11	*La Repubblica*	An assembly of traffic police causes a traffic jam. **Buses, an ultimatum from the drivers**. 'Change the agreement if no we stop.' Di Carlo asks them for a talk. Union 2: we would work anyhow to not punish the users. **'Strikes in public services must show solidarity.'**
20/11	*La Repubblica*	Buses, a new ultimatum from Union 1. **'Rutelli talk to us or strike.'** First meeting with the taxi drivers. **Tocci extends his hand but no apologies.**
24/11	*La Repubblica*	**Cease fire with buses at the end, two new strikes.** Rutelli's mediation not enough for the drivers.
27/11	*La Repubblica*	**Taxi drivers divided as to counterpropositions.** Councilor Tocci tries to mediate between different unions but finally postpones the whole thing.
28/11	*La Repubblica*	**Payday intoxication and traffic jams.** Blocks, queues and smog, with rain as an accomplice.
2/12	*Il Messaggero*	**Center and suburbs, a war about buses.** 'The first ring blocks 'our' jumbos; dangerous vibrations.' **Buses, the head of traffic police 'negotiates' with one of the drivers' unions**: After having assumed the new responsibility, Enzo Mosino tries to postpone the announced strikes. **Four years of life wasted in the traffic.** We use 15 days a year to park our cars. Big cities on trial. **Beauty cure for Subway A: beginning on the 14th, the last train at 22.**
4/12	*Il Messaggero*	**Black Friday, buses on strike.** Urban resistance: how to survive an nth bloc. The Greens at war: **'If municipal government as much as touches the blue line, they are finished.'**
5/12	*La Repubblica*	**A million cars trapped.** Rome, Black Friday – what with the rain and the bus strike. Rutelli: the capital cannot be taken hostage by a minority. **'Bullying the city.'**
6/12	*La Repubblica*	An alarm on Roman subway: **'Too many taken sick, no vacation days.'** Di Carlo cuts down Christmas holidays for drivers on Line B.
8/12	*La Repubblica*	Pietro Barrera, City Manager [*Eng. in original*] on the proposal of the Secretary of the Federation of the Public Employees' Union. **'OK to solidaristic strikes, we are prepared to meet the challenge.'**
15/12	*La Repubblica*	**ATAC, the day of the change.** Voting for turning it into a company, but AN [*an opposition party*] will fight.

Date	Newspaper	Headings
17/12	*Il Messaggero*	**Two ticket controllers from COTRAL assaulted**. A man who traveled without a ticket hurled himself at the two. **A crash at Portuense jams Tram No. 8**. Cars overcrowded. To find a place people go on foot to the first stop at Casaletto.
18/12	*Il Messaggero*	**Too much smog, one million cars at a stop**. Non-catalytic cars are forbidden to circulate from 15 to 20.
19/12	*La Repubblica*	Too many cars in circulation in spite of the prohibition. Municipality criticizes the traffic police. **Traffic, a non-working block produces jams and chaos**.
29/12	*Il Messaggero*	A grand project for the asphalt. **Soon a public tender on North-West passage**. Jumbo-bus even on Route 714, from EUR to the center. **At Square Agnesi you decide yourselves where to cross the street**.
30/12	*Il Messaggero*	**Too much smog: a new stop.** No traffic between 15 and 20. ATAC runs against the time. The 15th of January all public transportation on strike. A minor damages the jumbo-tram: perhaps he was 'sentenced' to clean buses.
31/12	*La Repubblica*	**The block of automobiles didn't work**. The traffic diminished only by 10 percent. **Benzene and carbon monoxide in 1998 – a year of a nightmarish smog.**
1999		
2/02	*Il Messaggero*	**Blocks without checks: special forces required**. Councilor De Petris: 'A team that will see to it that prohibitions are observed.' **Taxi drivers: 'Ready to strike.'** Carlo Bologna: 'We will set the letters from Tocci on fire.' **The rebellion of the Bus Unions is not over: further strikes confirmed**.

Roman traffic had turned into a battle ground.[13] It is superfluous to add that all projects, reforms, and changes in public transportation require a superhuman effort on the part of city employees, and that they often fail as much from bad publicity as from technical problems. Why was the war-frame so dominant?[14]

For one thing the war metaphor is highly dramatic, and, as rightly observed by Warsaw managers, the media is always on the lookout for the spectacular and the dramatic. Indeed, as Murray Edelman says, the main occupation of the media is the creation of a spectacle. Concrete news and information find their place but fail to incite enthusiasm. The most attractive spectacles are accidents, followed

---

[13] The reader should avoid the hasty conclusion that Rome's traffic is the most problematic in Europe. A recommended reading is the story of French lorry drivers' action in July 1992 (Otnes, 1997).

[14] The 'taxi-war' illuminates another peculiar effect of globalization. Although the deregulation of taxi services was definitely fashionable in big cities at that time, in Sweden it has been the taxi-drivers who have demanded deregulation against the wishes of public authorities. A taxi company from Lund that became famous in Southern Sweden for its active stance on deregulation was the first to go bankrupt after deregulation was introduced.

at some distance by celebrations and other positive events. The news undergoes a dramatization through metaphorization. As Edelman observed, 'Dramatization, simplification, and personification (including the personification of historical trends and social institutions into leaders and enemies) are common means, especially in lead sentences and headlines'.[15]

Journalists do not produce the facts alone, however. The process involves an intense co-production between journalists and other collective actors, a co-production not always based on cooperation, but an efficient co-production nonetheless. An enormous number of potential facts are produced daily – more than are generated in any of the sciences – but a great number of them are refuted daily, as well, because they don't correspond to the norms of veracity. It is a strongly agonistic production, a continuous battle over words and images. This eventful production of facts and reproduction of frames constitutes an important part of the action net called big city traffic.

The direct quotes in the newspaper headings given in the table clearly demonstrate that journalists were not the only people using war metaphors; all the actors in this collective drama helped in keeping the war-frame firmly in place.

An interpretation of this phenomenon points to a specific character of the events recalled. Most of them, and virtually all of them covered by the war metaphor, concerned industrial relations. Tourist coaches, for instance, were often described with the help of a naturalist metaphor – stampeding bisons. Union conflicts with the employers were described in military terms.

Interestingly enough, this is not a local frame. The Italian word for 'strike' is 'sciopero', which means a state of idleness, of ceasing to work. The military terminology is of an Anglo-Saxon origin, and does not have a long tradition in the Italian discourse on industrial relations.[16] This frame seems to be the result of an earlier imitation. There are two novel elements in this situation. One, 'the war' was now not only against the private capitalists, but against the public administration as well, and therefore, as Tatiana Pipan suggested, against the citizens. As she wrote in 1989:

The basic characteristics of a societal conflict are undergoing change. More and more often this conflict takes expression in demonstrative and spectacular actions, prone to produce results that were unthinkable in the past, involving the users, the citizens, and all kinds of consumers – against their wishes and interests.[17]

Vittorio Foa, in an introduction to Pipan's book, was quick to call attention to another novelty, closely connected to the previous one:

New and peculiar is the relationship in the media. They are not interested in tracing solidarity patterns, but in amplifying the clamor of the struggle, showing everybody the range of damage done.[18]

[15] Edelman, 1988: 80.
[16] The Nestor of trade union history in Italy, Vittorio Foa, denied any traditional presence of military vocabulary in the unionist discourse. 'Struggle' (*lotta*) used to be the most dramatic expression in this context (personal communication to Tatiana Pipan, October 22, 2001).
[17] Tatiana Pipan, *Sciopero contro l'utente*, 1989: 29 (my translation).   [18] Foa, 1989: 16.

At present there is a third novelty: the military frame of discourse. In Pipan's book, this frame was absent but for one quote from an interview: 'Inflicting damage is the last desperate weapon of those who are in the right: a war means shooting.'[19]

Although the last expression is proverbial (*la guerra si fa sparando*), it is possible to see how the new vocabulary creeps in. A new frame glides into place without any specific intentions. Strikes extend their influence beyond the employees and their families and it begins to concern the wider public; probably as a consequence, the media interest heightens. The media needs dramatization, and there is a dramatic vocabulary at hand, in the linguistic tradition of the English.

We therefore see another trace of globalization: globalization of the media. While Polish journalists were purposefully trying to emulate the US media, the Anglo-Saxonization of the Italian media was more mimetic in character. English words crept into the Italian public discourse, reframing it without any conscious effort.

Is it possible today to speak of labor conflicts within a non-military frame? Obviously it must be, for the public discourse in Scandinavian countries has, equally traditionally, framed it in the terminology of consensuality and problem-solving. This tradition has its consequences for traffic, as we shall see below.

Before we travel to Stockholm however, let me comment once again on the apparent stability of the war-frame in Rome. As the Warsaw example suggested, intentional attempts at reframing might succeed, although usually in an unexpected direction. A reframing does occur, but not toward the frame desired by the actors: 'a red metro' instead of 'a socialist renewal'. A reframing can, however, be an effect of historical contingency. In the days that followed September 11, 2001, to use war metaphors has become misleading, and also in bad taste. Real war has replaced the metaphorical war. Whether this event will contribute to the reframing of Roman traffic, however, remains to be seen.

STOCKHOLM: FIRE IN THE SUBWAY – A SOMEWHAT DRAMATIC EVENT?

The Roman war metaphor can be contrasted with the attitude of Stockholm media and city authorities, who present even truly dramatic events in pacifying, calm, understated tones, carefully avoiding extravagant tropes. A new line of a rapid tram was to be opened in Stockholm as well, and it had to be delayed because the traffic light system did not work properly. As a recompense, the citizens were offered a free ride on the tram on Sunday, October 17, 1999. Nobody commented. On the same day, a fire erupted on the green line of the subway, the most popular commuter line in Stockholm. I have followed the coverage of the Stockholm edition of two main dailies during October 7–27, 1999. This 11-day

---

[19] Pipan, 1989: 131.

coverage was necessary, because few articles on the matter appeared. One could say that Stockholm's traffic problems are relatively small and that public transportation works relatively well, so that there are few events to fire passions. A fire in the subway, however, should qualify as a dramatic event by virtually any criteria.

> *Dagens Nyheter*, October 18th
> **A stop at the green line is to be expected**. The green line remained closed until Sunday evening as a result of the morning fire. . . . The burnt cables nearby Central Station produced a great deal of smoke, and because of that the police and the fire brigade evacuated the station on Sunday morning. Two guards and an employee of SL[20] were taken to the hospital due to superficial injuries caused by the fire. Four people needed oxygen. **The fire brigade** received the alarm at 09.42 and at 10.31 the fire was already extinguished. The fire started close to the edge of the platform of the green line going in the northern direction, but the smoke did not enter the tunnels. The 'smoke divers' checked out the tunnels a hundred meters ahead. The fire was, however, so fierce that many cables were burnt. This has stopped all the metro trains. . . . Emergency buses had to be put into service. SL had many problems finding enough buses and drivers. **At 11.15 the blue and red lines were back in service**.
>
> **The fares will be raised**. The regional traffic councilor, Elwe Nilsson (Moderate) does not change his opinion because of the fire. – An accident like that is always *inopportune*. We do not know the reason yet. But we cannot permit an isolated incident to influence our decision.

There was no dramatization and no metaphors. 'An accident is always inopportune' – the epitome of understatement.[21] The report of the *Svenska Dagbladet* on the same day was almost identical, but it suggested that because the two guards drove to the hospital in their own car, they could not have been seriously injured. By the next day the issues had already changed:

> *Svenska Dagbladet*, October 19th
> **Every fifth subway delayed**
> SL wants to reach the target of 93% of punctual departures on the green line. It is almost two years since SL was close to that number . . . But the county traffic councilor Elwe Nilsson thinks that the subway functions better now than it did before and that it is time to raise the fares. The County Government makes the decision today.
>   – We have not raised the prices yet because the signal system did not work properly. But now it does and we can do it.

[20] The county organization responsible for public transportation in the area.

[21] Swedes are as fond of *meiosis* as the British are. The current slangish expression, equivalent to the American 'I adore jazz' is: 'I am somewhat enchanted with jazz' (*Jag är lite förtjust i jazz*).

> He quotes statistics showing that the number of extended stops
> has diminished. . . . The fact that every fifth train on the green line
> departs with a 3-minute delay is not so important for its passen-
> gers. . . . Neither are the accidents of the past year, including the
> most recent fire, in his opinion.
>   – SL has never decided the prices on the basis of accidents.
>   For Connex, the company that has managed the Stockholm sub-
> way since last summer, the fares are a political question that they
> cannot comment upon. But the company has its doubts about the
> councilor's idea that the improvement in quality must be post-
> poned. – We do not believe that the passengers will buy the story
> that the subway got better, says the representative of the press
> office at Connex, Henrik Kolga. The announcement about a rise in
> fares caused many protests from the political parties. . . . Even the
> parties in the center are saying that 'raising the prices should be
> impossible for anybody *who has a drop of honor left in their blood*'.
> And this week the Stockholm party began a campaign 'write to
> Elwe', suggesting that the Stockholmers should *bombard* the
> County with e-mails of protest (. . .)

Finally, some dramatic tropes and circumlocutions! Stockholm's media have
created a spectacle – but one that is much calmer than the Roman spectacle.[22]
The story of the fire ends with an anticlimax:

> *Dagens Nyheter*, October 19th
> **An umbrella caused the fire in the subway**. An umbrella that fell on
> the rails most likely caused the fire that consumed the cables at
> Central Station and stopped traffic on the green line for 24 hours.
> The umbrella caused a short circuit that ignited a pile of garbage
> nearby the cable. . . . – We are checking the cleaning timetable used
> in the subway this year and we will intensify the cleaning wherever
> necessary, says the head of security Johan Hedenfalk. In the
> autumn and during the winter we will also have containers to col-
> lect used newspapers at the station. The job of exchanging the old
> cables will start in the subway during the summer.

Nothing more on this topic appears until October 25th:

> *Dagens Nyheter*, October 25th
> **Subway problems already in 1933**. The fire at Central Station last
> Sunday caused total chaos. But already by 1933 the metro could be
> dangerous.

---

[22] Not that the Swedish press does not dramatize, but it dramatizes different events. The story
of Mona Sahlin, a Social Democrat candidate for the post of Prime Minister, who used her business credit card to pay for chocolate and diapers for her child, has become a tragedy of ancient
Greek proportions.

The *Dagens Nyheter* of October 26 contained a full-page advertisement from Connex, the company that is part of the corporation *Compagne Générale d'Enterprises Automobiles*: **The best subway in Europe in five years**. An expert was called in on the 27th.

> *Svenska Dagbladet*, October 27th
> **Competition is the villain behind the errors of the signaling system**
> The ferocious competition between the producers is to be blamed for the problems with the signaling systems in the transport on rails, says Bo Peterson, a professor at Lund University. The green line, the rapid tram, the airport train. . . . Putting in new rails has become a nightmare for transportation companies. The technology becomes more and more complex and the trial periods longer and longer. The companies do not dare to put the cars into service before they are sure that everything works. . . . Both the rapid tram and the airport train were delayed for just that reason. Time after time one discovers that the technology is much more complex than expected. . . . It does not help that the best companies in the world, such as Siemens, Ansaldo, or Adtranz produce it. . . . Why is this so? Is it not possible to avoid all this? Bo Peterson . . . believes that the competition between the system producers is the villain of the piece. Everybody promises very short delivery periods; otherwise they won't get the contract. The promises are untenable. The producers are willing to pay the fines in order not to lose the contract. – Stockholm is not alone in this. Copenhagen's subway has the same problems, and so have the rapid trams in Oslo and in Zurich. . . . I was on the automatic subway train in Docklands in London to celebrate their 10-year jubilee. The train stopped twice.

Here, we have a scientist of a more dramatic bent than the journalists, but at least we have learned that neither technical problems nor the procedure of public tenders differentiate Stockholm from Rome and Warsaw. The users' habits are different, and so is the tone of the public debate, including that of the press.

The students of European politics and public administration claim that they see the signs of convergence. While Robert Putnam maintains that Italian politics are more and more closely approaching the European norm, which is supposed to be consensuality, the Stockholm councilors claim that Swedish politics are increasingly moving toward the European norm, which they interpret as confrontation.[23] Let me now turn to an example of an actual political fight about traffic in Stockholm.

On October 3, 2001, the Social Democratic councilor Annika Billström (who was a member of the opposition at that time, but in charge of traffic at the time of my study) wrote the following article in a debate column in *Svenska Dagbladet*

---

[23] Putnam, 1993; Czarniawska, 1999.

(I have quoted the excerpts put in bold by the editors):

> **End the bickering about traffic!**
> We Stockholmers now have a fantastic opportunity to dissolve all traffic jams in the region. It is necessary, however, that the regional politicians forget prestige and bickering and show a willingness to collaborate with the [*Social Democratic*] government.
>
> Three years of bourgeois governance has created a total paralysis of decisions concerning infrastructure. Instead of those, the attention focuses on old-fashioned measures such as privatization and tax reduction – traffic problems are blamed on the central government.
>
> Social Democrats understood very early that growth and justice go together. Unfortunately this is not clear for the Left Party and the Greens.
>
> If the traffic crisis is to be solved, we need to invest in ring roads. Many, including the environmentalists, are going to oppose this measure and demand more transport on track. We need to be clear on one point: there is no possibility of solving the crisis through environmentally optimal solutions.
>
> Can we all agree on what is best for Stockholm?

On October 5, 2001 there was an answer from one of the criticized parties, the Left Party, in the person of councilor Margareta Olofsson:

> **Blind hen Billström**
> Annika Billström has apparently missed the debate of the national environmental goal – especially the utterances of many traffic experts who have repeatedly shown that further construction of motorways engenders more rather than fewer cars, making environmental goals more difficult, or perhaps even unattainable.
>
> If Annika Billström really wanted to take responsibility for the increasingly difficult traffic situation in our city, she had ample opportunity to do so through a cooperation with the Left Party, Environmental Party, Christian Democrats, and the Stockholm Party.
>
> Had Social Democrats accepted the 'crowding fee' proposed by [*the above mentioned parties*], the Moderates and the Liberals would be completely isolated. The Stockholmers could have enjoyed a functioning city even today.
>
> If you, as the elector, wish to live with traffic jams, exhaust fumes, and noise for 10–12 more years, until Billström's motorways are built, at the same time spending 45 billion of our common resources, vote for the Social democrats – but only if you are a middle-age man with a car.

Being called 'a blind hen' is not particularly pleasant, but it is a far cry from being called a Pol Pot, and Stockholm's 'battle' is a far cry from the Roman 'war' (the last and perhaps the first strike on public transportation in Stockholm took place in 1980). The Roman traffic is not only a transportation system, but also a magnificent public drama, one among other public dramas. Even if the war-frame vanishes, it can be replaced by another dramatic one. (The story of Tram No. 8 was framed as a thriller.) Convergence is still far away, and the frame of solidaristic effort and pragmatic problem solving is highly salient in Stockholm. The only clear reframing happened in Warsaw.

FRAMES, FACTS, OR METAPHORS?

As mentioned earlier, it is not my intention to criticize the media; I am interested in the role that the press actually performs in the organization of the traffic in big cities. Researchers, like journalists, use tropes and simplify. But the ends are different, and also the means. Research on organizing, at least in the form I prefer, concentrates on collective actions rather than actors. It is not that people are not important or that there are no heroes and villains in organizing. But in order to understand organizing, it is not enough to understand the actors. Neither Sir John Gielgud nor Sir Laurence Olivier hold the key to understanding Shakespeare; nor is this key to be found in Shakespeare's biography. The CEOs of ATAC, for example, changed five times in recent years, but the traffic in Rome continued to (mal)function. The actions of the media are part of the complex action net that constitutes the traffic in big cities, and as such they deserve our attention.

Whatever the principal frame, in all contemporary big cities there is a competition, if not a struggle, that has not been studied thoroughly: the competition between various parties, including city authorities and the media, for the right to represent the city. Whose representation has the right-of-way in this traffic of images? Which is 'true'? Which is legitimate? Which wins? And for how long?

For any audience . . . an account is an interpretation of an interpretation. An adequate analysis would see it as a moment in a complex chain of interpretations, each phase of the process anticipating later interpretations and helping to shape them. Ambiguity and subjectivity are neither deviations nor pathologies in news dissemination; they constitute the political world.[24]

A representation of the events taking place in a city may be expressed in many media – photographs, pictures, films, novels – but most obviously through official documents, scientific reports, and the mass media. Although the first type of representation has the license to resort to imagination, the second should be

---

[24] Edelman, 1988: 95.

based on facts. But what counts as facts? There are at least two answers to that question. One is based in the correspondence theory of truth, where facts are utterances that correspond (preferably in a 1:1 relation) to the reality (knowable, presumably, beyond the utterances). The other is based on the pragmatist theory of truth, wherein *facts are utterances expressing collective experience in a manner that does not produce too many protestations.*[25] In any case, as the etymology of the word indicates, the facts must be produced (made),[26] and the mode of their production is the key to their credibility.

The production of facts that follows the forensic model of science[27] depends on producing witnesses and proofs, checked by procedures of validation, primarily through repetition. Journalists produce facts through a weak version of the procedure used in history: the sources are the witnesses and the documents, which are validated through confrontations with the opposing version of the events. The social sciences live in the world between these two, mixing ad hoc the methods of validation from natural sciences and from history.

The city managers in Warsaw, Stockholm, and Rome had the same wish: to be correctly represented in the media, with both successes and failures, and with a strong presence. But only the Warsaw managers, wiser by their peculiar experience, knew under what circumstances such dreams can be realized. The media in the democracies dramatize, metaphorize, exaggerate, and create a spectacle. It is in this context that the full meaning of the Aristotelian notion of *catastrophe* comes to light – not necessarily a disaster, but a resolution of the narrative tension, without which no story is interesting. Therefore, the dream of 'reforming' the media is unrealistic, at least when one is otherwise occupied with a project of such imperial proportions as the restructuring of Roman traffic. The city authorities in Rome might wish and try for a situation like the one in Stockholm – less presence in the media while the most urgent difficulties are being resolved.

But the opposite tendency is very clear – the irresistible temptation to use traffic as a stage for grand dramas. Indeed, traffic is more easily utilizable for this purpose than any other issue because it involves so many of the city's dwellers. The battles fought inside the walls of Campidoglio, where the city council resides, are not equally attractive, but this attractiveness, profitable in political terms, is very costly when a technical innovation is to be introduced. The different chains of translation collide: the city council imitates other city councils and the newspapers imitate other newspapers.

Although this observation alone should elicit little surprise, it requires completion with another conventional remark: there is a long historical connection between big cities and the media, especially newspapers. Robert Darnton, in his project on the history of communication, suggests that Paris in 1750 was an early model of the Internet: the city-network operating in opposition to the state-controlled journals, elaborating and distributing the news to the provinces.[28]

[25] Rorty, 1991.   [26] Knorr Cetina, 1994.   [27] Mary Douglas, 1986.
[28] Darnton, 2000.

A contemporary example is *Metro*, a free daily that was started in Stockholm but which is now printed and distributed in several European capitals.[29] *Metro* has two interesting traits: it is not a city newspaper, in that it reports general rather than local news; but it is limited to big cities, and is usually distributed through the network of public transportation.

Let me reiterate something I suggested earlier: media reports are part of the organizing of a city, a truism that is perhaps most visible in the case of public transport and traffic. However, journalism and city management belong to two different organization fields. The direction of imitation in one might not coincide with the other.

In Warsaw, the press openly declared that US journalism was their model. For solutions concerning city traffic, however, they swung to the European model: public transport rather than private cars. Will the two be a good match? Or will a still older tradition, that of French journalism re-emerge, to stand on the side of the collective citizenry against the state and against powerful individuals?

In Rome, there was a somewhat surprising imitation of the British media, at least in the reporting of industrial conflicts. Perhaps incidentally, the former head of the London subway has been employed as a consultant for the metro construction in Rome. As Berlin is still Rome's formal model for the traffic system, the interest in London may be explained by the long history of the London Tube (which is now, however, in dire straits) or the general tendency to follow the UK in its public administration reforms (again, the recent talk of a re-nationalization of British Railways introduces an interesting complication). Much as I am aware of the dangers of overinterpretation, my main goal here is not to define trends, but to pinpoint connections between seemingly unrelated actions and actions that are related one-sidedly. The press, supposedly, is only re-presenting the actions of city management; I claim that this representation is in itself a part of this very management.

As for Stockholm, the Swedish tradition of journalism is somewhat peculiar, as it is still influenced primarily by the construction of the welfare state in the 1930s, where press was part of a popular education program; the main role of the press was to explain to 'the people' the ongoing societal reforms. Until the late 1960s, journalism was a craft, not a profession.[30] More recently, the Swedish media began to develop under the influence of the Anglo-Saxon – especially the US – tradition, but it still preserves its educational character.

Mimesis is as complex in journalism as in city management. The *Metro*, which conquers more and more big cities, has borrowed its idea from the now-defunct *Information* in Paris, and some of its typographical details from the *USA Today*,

---

[29] As of December 3, 2001, the *Metro* was distributed in Stockholm, Prague, Gothenburg, Budapest, Helsinki (two versions), Santiago de Chile, Philadelphia, Barcelona, Madrid, Boston, Zürich, Toronto, Buenos Aires, Milan, Rome, Warsaw, Athens, Montreal, and Copenhagen. The *Metro* also has regional (Scania) and national versions (Holland, Hungary), which recalls the fact that many cities are bigger than some countries.   [30] Stockholm, interview 22: 13–14.

but it claims complete originality in its organization. The lack of a strong professional tradition permitted *Metro* to borrow models from the virtually unrelated organization field of industrial companies; and borrow it did, focusing especially on the practice of outsourcing. This strategy means that the imitation of practices can be separated from the imitation of form, and that both can cross the borders of organization fields. Globalization works from many different angles.

4

Europeanization: Coercion or Mimesis?

Our social life includes a thick network of [imitative] radiations . . . with countless mutual interferences.[1]

The concept of reframing is not limited to a cinematic metaphor. It is also used literally, signifying changes in the legal framework. Many processes initiated by the EU are of this kind. Apart from global and European tendencies that city managers adopt spontaneously or as the result of local political decisions, there exist obligatory (coercive) unifying tendencies in the form of EU directives. These general directives are subsequently translated into their local versions. Chapter 4 presents an example of the introduction of an EU directive and its consequences for Warsaw, Stockholm, and Rome. The directive concerned public tenders, specified by the EU as the appropriate form of contracting suppliers of services and products within the public sector. The concrete text of the law was to be decided by each individual country, but the recommendation was that all external contracts above a certain level of expenditure to the public purchaser should be announced publicly within the country and, whenever applicable, within the EU; and that the contractor must be selected from among the submitted tenders through certain transparent procedures. By 1994, Poland, Italy, and Sweden had an appropriate law, and the three capitals whose management I studied were obliged to follow it.

PUBLIC TENDERS AS SAVING GRACE: WARSAW

While actions such as privatization, marketing, and public tenders were provoking less-than-hidden ridicule in Stockholm and somewhat better-hidden skepticism in Rome, in Warsaw they were revered. In Warsaw, the 'marketization' of the

---

[1] Tarde, 1899/1974: 101.

public sector was not just one managerial fashion among many; it was heralding the dramatic change of the political regime. There was no question of the market's absolute superiority to all non-market mechanisms and actions; the question concerned only the correctness of its enactment. It often happened that some European organizations were teaching their Polish equivalents the art of becoming market-oriented. For example Company South, a construction company working on a new water treatment plant, learned the proper procedures from its sponsor, European Investment Bank.

The task of building a new plant was first alloted to a construction enterprise building a new water system in Warsaw. The enterprise announced a tender for the design and technology of the plant, which was subsequently won by a team consisting of a French company and a Polish civil engineering office.

The difficulty lay in financing the project. The French company had promised to raise 60 percent of the required capital, a promise that had won them the contract. It was based on a hope of *ecoconversion*, an idea launched by François Mitterand, the President of France at the time. Ecoconversion meant the transformation of foreign debt into ecological investment. The French company, Degremont, counted on 10 percent of the Polish debt in France being reduced, if that money were to be invested in an ecological project. Additionally, the *Société Generale* promised advantageous credit conditions for all deliveries and services provided by French companies.

Reality soon soured those hopes. The rate of ecoconversion was established at 1 percent rather than 10 percent of the Polish debt. Additionally, the credit had to be insured at 11 percent, for Poland was then seen as a high-risk investment country. The impasse was not solved until 1993, when the French company named the European Investment Bank (EIB) as a potential partner. The same year a single proprietorship company was founded by the City of Warsaw, under the name of 'Company South', and it contracted a French company and a Polish engineering office to begin work connected with the building of the treatment plant. A year later, a credit agreement was signed.

There was frantic activity during the year between the creation of the company and the signing of the agreement. As one of the company directors said, 'It was really tough. This last year I worked very hard. The EIB is a very demanding institution. You have to do simulations, propose multivariant programs, do lots of homework, as usual in the West. But, if you do your homework properly, you see the results.'[2]

During the first visit of the EIB team, which was headed by a project manager, the cooperation schedule was established. It was to consist of three 'evaluating missions', each preceded by almost weekly visits from the five-person cross-examination team, which, apart from investigating the circumstances of this particular project, broadly monitored Warsaw's budgeting practices. After the last session, a final report was sent to the Board of Governors, and the credit agreement was reached, as promised, in November 1993.

[2] Warsaw, interview 2: 8.

During this time the Polish side collaborated closely with the bank's team. 'Homework' was complemented by information, help, and advice delivered around the clock by the EIB personnel.

Both sides were pleased with the cooperation. The bank had had the good fortune of meeting Polish partners with fluent English and experience abroad; Company South had had the good luck of dealing with an international finance institution, which, unlike most commercial banks, had the patience and resources needed for a close cooperation. The EIB advanced the project to the rank of a pilot project for similar infrastructural investments in central Europe.

This 'reframing under special supervision' became especially visible when Company South prepared its own tenders:

Now we are in the process of preparing a tender for construction and assembly works. This tender is divided into two phases. The first phase is a so-called prequalification, a collecting of references and a standing financial evaluation. There are about 10 elements that have to be evaluated: substantial and geographical experience, engineering and technical staff, equipment stock. This shows the company from the financial point of view and in terms of what it does.

The European Investment Bank requested that the announcement be placed at their expense in both the Polish press and in the European Union Official Journal. A total of 26 companies responded: 14 foreign and 12 Polish companies. I have to say that it was a wonderful group; one should really hang such a list above one's bed next to the picture of the first Holy Communion.

Then we organized a tender commission, completely independent, with a prevalence of people from the Warsaw Polytechnic. The commission decided the tender regulations, which were sent to EIB for acceptance. Next, the commission asked a consulting company to calculate the evaluation points in order to make a ranking list. The short list included ten companies – five foreign and five Polish. Of the foreign companies four were German and one was French. Those companies received detailed tender documentation, and they have to present their commercial offer with costs specifications within three months (Warsaw, Interview 2: 10).

Things did not work quite as well in the case of a tender for the metro ticket control machines:

Gazeta Wyborcza April 1 1994
The City of Warsaw decided to introduce, as the first city in central Europe, a unified Automatic Ticket Control System for all means of public transportation. New tickets will be introduced first in the metro and then in buses, trams, and parking facilities.

Eleven companies participated in the tender organized at the beginning of 1993, and in its final stages two candidates emerged: the French Monotel and the German–US Siemens-Cubic. The final choice was Monotel, which already had had experience introducing such systems in Toulouse, Mexico City, Seoul, and Adelaide. Monotel also produces ATCs for the Paris Metro.

The competitors did not take the decision calmly. The tender became the center of attraction as the participants continued to disclose more and more spicy details about the tender.

Gazeta Bankowa, no. 17, April 23, 1994
Anything goes in the quest for a dozen or so million US dollars?
Members of the tender commission . . . quite quickly decided that their knowledge of ATC systems was only superficial, so the technical expertise of the project should be turned over to specialists.
[*Only one was found*]

The first specific decisions of the tender commission were made at the beginning of the year. They were preceded by visits of the commission members and of the expert to the headquarters of the competing firms. The result of these trips was the final choice of two firms – the French Monotel and the German–US Siemens-Cubic. Neither firm missed a chance to tarnish the other's reputation, each accusing the other of excessively long and hearty (read: interested) entertainment of the Polish guests. . . .

The finalists presented two similar concepts of ATC systems . . . It is difficult to decide which one is better: the word of expertise is divided on that issue.

The introduction of the solution proposed by Siemens would cost the City about $21 million. The creditor would be the Polish Development Bank. The loan would be repaid only from the moment when the system became profitable. Besides, Siemens-Cubic found a national partner – Raczka & Gasior from Mielec. On the other hand, Monotel proposed a system that was cheaper by $3 million, without, however, being willing to clarify the details of the financial aspect of the matter. The French found a company – Syntax – that could play the same role for them as Raczka & Gasior did for Siemens.

'Monotel proposed a cheaper solution, realistic and totally satisfactory as far as the capital's needs are concerned', said the director [*of the Transportation Department*]. The Siemens' representatives were speechless, but not for long. Their Polish representative started by sending intervention letters to the President and the Prime Minister, trying to argue that the contract with Siemens would bring hope to the unemployed in Mielec. Siemens-Cubic made an official statement that Monotel lags behind Siemens technologically. Then Siemens announced that Monotel is merely a producer of turnstiles, without the slightest idea about ATC systems, and that it is also bankrupt.

The aim of this article is somewhat ambiguous: did the journalist wish to convince the reader of the correctness of the decision? (Siemens, who lost the tender, was mocked more than was Monotel). Did he wish to expose the unethical practices of foreign contractors? There is no doubt that the game was rather rough here, unlike the fair play appreciated by the EIB. A school of life instead of a school of capitalism? This episode was not the end of the story, however. A Polish competitor entered the stage.

> *Gazeta Wyborcza* May 24, 1994
> **A lost chance?**
> New turnstiles and ticket sale and control machines could be produced by a Polish factory. The capital's authorities, however, preferred to sign a $20 million contract with France – complain representatives of Mera Plant in Warsaw's suburbs. Warsaw's councilors and government claim, however, that Mera's offer was uncertain and arrived too late.
> 'You will have to explain yourself to authorities, who won't take just any answer', we read in the letter of Mera Blonie to the City Mayor.
> 'The contract signed with the French is another lost chance for Polish industry', roared the Managing Director of Mera Blonie during yesterday's Council meeting, adding that the rejection of Mera's offer means fewer jobs and less tax paid to the Treasury.
> 'I would like to remind everybody that the tender for the new ticket system was opened at the beginning of 1993 and that an offer from Mera Blonie was submitted in April 1994, a day before the final decision by the Warsaw Council', answered the Deputy Mayor.
> 'Nevertheless, the Transportation Department sent to Blonie the members of the tender commission. It turned out that Mera wanted to introduce ticket machines produced in cooperation with a French company, Dessault.
> Dessault is a known company specializing in the production of metro turnstiles; whereas 90% of ticket machines in Warsaw will have to be installed in buses and trams.
> Unlike Monotel, Mera Blonie did not present proposals for financing the contract. A lack of experience with the installation of urban ticket control systems at both Mera and the cooperating firm Dessault raises doubts as to their ability.'

The issue at stake was not so much one of patriotic investment as of a 'blackmailing bankrupt giant', one of the gigantic state debtors. It seemed, however, that the matter had already been decided.

> *Gazeta Wyborcza* June 9, 1994
> 'Very likely as early as June, the Warsaw government will sign a contract with the French firm Monotel for installation of the urban

> ticket system. The opening of the Metro was an occasion we could not miss. . . . I was acclaimed a grave-digger of Polish industry for having chosen Monotel', complained Warsaw's Deputy Mayor yesterday. 'But I could not ignore the opinion of the commission, which has been working for a whole year, simply because Mera is close to Warsaw.'
> The Deputy Mayor added that Monotel would be responsible for the contract, but domestic companies, which would also see to the installation and guarantee service of the equipment, would produce at least 30% of the orders. Also, the new tickets will be produced in Poland.

Note the typical beginning of this account: 'The Warsaw government will sign the contract'. The opinions and actions of the officials dominated the picture; the councilors' function seemed to be advisory. In Stockholm, the officials' proposals are anchored with the councilors and made public only with their consent. It often happens that the councilors refuse to accept the officials' projects, and therefore it is the councilors who speak to the press about the future. When the officials meet the press to speak of future plans, they use careful formulations like: 'One should hope that the councilors will accept the government's proposal and that it will be possible to sign the agreement as early as in June . . .'. In Rome, the officials do not express their judgments and opinions to the press; this is entirely the privilege of the commissioners.

True to this picture rather than to that of the deputy mayor, the new Warsaw council was in no hurry to sign the contract. The council, preoccupied with vociferous public opinion, appointed a special councilors' committee to study the problem.

> *Gazeta Wyborcza*, September 1, 1994
> Warsaw authorities were severely criticized, among other places, in one of the TV talk shows, 'A Matter for a Reporter' and in 'Tribune'. Deputies from the industry committee considered the contract with Monotel suspicious. And the Deputy Industry Minister . . . threatened to withdraw the State's credit guarantees and tax reductions for imported machines.

One forms an impression that the autonomy of the local government *vis-à-vis* the central government was precarious and that TV talk shows, a novelty of recent years, were more important than were expert committees – a fact that might be interpreted both optimistically and pessimistically. The socialist vocabulary seemed to have returned – the minister 'threatened to withdraw'. But it is also true that many of my interlocutors used the pronoun 'I' when speaking of the activities of the organization they represented: 'I will not pay', 'I will not give them', and 'I will show them'. Perhaps the minister used the same rhetoric.

> *Gazeta Wyborcza*, October 4, 1994
> A special councilors' committee decided a week ago that the capital needs a new ticket system; whereas the contract with Monotel does not sufficiently ensure the capital's interests. On this basis the Warsaw Council broke the contract and decided that a new tender for the modern ticket system will be published.

> *Gazeta Wyborcza*, October 10, 1994
> Monotel estimates its losses at half a million dollars. It threatens a lawsuit if the city authority officially breaks the contract...The Council's decision was influenced by the opinion...of the Information Center and Legal Services Director of the National Economic Chamber. According to him the contract was disadvantageous for the city.

On April 14, 1995, the metro went into operation – without turnstiles and with bus tickets. Many people (and I was among them) expected the travelers to freeload. But that did not happen. When I tried to visit the newest metro station with its designer in 1998, we were stopped by one of two armed guards (equipped with all kinds of communication technology). They were suspicious when they learned that we did not intend to ride anywhere; they never took their eyes off us during our visit. These human turnstiles were very effective indeed, although they were probably costly. Eventually, it was Monotel who installed the turnstiles; they took the case to court and won, but it took them until 2001. A happy end seven years later...

The example of the ticket control machines gives food for thought. The under-the-table fights and below-the-belt blows are not unknown in tenders. But unless the issue concerns a major state contract, it is highly unusual for an unsuccessful bidder to write letters to presidents and prime ministers. It is symptomatic that it was the Polish representative of Siemens-Cubic who undertook this initiative.

In Sweden, at this time, many consulting companies employed Polish immigrants to help the Swedish entrepreneurs cope with 'the Polish culture'. Although their help was no doubt valuable, if only in terms of language, it is also clear that they helped perpetuate the old order by resorting to the 'ways things were done in Poland'. Paradoxically, the foreign partners unwittingly helped to reproduce the very system that annoyed them. Such phenomena were by no means limited to this particular case, as Janusz Beksiak pointed out in his article evaluating the introduction of capitalism in Poland: '... instead of competing on the market and making deals there, ... the economic actors attempt to influence the state apparatus, using mostly political arguments and other means of political pressure'.[3]

One such action increases the probability of similar reactions. Once the tender was questioned and put under public scrutiny, and once the state authorities were involved, all parties concerned eagerly reenacted the old order. The managing director blackmailed, the minister threatened, and the socialist vocabulary

---

[3] Beksiak, 1994: 27.

resurfaced. The new council, intimidated by this public critique, did not respect the decision of its predecessor.

It is obvious that the city's decision was not properly *anchored*. It hung in the air, with no serious consequences, and could simply be revoked. One possible reason for the lack of anchoring is an exaggerated belief in the power of the tender as an institution. It becomes ritualized. Once a tender has been concluded, nothing can influence its results. The practice showed, however, that the situation could be altered. Tenders are, no doubt, rituals, but they do not involve magic. Once concluded, their results must be anchored and incorporated in subsequent organizing.

As these examples show, a purposeful reframing does not eliminate interference from the previous worldview. Frames cross. Sometimes the conflict is obvious, as when a new political team has different preferences. Usually, however, it is a hidden conflict, in that actors do not realize that their way of thinking, which seems natural to them, is the result of an applied frame. What prevents them from seeing their way of thinking as a frame is the strong modernist illusion that it is possible to see the world 'as it really is', completely and without delusions. The frame is, then, only a defect of perception suffered by others (in everyday language one talks about 'blinders', like those put on horses in order to limit their side vision). The following reasoning was typical of many actors who participated in the public discourse: 'I am all in favor of changing the previous order, but *surely* effective organization requires a concentration, and patriotism requires favoring local investors.'

PUBLIC TENDERS AGAINST BRIBECITY: ROME

In Rome, the institution of tenders also caused problems for public transportation. But in Rome the integration of all Roman tickets into one, *Metrebus*, was a low-technology, high-politics operation; 'supertrams' rather than turnstiles became the issue. On March 25, 1998, a new line of rapid trams was inaugurated on the Casaletto-Largo Argentina line. The vehicles did not live up to the title of 'rapid', however, because they had been 'borrowed' from other lines at the last moment. The winning bid was FIAT's, and it was to deliver 28 new trams in time for the opening of the line; in the meantime, however, the Regional Administrative Court invalidated the tender. One of the competitors questioned the correctness of the procedure and the appeal was recognized. I discussed the event with one of my interlocutors, a top manager in one of the municipal transport companies:

> I: Nowadays, all competitions are announced in Europe, but there is always somebody who appeals and who wins the appeal. After all, the matters concern interests and politics.

> BC: The public administration tries to live up to the ideals of market that private companies cannot afford . . .
>
> I: Exactly. That's the paradox. We need to be quicker and leaner, and instead we have many more harnesses, encumbrances, and impediments compared to the private companies.
>
> BC: Thus it seems that the market instead of liberating the public organizations placed it under new rules . . .
>
> I: Yes, this had to do with the scandal of Bribecity.[4] Now it is almost impossible that those acts of corruption could happen, so private interests use the money that previously went to bribes in order to pay the lawyers to cancel the results of the tender. But it will be better; it takes time. Italy is in a period of transition, and there are many contradictions, many difficulties. (Rome, Interview 15: 7).

This opinion was shared widely: transition has its costs, and things cannot change quickly.

> I foresee great changes. Well, we want those changes. We dream about a legal simplification of all the norms that govern us – norms that were undoubtedly created with the intention of guaranteeing a correct procedure, but that are an impediment. It's the cost of transparency, you know. If we need to print a flyer, it costs us 20 to 30% more than a private company, as we have to have a public tender, publish the announcement, which costs at minimum LIT 1 million, and so on and so forth. Transparency is probably much more expensive that any other thing. (Rome, Interview 8: 3)

Please keep in mind the issue of producing a flyer, because I shall return to it in the example of Stockholm. There were also more pessimistic voices in Rome, although there was a common recognition of the necessity for a law like the 'law Merloni' on public contracting:

> In contrast to what has happened many a time during grand events such as Olympic Games or World Championships, the Jubilee of Christianity in Rome is prepared entirely via public contracting, according to EU directives. The announcements must be published as they should: in the Official Gazette, in the EU bulletin and, if you go beyond requirements, in local and national newspapers. The publicity is in place, and no private deals. The net result is that all

---

[4] *Tangentopoli*, a bribe scandal in the Italian public administration, was revealed in 1992 by Judge Antonio Di Pietro and other lawyers from the group *Mani Pulite* (Clean Hands). Their estimate of bribes paid to the state and municipal functionaries was $100 billion in 20 years.

takes more time. You can get a private agreement in 15 days; whereas the institution of public tenders, rightly guaranteeing the occurrence of competition, drags everything into eternity.

Then, the winner is always the one with the lowest costs, as any attempt at introducing quality evaluation leads straight to discretion and therefore prepares the ground for bribes. In order to save some common sense one uses mixed systems, introducing additional quality evaluation, estimates of time of execution, of company's status at the time of entering the competition, but that makes public tenders a fiction. . . .

The opportunity is no doubt of historical significance: for the first time in this country the public administration does public contracting, but if this guarantees competition, it remains to be seen. . . . There are cartels and there are agreements; they are, however, not visible and nobody denounces them. If not, the cheapest tender is chosen, with incredible results: some companies declare that they can have zero profits as long as they can have the contract. A public contract means that they can get a loan in a bank, and survive in a situation of certain bankruptcy, so they work for us in order to gain the trust of the bank, and this triggers a chain of pathological motivations. . . . (Rome, Interview 51: 19–21)

The description of the process given by this interlocutor is well known from studies of private tenders, especially in the construction industry.[5] What we witnessed is interesting indeed. The EU forces its members to adopt a certain procedure: a certain form of organizing. But it is only in the case of the Warsaw tender supervised by EIB that the coercion (already translated into an attractive ethos) extended to actual practice. The EIB people saw to it that Company South followed the prescription step by step. One could speak of isopraxism, if it was not doubtful that such a practice exists in anyplace, without such supervision.

In the case of the Warsaw metro turnstiles and the Roman streetcar producers, coercion ended with the law. The form had to be observed, but the contents, that is the practice itself, succumbed to local mimesis. In the case of Warsaw, a conflicting situation made everybody regress: when in doubt, fall into old routines. In Rome, mimesis occurred by proximity. The last quote describes tenders in construction projects; public sector contracts are copies of construction sector contracting, where such tenders have a long tradition – and a long list of problems.

---

[5] See Anna Kadefors, 1999, on mistrust between clients and contractors in the construction industry, and also a quote concerning tenders on public transportation vehicles in Chapter 3. Kadefors also notes an important difference between Swedish contractors on one hand, and Polish and Italian contractors on the other. In Sweden, an appeal against the results of a public tender is not *comme il faut*. Construction companies are afraid of acquiring a reputation of being quarrelsome and impossible to cooperate with (personal communication, March 2001). No such fears exist in Poland and Italy. This can be partly explained by the sheer size difference of the three countries: as of 2000, there were 8.9 million inhabitants in Sweden, 38.6 in Poland and 57.6 in Italy. It is difficult to hide in Sweden.

STOCKHOLM, OR BEING PRAGMATIC ABOUT IT

Here is a conversation of the kind I have heard many times during my observation days at the Stockholm city administration offices and companies. In this case it concerned the production of a flyer representing the office's work:

> Head of the Office: We need to do it well. Talk first to Karin, who was responsible for this publication before. You need not worry about practical details as they usually work OK, with the exception of the printing company. We need new contracting. Possibly not public.
>
> New Co-worker: Is this legal?
>
> HO: Oh yes it is. We used to contract the whole thing from an advertising company, so it is not just printing, but a complete service. . . . You can start right away, and if you don't find anybody we can use some printing office that was contracted centrally. But I would like you to contract a complete service, an advertising company, and it wouldn't be completely wrong to keep the guys we had before, if you can convince them to give us a better price. I remember when Stockholm Energy lost their advertising company and it was a catastrophe.
>
> NC: Not to worry. I know exactly how to do it, how to get the best deal.
>
> HO: In terms of money?
>
> NC: No, in terms of quality. If you choose to focus on money the quality goes down the drain. (Stockholm, Observation 1/7)

The two people did not seem to notice anything special in this conversation and neither did I. In fact, as mentioned earlier, I heard many similar conversations during my observation days. Then, I read with great interest an article in my local daily, *Göteborgs-Posten (GP)*, in a series under the title 'Competition Put out of Game'. The article heading was: 'This Is How They Waste the Taxpayers' Money: Municipal Companies and Administrations Don't Give a Damn About the Law'. The article series and the investigation on which it was based could have been provoked by a letter sent to the *GP* by a lawyer, published on May 3, 1999, wherein the author claimed that Sweden could save SEK 20–25 billion a year 'through effective and loyal purchasing'. According to the information gathered by the *GP* journalists, the actual contracting and purchase were neither effective nor loyal. The article contained a short presentation of the law on public purchasing, which was enacted in 1994.

> *GöteborgsPosten*, May 22, 1999
>
> It was meant to guarantee that all suppliers on the market have the same opportunity to compete for contracts with state and municipalities and that nothing unfair happens. The law is also intended to guarantee the free circulation of goods and services within the EU.

Alas, the practice was far from this ideal, and *GP* compiled a list of the most common arguments made by municipal politicians and officials to justify their disregard for the law:[6]

- We had an old general contract with him and did not think we should seek new tenders again. Even if it were a matter of several millions.
- We were thinking of doing it properly, but alas, time was extremely short.
- We would not have chosen any other consultant. Our guy knew the question from its very inception.
- We didn't think it was a good idea to announce this within the EU, even if we know that we should do so when the contract is above the threshold sum. After all, nobody from abroad would apply for such a thing.
- We have a general contract with two consultants whom we think are very good. We always use them. We do not see the point of getting more information. We have done it for many years now.
- The first job the consultant did for us was not so expensive that we needed to seek tenders. After a while it became much more expensive, but we didn't know that from the beginning. We sort of ended up in the hands of the consultant.
- We took a former councilor/official whom we know very well, without seeking tenders, because we know that he knows this job.

Although *GP* claimed that this disregard for the law happened in such areas as planning, construction projects, maintenance of streets, roads and illumination, real estate, energy production, and IT, their examples concerned only consultants (and only male consultants at that). It is worth pointing out that the Italian law on public works did not extend to consulting: consultants were contracted without the procedure of public tenders.

The tone of the article is clear: the excuses are ridiculous; public tenders should be the only method of contracting; and municipal governors and managers are wasting money and disobeying the law by insisting on their old practices. The journalists, and the lawyers they quoted in their support, did not see any problem applying the institution of public tenders literally and, as they called it, 'loyally'.

The practitioners did not share their ideas: in the cities under study they appreciated the letter of the law and considered it necessary, despite seeing the paradox of its applications. But then paralogisms are a form of knowledge and self-knowledge that are well-spread in public sector organizations.[7] In the face of paradoxes, most practitioners do not try to 'resolve' them, but are able to appreciate the reasons for their emergence and the often positive and unexpected

---

[6] The information could have come from the region around Gothenburg, but the Head Lawyer at the State Office for Public Contracting confirmed the commonality of such practices and such arguments.

[7] Paralogy is a form of knowledge that accepts contradictory statements about reality. Traditionally considered to be a logical fallacy, it has been suggested by Lyotard (1979) to be the source of innovation in language. On paralogy in public administration, see Czarniawska, 1997.

consequences of their existence. As I mentioned earlier, the practitioners in Stockholm were well aware that the law was not observed to the letter, but, unlike the journalists, they did not see anything alarming about it. Indeed, Stockholm was spared any major contracting scandals, although there were some minor, local ones. They admitted the tendency to contract old, well-tried suppliers, but pointed out that the law permits them to renegotiate the prices. They advertised abroad when it seemed sensible to do so, and they were aware of the conflict between cost and the demand for quality.

Non-normative researchers would tend to be in accordance with the practitioners. Let me address one by one the excuses that the practitioners gave for not employing the procedure of public tender.

'We had an old general contract with him and did not think we should seek new tenders again.' Indeed, why should they seek new tenders unless they were dissatisfied with the consultant? My Institute is still smarting from a similar move our University made in this respect: they abandoned the travel office that we used for years, and contracted several others that were cheaper. They were cheaper, it transpired, because they did not have enough personnel and resources to deal with the job, and an endless procession of problems has ensued. This is a situation that is very well known in Italy.

'We were thinking of doing it properly, but alas, time was extremely short.' This is a typical complaint against public tenders – especially because they can be invalidated, as we have seen before. The losses are usually very high.

'We would not have chosen any other consultant. Our guy knew the question from its very inception.' Here, it is important to return to the fact that all the GP examples concern contracting consultants, whereas my examples do not. Consultants, more than any other suppliers one could imagine, also supply a certain kind of relationship; indeed, their services are relational in nature.[8]

'We didn't think it was a good idea to announce this within the EU, even if we know that we should do so when the contract is above the threshold sum. After all, nobody from abroad would apply for such a thing.' Announcing within the EU automatically raises the costs of the procedure itself. One would imagine that it is not very difficult to estimate if a certain specialty can be represented outside Sweden.

'We have a general contract with two consultants whom we think are very good. We always use them. We do not see the point of getting more information. We have done it for many years now.' Here, at least two important schools of thought are evident. The Uppsala network school shows convincingly, and for years, that markets are composed of nets built on trust.[9] They may turn into 'nasty networks', run on nepotism, but not necessarily so. As to 'more information', in spite of Nobel-rewarded work by Herbert Simon on satisfying rather than optimizing criteria in decision-making, the faith in 'complete information' persists.[10]

---

[8] Gergen, 1994.   [9] See, for instance, Brunsson and Hägg, 1993.
[10] See, e.g., March and Simon, 1958.

'The first job the consultant did for us was not so expensive that we needed to seek tenders. After a while it became much more expensive, but we didn't know that from the beginning. We sort of ended up in the hands of the consultant.' Again, investment involvement, while not laudable, is certainly a very well-known phenomenon.

'We took a former councilor/official whom we know very well, without seeking tenders, because we know that he knows this job.' During my study of Stockholm, I was told a great many stories about the failures of managers who were recruited into the city from private companies – managers whose brief appearances in the role of the saviors of the public sector were well documented by the press. Although the recruitment of new employers from another sector might be done in the name of renewal, recruiting a consultant who does not know a given type of activity seems rather risky.

In short, the practitioners seemed to be much more anchored in reality, and therefore much more pragmatic, than the journalists were (which is probably why they belong to two different professional groups). However, my reasoning is meant neither to defend the practitioners nor to criticize the journalists, as they both act from a profession-specific standpoint. It is to show the complications and the paradoxes of the procedure – that could also be called a ritual – of public tenders. The first question is, however, why were public tenders ever introduced into the European public administration? What was the nature of the remedy and against what malady was it applied?

WHY PUBLIC TENDERS, OR CITIES ON THE MARKET

The politicians and administrators in most European cities, and especially European capitals, are of the opinion, strongly supported by the European Community offices, that city administrations, like the other units of public administration, must change their identity from that of tax-financed money-spenders to that of self-financed participants in the global city markets. Marketization is a slogan that is common to all of them, and it includes such things as proper privatization, company-ization, increasingly allowing private companies to participate in the running of cities, marketing (even 'branding'), competing on the city markets, and imitating or incorporating all kinds of market rituals.

The postulate of marketization, formulated from outside as well as from inside the city, results in a great deal of enthusiasm and even more prescriptions as to the necessary and appropriate actions. As to the reasons for the enthusiasm, it may well be that the cities activate their collective memories and revive the times when cities were markets,[11] and when cities competed with one another on

---

[11]   Two alternative or complementary hypotheses concerning the origins of the city are those of ceremonial centers and military strongholds (Braunfels, 1988).

political arenas, free from the heavy hand of the state. Prescriptions and proscriptions are not only free advice (although there is much consulting work involved), but also in many cases legal directives, issued by the EU and implemented by local jurisdictions. But what are the consequences for action programs in the 'marketization' of these cities?

One major prescription resulting from the market orientation is the special cultivation of the institution of competition. The city authorities are indistinguishable from other public administration sinners in that they bear historical blame for an innate tendency toward monopoly. (This allegation is difficult to explain, as both monopoly and various kinds of oligopoly are the products of a free market – a market before the entrance of anti-trust laws and other regulations.) The public administrators are allegedly guilty of squandering taxpayers' money, although this differs from one country to another depending on the right of the city to autonomous taxation. The cities, however, have a long tradition of taxation and of using the tax money for collective consumption. The cities, compared with other types of public administration units, also have a more distinct tradition of marketing themselves,[12] a long tradition that needs only to be modernized.

But the sharpened demand for conscious competition unavoidably increases contacts among cities. They all want to know what the others are doing, and are engaged in variegated attempts at imitation. This paradoxical face of competition is, of course, well known to market analysts, who coined the expression 'the competitive edge'[13] just to capture this urge to distinguish oneself by following similar routes. When this urge is accompanied by formal institutions, the effects can be very visible.

This case of public tenders also illustrates the embeddedness of big cities in their regional and national context, the latter being especially obvious for capital cities. The big cities set examples, but they also collect experiences from their region or country and re-present it in other contexts. Thus, Stockholm has a duty to re-present 'Swedishness' to foreigners (the fulfillment of which is often questioned by small towns and by its main competitor, Gothenburg), but also attempts to launch innovations within the country. Warsaw is equally intent on re-presenting 'Polishness' and launching innovations. Rome, on the other hand, cannot represent 'Italianness', for such a concept hardly exists in that strongly regional country. It can be said, however, that it represents all the sins of public administration and that it thereby focuses the attention of foreigners and Italians in the same direction, albeit for different reasons than the other two capital cities. Briefly, a reframing can either start in a capital or, initiated somewhere else, find its most extreme expression there.

The capital is a laboratory of fashion (to be condemned or admired in the provinces, but always imitated) and hosts most of the national representation work. It is, therefore, only natural that the duty of modernization resides in the

---

[12] See, e.g., Sahlin-Andersson, 1996, on the difficulties that, e.g., debt collectors have in introducing a market orientation into their activities.　　　　　　　　　　　　　　[13] Porter, 1985.

capital. An understanding of how this duty is fulfilled is a key to an understanding of the ritual of public tenders.

MODERNIZATION PROCEEDS BY RITUALS

Societies vary by factors of one hundred to one in resources, and enormously in their own traditions. But they adopt surprisingly similar forms of modernity.[14]

In many respects, the procedure of public tenders has the same value in all three cities: it is a ritual of the market that symbolizes modernization, staying ahead through the introduction of global novelties. Also, in all the three cities, it produces complications because times are prolonged, quality may easily suffer, and costs are high. This is, however, typical of rituals: they are usually ornamental and are therefore costly, they tend to demand a great deal of time, and they are hardly functional in the narrow sense of the word.

Edmund Leach defined ritual as a stereotyped behavior that is potent in terms of the cultural conventions of the actors, although not potent in a rational-technical sense, and which serves to communicate information about a culture's most cherished values.[15] In other words, functionality in rituals is subordinated to the symbolism of power. Steven Lukes defined a political ritual as a 'rule-governed activity of a symbolic character that draws the attention of its participants to objects of thought and feeling, which they hold to be of special significance'.[16] The market and competition are at present the cherished values of the common European culture as it tries to construct the objects of thought and feeling that are of special significance.

Nevertheless, this global or rather transnational culture is translated in accordance with the local context (where context is re-invented during the translation). In all the examples above, it has been obvious that, over and above the shared wish to appear modern and global, the procedures of public contracting were tied to local history. Indeed, as the proponents of the garbage-can theory would say, the solution found local problems to solve.[17] Thus, in Warsaw, the public tenders were the means to bring about an increased effectiveness and efficiency in the public sector, previously burdened with the verdict of extreme inefficiency. In Rome, the most important problem addressed was transparency, or rather the infamous memory of Bribecity. In Stockholm, public tenders were applied as a Band-Aid on the Swedish sore, which was supposed to be the overspending of the welfare state. The major worry of the journalists was the wasteful spending and the savings that would result through the proper observance of the procedure. Hence, while the other problems were also being connected to the proposed solution, one of them – the local one – was given precedence.

In the same vein, these solutions produced new problems, or new versions of old problems, in terms of unexpected consequences. In Warsaw, the problems

---

[14] Meyer, 1999: 15.   [15] Leach, 1968; Turner, 1982.   [16] Lukes, 1975: 291.
[17] Cohen et al., 1972.

were technical and operational: things did not work very well, even if procedures were applied correctly. The desired reframing has not been achieved. In Rome, the main worry was time, a problem that is traditionally attributed to bureaucracy: here, however, the red tape of the administration was easily replaced by the red tape of the market. And although bribes were no longer a problem, the lawyers' growing fees were seen as a societal waste. In Stockholm, the efficiency problem was noted, but transparency was not a special benefit in the light of the traditional law on public transparency, which had been in place for a very long time. The problem was the quality of contracted goods and services and the imperative of proceeding pragmatically, often hampered by a demand for a literal application of the law. In a sense, the old problems – against which the solution was applied – were reproduced in a new, 'modern' form. This observation recalls the investigation by Joan Acker, who studied the modernization of Swedish banks from a gender perspective and discovered that the reform wiped out the old forms of gender discrimination and created new, 'modern' ones.[18]

The differences in the actual enacting of the ritual can also be attributed to the differing attitudes towards the value that it was supposed to represent.[19] In Stockholm, the feeling was that modernity had been achieved long ago (see Chapter 5), and therefore the ritual's technical rules need not be observed to the letter. The management in Warsaw and Rome, like its public – the media and the citizens – was not quite sure about it. Rituals of modernity were to ward off pre-modern vices of sin (corruption) and sloth (inefficiency). A faithful following of the ritual was therefore of importance.

These phenomena would be less startling if we paid greater heed to the work of the anthropologists who have registered them repeatedly. This has not happened because of the modernist wish to achieve a rupture with the past that would allow societies to be divided into 'primitive' and 'modern', and to study 'modernization' only in the context of 'primitive' societies. Now, however, we might be ready to admit, with Bruno Latour, that 'we have never been modern', and, with John Meyer, that modernization is a process that never ends.[20] Thus, the pre-modern sediments are always present: the European Community is as much in need of common rituals as the Roman Empire, although the rituals differ.

'Modernization' proceeds in the same way at all times: an abstract, translocal solution is applied, in a local translation, to local problems, redefining them in a new, 'modern' way.

MIMESIS AS COPY AND CONTACT

If this analogy is accepted, new ways of interpreting the strange fate of public tenders emerge. Michael Taussig, inspired by James G. Frazer's distinction

---

[18] Acker, 1994.
[19] I am indebted for this insight to John W. Meyer (personal communication, 15 September 1999).   [20] Meyer, 1999.

between contact and imitation, distinguished between *copy* and *contact*.[21] Although the two usually go together, the case of public tenders shows why it can be useful to separate them, in order to understand the events.

It can safely be said that the coercive element in the introduction of the procedure, although undoubtedly present, was of little importance: the wish to imitate can be described as normative as well as coercive.[22] Although it is obvious that coercion produces obedience (and if so required, imitation), it is a condition that is rarely met in non-totalitarian societies. As Terry N. Clark has pointed out in his commentary on a Tarde-Durkheim debate, where Durkheim stood for constraints and external norms and Tarde stood for imitation:[23]

. . . certain social realities . . . once formed . . . impose themselves upon the individual, sometimes, though rarely, with constraint, oftener by persuasion or suggestion or the curious pleasure that we experience, from childhood up, in saturating ourselves with the examples of our myriad surrounding models . . .[24]

The unclear character of this 'curious pleasure', although well-known through introspection, seems too fickle to be included in serious social science reasoning. At any rate, the relative weight alloted to the coercive and normative isomorphism by, for example, Paul J. DiMaggio and Walter W. Powell, seems to stem from the continuation of a Durkheimian way of conceiving the social action.[25] Although examples of such influence can no doubt be found, it might be more appropriate to treat them as residual categories, and to concentrate instead on the mimetic processes.

In the case under discussion it is, however, difficult to speak of *contact* with the EU, as there is no such thing: Brussels does not necessarily practice what it preaches. As the joke goes, if the EU applied for admission to the European Union, it would not be accepted.[26] The city authorities were, therefore, to *copy* a certain procedure that is transferred in the form of abstract rules. These abstract rules needed to be translated into local practices, and the conditions for a complete mimesis were in place: the contact – with other fields of practice, or with one's own past – was immediate and unavoidable. A translation that aims at copying abstract ideas is bound to be influenced by that with which it has a direct contact. This observation is further corroborated by the case of the South Company in Warsaw, where EIB ensured that copying was taking place through continuous contact.

---

[21] Taussig, 1993: 22. Taussig himself would probably not appreciate my poaching of his terms. In spite of his declared preference for a symmetric anthropology, he applies symmetry only to direct encounters between 'the savages' and 'the Europeans'. The world of global economy, with its 'Truth as Accountability', is for him a disenchanted world where mimesis is dead (p. 97). Frankfurt School's emancipatory reading dominates the picture, although now and then Taussig acknowledges that things have changed since Benjamin's times.

[22] Bengt Jacobsson (1997) shows that Sweden introduced most of the EU regulations long before joining the union.   [23] Clark, 1969: 17–18.

[24] Tarde, 1899/1974: 184.   [25] DiMaggio and Powell, 1984; Powell and DiMaggio, 1991.

[26] Giddens, 1999.

In sum, one could suggest that, if the aim is to imitate a practice (which it rarely is, as we shall see in Chapter 5), the way to enhance mimesis is to create possibilities for both contact with and copying of that practice. It is no accident that an important part of the traditional occupational training was a 'practicum' – literally, doing what was supposed to be learned in the context where a given practice was well developed. In times of mass education, mechanical reproduction, and electronic communication, this strategy is not considered to be feasible because of its cost. Shortcuts are introduced, and take such forms as embodying practices in people and machines, sending them from one place to another (which provides a limited contact, especially if the 'imported' practice is to compete with local practices), and relying completely on 'mimetic machines' to simulate a contact.

Another point can be made by introducing the literary meaning of mimesis as description, in contrast to narrative. From such a point of view, there is an excess of mimesis compared to narration in modern organizing. The descriptions of how things should be done go on forever; while the narratives – how we have done it this time around – are fewer, especially in formal education situations. Yet, narration can make up for a missing contact, aiding mimesis-as-copying, as it mimics social practice better than description – better, that is, in the sense of being able to provoke a reenactment via dramatization, via movement.

In an ideal world of organizing, a complete mimesis – a contact and a copy – would be stabilized and reinforced by repetitive narration. In the actual world of organizing, however, the picture becomes complicated, and not only because it is difficult and costly to strive for ideal conditions. Another phenomenon worth noticing is an ambiguous attitude to imitation among city managers, an issue which I discuss in Chapter 5.

5

The Invention of Tradition and Social Memory[1]

All beginnings contain an element of recollection. This is particularly so when a social group makes a concerted effort to begin with a wholly new start. . . . The beginning has nothing whatsoever to hold on to; it is as if it came out of nowhere. For a moment, the moment of beginning, it is as if the beginners had abolished the sequence of temporality itself and were thrown out of the continuity of the temporal order. . . . But the absolutely new is inconceivable . . . in all modes of experience we always base our particular experiences on a prior context in order to ensure that they are intelligible at all.[2]

The three cases of city management described here have a strong element of a 'beginning', of what I call reframing in this book. The case of Warsaw is the most obvious: the ambition was to start anew and break the links with the immediate past. The case of Rome resembles that of Warsaw, although the rupture was not so dramatic. The evil tradition of Bribecity had to be discarded, possibly in a spectacular way, in order to furnish examples for others. And although Stockholm had no tradition to break away from, part of its profile is constant renewal, achieved by various oblivion mechanisms that permit people to forget that a particular 'novelty' had already been introduced ten or twenty years ago.[3]

But as the absolutely new is inconceivable, some type of prior context must be chosen as a starting point. One obvious possibility is to look elsewhere. Thus, cities imitate one another, translating into concrete practices the abstract ideas that arrive in the form of regulations or consultations, and thereby adding fuel to the globalization machines. Another possibility, especially attractive to those who wish to resist globalization, is the imitation of their own city traditions. One might assume that traditions are, by definition, an inappropriate source of imitation models for the purpose of modernization. This is not so, however, as I hope

---

[1] A part of this chapter has been used in Czarniawska, 2002.
[2] Connerton, 1989: 6.
[3] See Karin Brunsson, 1998, for a detailed description of such 'oblivion mechanisms' in the Swedish public administration.

to demonstrate later. Apart from intentional associations to one's own tradition, there exists a persistence of habitual practices, a 'social memory',[4] which further excludes a possibility of 'the absolutely new'.

WARSAW: INVENTING THE TRADITION OF MODERNITY

Warsaw's problems, as reported by my interlocutors, can be seen as both typical and unique. The city finances, transportation, and water and waste systems are characteristically problematic areas in big cities. Warsaw was, additionally, a big city managed during the transformation of an institutional order. *Institutional order* here has a wider meaning than a set of formal institutions; it is a set of social practices considered to be legitimate in a given place and time. It was against the background of such a changing institutional order that the management of Warsaw was taking place in 1994–5, which was the time of the study. A common way of transforming practices and institutions is by imitating desirable models, abstract or concrete, copy or contact. This was not, however, the way chosen by Warsaw's councilors and officials.

The Sin of Imitation

'O Poland! You were the peacock of the nations – and their parrot!' said the Polish Romantic poet, Juliusz Slowacki in 1839 in *Agamemnon's Grave*. As in other European nations, imitation was historically seen as negative – as a 'primitive' trait of a society,[5] and poets and novelists took it upon themselves to denounce a supposedly Polish proclivity for unreflective imitation. An elderly nobleman in *Master Tadeusz* (1834) – an epic poem by another Romantic poet, Adam Mickiewicz – tells the story of how 'Frenchness' arrived in Poland for the first time and how people of his generation felt afraid to criticize all the 'aping' that took place under the label of 'progress'.

This ambiguous attitude toward imitation persists. Experimentation was limited because of the strong assumption of 'uniqueness'. Alterity was given priority over identity: the 'uniqueness of Warsaw' was a topic that returned often, as described in Chapter 2.

'Aping' is hardly a correct way to summarize that which goes under the label of organizational imitation. Guje Sevón, who studied this phenomenon in many

---

[4] Connerton, 1989.

[5] Taussig (1993: 74) attributes the connection between 'primitivity' and imitation to Walter Benjamin, but such a connection has been taken for granted in Polish literature since the fifteenth century – that is, since the usually assumed beginning of modernity (Toulmin, 1990). Indeed, the 'primitive' could hardly exist without the 'modern'.

contexts, claims that similarity is a result as much as a cause of imitation.[6] Organizational imitation, in her view, is a creative operation of identity formation consisting of a chain of translations. It starts with a self-definition: 'Who are we? What situation is this?' It continues examining the existing repertoire of organizational identities in order to ask: 'What or who we would like to be?' The 'existing repertoire' varies according to an organizational span of attention, but this span is usually contained within one's organization field. An interesting complication was the case of Warsaw, where an institutional order was in shambles. The organization fields were redefined within Warsaw's city management, which left the cozy harbor of public administration and ventured into business.

The picture of imitation as sketched by Sevón should assuage the fears expressed in the Polish tradition, as it is closer to *emulation* than to *mimesis*; indeed, it is an imitation of desires. But emulation is more difficult than mimesis: it is purposeful and aims at excelling or at least at equaling that which is emulated. And although emulation is, I would claim, a common phenomenon in the business world, it acquires a doubtful ring in the context of public administration. Since Veblen's use of the term, it has been seen as a morally problematic tenet of an action.[7]

In Warsaw, the unwillingness to either emulate or copy foreign models was accompanied by a positive attitude toward one's own distant past, toward historical models. Such an attitude is not unknown in the organizational context. Birgitta Schwartz, who studied Swedish companies, observed that organizations preferred copying their own successful actions over using examples from other organizations in the field. Schwartz called this tendency *automorphism*,[8] an isomorphism of a structure with itself, in contrast to isomorphism as so often postulated in organization studies.

Automorphism is but a metaphor for what takes place in organizational contexts. There is no constraining force, either mechanical or organic, requiring that structures repeat themselves. It is an inventive process, where the past serves as a source of inspiration. But what can be found in Polish history that might be used as a model or an inspiration for city management in the twenty-first century? The relevant models can relate either to the economic enterprise typical of the capitalist institutional order, or to the city administration typical of democracy.

The Repertoire from the Past

Janusz Beksiak performed a historical analysis of the Polish economy, concluding that capitalism never fully took root in Poland.[9] The estate economy of the sixteenth and seventeenth centuries was supported by an anticapitalist institutional order that limited the conditions for entering the market, attempted to

[6] Sevón, 1996.   [7] Veblen, 1899/1994.   [8] Schwartz, 1997.   [9] Beksiak, 1994: 14.

control prices, supported autarchy, spread a negative attitude toward invest-ments, and encouraged the creation of monopolies by the landowners and Gdansk merchants. This situation stabilized due to the increasingly better terms of trade. The Dutch, Spanish, Portuguese, and British empires were busily con-quering the world and could spare no time for grain production. One after another, generations of Polish landowners learned that with no need to calculate, invest, innovate, or to market their product, they could count on their profits increasing automatically. Beksiak failed to mention the cultural and religious aspects of the process that corroborated the disapproving attitude toward capi-talist enterprise if it was undertaken by ethnic Polish actors, but he did show how the Polish 'anticapitalist phobia' took form.

After the partition of Poland, the situation varied in the parts that were under foreign rule; but a common factor was that the main economic institutions did not support and encourage native economic initiative and often actively prohib-ited it. Capitalism was a foreign phenomenon, a view that began to change only after 1919, when the Polish Republic was created. Beksiak has said, however, that the period between the wars was too short for any decisive capitalist order to take root, and that the economic statism of the Second Polish Republic, hostile toward foreign capital, inadvertently impeded the development of domestic cap-italism. Beksiak ended his analysis thus:

The economy was no doubt of a capitalist type, but it was an old-fashioned and discordant variation of capitalism. It was capitalism of a poor country, where the natural economy dominated, where anachronistic action patterns typical of the great estate owners and their peasants were still very much alive, where defensive attitudes won out against expan-sive ones, and where the state ruled over the whole economy.[10]

The management tradition in the city is even more feeble. One must remember that Poland is historically an agrarian society: even as late as 1840 'the citizens of the towns formed only a small part of the Polish population as a whole'.[11] The first models of city management that could be characterized as modern appeared in the second half of the nineteenth century, when Warsaw belonged to the Russian Empire. The management of the city by Mayor Sokrates Starynkiewicz could easily have been a reason for pride, if only Starynkiewicz had not been Russian. This fact is subject to the implicit but firm interpretation that whatever he did, he did to support the Russian Empire and not for the benefit of the inhabitants of Warsaw. Similarly, yet another occupant – the German General Governor Hans Von Besseler – organized the first City Council elections in 1915. The elections were patterned after the Austrian system, probably because the Austro-Hungarian empire had a patent at the time on 'modern bureaucracy', just as New Zealand today has a patent on 'New Public Management'.

But the nuances of historical analysis were ignored in the popular *historiogesis* – the reading of history. 'Warsaw between the wars' was an ideal to emulate, and in

---

[10] Beksiak, 1994: 17.   [11] Niederhauser, 1982: 16.

this matter there was an amazing accord between councilors, officials, and the media. The period evoked a symbol of the centralized city government run by a strong landlord, but also allowing local autonomy. Its methods of management were considered to be a source of inspiration, if not imitation. I have seen a small booklet describing the organization of Warsaw Waterworks between the wars, religiously perused by its present executives. 'Warsaw between the wars' was modern and prosperous; the task was to bridge the gap of 50 years and to continue what was successfully initiated then. Few voices intimated that these 50 years were dedicated to a forceful modernization, and even these voices were dismissed as being those of 'the old guard'. Professional family connections transcending half a century were recalled with fondness; professional careers forged during 1939–89 were not. This situation prompted my interest in the official history of the between-the-wars period in Warsaw management.

Warsaw Between the Wars

After the elections of 1915, Von Besseler instituted a city council of limited autonomy on July 24, 1916. This council was granted full democratic rights by the Polish state on February 23, 1919. On March 2, 1934, however, the Council of Ministers dissolved both the city council and the city government.

This event did not happen suddenly. According to Drozdowski, whose study forms the basis of my reading of the situation,[12] Warsaw had served as a political arena for fights inside the national government since the end of the First World War and the recovery of national independence. The city's autonomy lasted only as long as the Warsaw authorities reflected the structure of power in the central government. When these two no longer corresponded, the crisis in the city's finances became a pretext to invalidate its council (the formal reason was: errors in the preliminary budget). Command rule was taken first by Marian Zyndram-Koscialkowski, and after August 2, 1934, by Stefan Starzynski, who until then had been the Deputy Chief Executive Officer of the National Economy Bank.

Starzynski announced 'an activation of the neglected peripheral districts of Great Warsaw; a turn in the capital's urban development so that it "faces the Vistula"; a stable, balanced budget; and the encouragement of affection and pride for the city among its inhabitants'.[13] He thoroughly disliked the command mayoral position he held and hoped that his political activity in the Camp of the National Union (CNU)[14] would contribute to the political stabilization necessary for the reconstruction of an autonomous local government. In spite of his enormous efforts, his influence in the CNU was not enough to turn the tables,

---

[12] Drozdowski, 1990.   [13] Drozdowski, 1990: 212 (my translation).

[14] An informal interparty coalition that worked to diminish the dissention between political opponents.

and the government commissar, Wladyslaw Jaroszewicz, effectively opposed his moves. One could say that Starzynski's strategy was to help the city by placing himself in the right spot in the big power game. He did not succeed, but it is difficult to imagine an alternative strategy, given the lack of tradition in Poland's local government at that time and the exercise of command rule.

Still, it was possible to take a very important step – the Self-Governance Act of August 1938, which made the city independent of the central government. The elections took place on December 18, but until March 1939 the council failed to elect a mayor, and Starzynski was once more appointed to the post by the Council of Ministers. The Second World War broke out on September 1, 1939. The city council transformed itself into the Citizens' Committee, and its members, including Starzynski, were arrested on September 28. Starzynski died in a concentration camp in 1941.

Another relevant aspect of Warsaw's city management between the wars is the economy of the city. It is obvious that Warsaw's economy constituted part of both the regional and national economies. Drozdowski listed five periods of economic development in Warsaw between the wars:

- 1918–23: reconstruction of the autonomous national economy, in which Warsaw played an important integrating role.
- 1924–6: the stabilizing currency reform; the recession of 1925–6.
- 1926–9: boom; the rapid growth of Warsaw and the Warsaw Industrial Province.
- 1929–34: recession, crisis, depression.
- 1935–9: boom resulting from the mobilization of the Polish army.

The relation between the economy of Warsaw and the economy of the country is clear. The balancing device was the crafts and small industry, which were not so easily influenced by the fluctuations in the global economy.

The Warsaw authorities were actively involved in the economic life of the city and assumed many tasks and roles. The story told by Drozdowski, in fascinating detail, reveals how irrelevant the division between private and public was at that time. Two such sectors simply did not exist as separate organization fields. During 1918–21 the Procurement Department of the City was the biggest wholesaler and retailer in the country; but when it started suffering losses after 1925, it was transformed into several small companies. What belonged to the city yesterday could be sold to a private owner tomorrow, and vice versa. Similarly, the appointment of a bank executive to the position of mayor raised a few eyebrows at the time.

State control was nevertheless distinct. The government commissar approved the budget proposal, loans, capital investment, real estate decisions, fees, and taxes. The galloping inflation of 1922–3 consumed the city's income, leaving Warsaw at the mercy of state subsidies. During the currency reform period, self-management in the city practically ceased, but, as Drozdowski claims, the first two terms of the city council were nevertheless enough to rebuild what had been destroyed in the First World War, and to stabilize the city's economy. The true troubles started only after 1928, when the national government introduced a new act that strengthened the state governance of the capital, and curbed local authority over the city. Although the boom that followed permitted several investments, 1930 marked a period of serious economic crisis in Warsaw. In spite of protests against the city council, the government extended its term. The third council ruled (in a very limited sense of the word) Warsaw until 1934.

When the council was dissolved, the city's coffers had a deficit of 76 million zl.[15] Political appointments went far down the hierarchical ladder, and virtually no control was exerted over the public utilities. The situation invited fraud and mismanagement, or at least evoked suspicions of fraud and mismanagement.

With the financial help of the state, the first of the two mayors appointed during the command rule paid the wages and the salaries due, and introduced serious savings intended to balance the budget; however, public pressure forced him to lower the prices of gas and transportation. Starzynski continued this renewal program of balancing the budget and developing investments. Although the common belief then, as now, was that the crisis stemmed mainly from the lack of professional expertise on the part of city authorities, Starzynski did not share this opinion. In December 1938 he wrote an article on Christmas trees in which he said:

'The magistrate's Christmas trees are the symbol of magistrate management, which undoubtedly achieved the results that are visible far and wide, and therefore create a great effect. But it needs the mirror of public control, control coming from the independent representatives of the city's inhabitants, that is, from a city council established by free and open elections'.[16]

Although this statement can be seen as a preparation for an electoral campaign, the fact that Starzynski fought for the resurrection of self-government and that he liberated the city from the state to a significant degree, convincingly demonstrates his belief in self-governance. Of course, it is possible to argue that Starzynski confounded cause and effect. Was command rule not saving Warsaw from the troubles in which self-government had landed the city? This question, or rather the proposal of the reintroduction of command rule, was heard again in the 1990s, as were so many other questions – and answers – inherited from the past.

Half a Century Later

The similarities between the political situations of 1919–39 and 1990–4 are striking. Then, as now, there was a dramatic transformation taking place, revealing

---

[15] I am not sure how Drozdowski arrived at his calculation. Starzynski's deputy, Kulski, spoke of a planned deficit of 7 million, a liquid debt of 61 million, liabilities of 45 million, and costs of debt servicing amounting to 19.7 million. Kulski also adds that Warsaw's debt was significant but not dramatic compared to the other big cities of that time (Kulski, 1990: 45).

[16] As quoted by Drozdowski, 1990: 247.

a lack of compromising skills and an uncomfortably close connection between the national and city governments, an arrangement that constantly threatened self-government. According to Drozdowski, the successes of the last council before the outbreak of the Second World War can be explained by the fact that it functioned more or less in opposition to the increasingly autocratic central government. The link to the central government remained, although it changed from positive to negative. Interestingly enough, Starzynski, who is now seen as the prototype of the 'strong master' as presented by Drozdowski, certainly perceived himself as the defender of self-government. One might form the impression that public opinion jumped to conclusions in its interpretation of the past. The authoritarian position given to Starzynski has been interpreted as reflecting his management philosophy. This interpretation might have additional roots in Starzynski's personality; apparently, he was very strong-minded.[17] Drozdowski demonstrated, however, that Starzynski was disappointed by the limitations imposed on self-government, and that he took it as a personal failure that his dream – to become the elected rather than the appointed Mayor of Warsaw – never came true.

As to whether a city gains more from self-government or from command rule, historical reasoning based on the assumption of a one-way, clear-cut, cause-and-effect connection must invariably be incorrect. The developments that I am summarizing here clearly show one thing only: that Warsaw's political and economic problems and solutions were always more dependent on the global economy and national politics than on any specific form of management. Thus, it is easy for me to agree with Starzynski and some of my interlocutors: that self-government is valuable in and of itself as a form of democratic rule rather than as an instrument for achieving short-term economic goals.

Is automorphism a problem or a solution? One could say that the picture of prewar Warsaw is the least attractive model to be imitated. Its main traits – short-lived solutions and the constant feeling of a threat – are exactly what should be avoided at present. And yet they are repeated in discontinuous policies, revoked decisions, and a dominating 'emergency management'. This view is correct, but there are different ways of imitating, as I have endeavored to demonstrate throughout this book. After all, both self-government and effective city management were in the formation stage at the time the war intervened, and only the tragedy of history prevented their full development. But several city institutions existed and functioned with some success. Their heritage is not lost. One can perhaps paraphrase what Beksiak said of Polish capitalism between the wars: city management between the wars was not extensive, it was not the best kind, and it did not last long, but who knows if it was not enough to begin with?

It is important to note that no matter what the historians and economists say, today's city managers did not perceive the period 1919–39 as problematic. They saw it as a time when the seeds of modernity had been sown, and expected that

---

[17] Kulski, 1990.

cultivation of that tradition would permit Warsaw to join other modern big cities. How could they be so mistaken? This question has been brilliantly answered by Eric Hobsbawm. *Invented tradition*, writes Hobsbawm, is

a set of practices, normally governed by overtly or tacitly accepted rules and of a ritual or symbolic nature, which seek to inculcate certain values and norms of behavior by repetition, which automatically implies continuity with the past. . . . [T]hey are responses to novel situations which take the form of reference to old situations . . .[18]

In this case, I speak more of forms than of practices, but the tenets of modern organizations assume that practice follows the form, that action follows structure, and that isomorphism leads to isopraxism. Hobsbawm, however, would probably object to the application of his concept to a modern organization. In his text, he contrasts technology to ideology, and states explicitly that ' "traditions" and pragmatic conventions or routines are inversely related'.[19] They are inversely related in theory, or rather in ideology; but not in practice, answer Meyer and Rowan:

Formal structures of many organizations in post-industrial society dramatically reflect the myths of their institutional environments instead of the demands of their work activities.[20]

The received dichotomies such as ideology–technology or symbolical–practical can no longer be sustained. Organizational forms are rituals of modernity. They tend to be loosely coupled or decoupled from practices, but are legitimized by a modern, technological assumption that the content of a practice is determined by its form. In their invention of tradition, Warsaw politicians and city managers seek confirmation of a tradition of modernity, implied by a continuation of organizational forms.

AUTOMORPHISM OR THE COMPLEX RELATIONSHIP OF CITIES TO THEIR PAST

Is automorphism to be found only in Warsaw? Is Warsaw unique? As usual, the answer is both yes and no, for the past can be put to varied and complex uses.

Rome: Continuity and Rupture

In Rome, the emphasis was on modernizing the city management, and that meant a break with the past – especially with the recent past. In this sense, city management shared a common predicament in Rome and Warsaw, for entirely different reasons. In Warsaw, to break with the past was to break with the totalitarian

---

[18] Hobsbawm, 1983: 1–2.   [19] Ibid, p. 4.   [20] Meyer and Rowan 1977/1991: 41.

regime, leaving the road to the more distant past standing open. In Rome, to break with the past was to break with Bribecity, a difficult rupture that could not have been achieved by inventing a successful past. The closest successful past was the Roman Empire, and although Roman aqueducts were often mentioned, it would have been difficult to claim those times as a source of a modern management tradition. Not even the relatively recent cases of successful management could be used as models for present developments, as pointed out in the context of organizing the Third Jubilee of Christianity:

> The problem that the technical committee for the reception of the pilgrims had to tackle, in, let us say 1950, was the pilgrims' shoes. There was a reception center in Ostiense where the pilgrims could wash their feet and put on new shoes. Today the world is different, the means of communication are different, and mobility is different. Everyday the Fiumicino airport is vomiting out thousands of people. Europe is on the move; the people from the East are coming with all possible means of transportation to the City. (Rome, Interview 35: 3)

But a city with a cultural capital like Rome cannot permit a rupture from its past; indeed, one cannot even imagine such a desire. The city councilors and officials in Rome were therefore performing a difficult act: modern management was to begin, and was to rely on a decisive rupture from the immediate past. The success of this management was to be grounded, however, in an effective preservation of past heritage and of accessibility to the tourist in the most modern way. To keep one's cake and to eat it too, would not be easy, but it was deemed feasible. A rampant modernity was as unwanted as an unreflective continuity:

> Visiting Baghdad many years ago, I expected to find the capital of the Islamic world, and I found instead a beautiful modern city that would not be out of place anywhere in the USA. Why do the same to Rome? Why deprive Rome of its artistic potential that is not completed, but continues to evolve? The excavations along the Imperial Fora will create a new aspect to the city, while at the same time conserving its antique character. The large squares constructed by the emperors, like the Traian Forum designed by Apollo d'Oro from Damascus, will become more visible. All this will be completely in the open. In this way, I would like to project an image of Rome as a very modern city that knows how to conserve its riches. (Rome, Interview 48: 7)

This ambitious program can be exemplified with excerpts from a beautiful brochure published by the Department of Territorial Policies, Municipality of

Rome.[21] The introduction by Mayor Rutelli was summarized in an appeal: 'Re-stabilize rules, restitute certainties' (this from the man who deregulated taxi services). Some of the headings read: 'New instruments to design a modern metropolis', 'Programming the future while constructing the present'. The text of the brochure ends with a peculiar declaration of uniqueness:

Our goal is to modernize Rome. We start from conditions that are profoundly different from those in any other European city, for in none of them exists such a complex interlacing of powers and norms; an interlacing that often translates into a labyrinth of vetoes crossing one another.[22]

A powerful affirmation of difference, but a difference that is to be partly obliterated: the labyrinth of old power games and regulations requires a decisive rupture, while the labyrinth of old monuments and underground archeological treasures must be preserved and maintained with care.

Stockholm: the Continuity of (Modern) Tradition

Yet another version of the relationship with the city's own past was to be observed in Stockholm. The city management was presented as a continuation of a tradition, but this tradition was already that of modernity. Let me quote a story that one of my interlocutors told me in the context of water and sewers management. Like all stories, it starts with a description of a state of affairs so bad that it had to be changed:

> In the nineteenth century Stockholm was besieged with sickness, with epidemics. People had all kinds of stomach diseases and the cause was clear: the primitive handling of water, and drinking of dirty water. Thus the city witnessed epidemics of cholera and many other diseases that today are to be found only in developing countries, high infant mortality etc. The solution was to build waterworks, which was accomplished by the turn of the century. The next step was the sewers, and this was a revolution, a revolution in hygiene.

The actions were successful, and for a while it seemed that all was well. As often happens, however, after a time unexpected consequences began to surface:

> It was fantastic, the way one solved society's hygiene problems. But later on it became clear that the problems were pushed away, and not really solved. Water in lakes and the sea had become so polluted

---

[21] *Modernizzare Roma*, 1995.   [22] Ibid: 49.

that it was impossible to bathe there anymore. It was then that the first purification plants started to be built.

The first purification plant, using mechanical devices, was opened in Stockholm in 1934. In 1950 a second, bigger one was built; the third in 1950. After that, purification techniques became better and better. Later on, water treatment has been built up and improved.

The situation was under control, but the heroes did not remain idle. They dedicated themselves to improvement and were successful.

In the 1960s the focus fell on environmental issues. The first environment protection law was enforced in Sweden in 1969. It was extremely helpful for improving the situation of discharges and consequently diminishing the pollution of nature in general and water in particular.

While the heroes were busy, so were their antagonists: society and nature. The growing complexity of knowledge was always a step behind the growing complexity of the situation.

But society was becoming more and more complex. You can see yourself how the traffic increases all the time, and how elements dangerous to the environment – biocides and fungicides – create more and more problems. All this has found its expression during the famous Rio-conference that adopted the concept of 'sustainable development', coined by Brundtland-committee. All participating heads of state signed the Rio-declaration, so that the attention paid to the issues of environment became quite different.

The contest continues, but the gap does not widen. Each change in the state of affairs is matched by an appropriate action, and so on.

Today we talk not about environmental protection, but in terms of sustainability, in terms of circulation and natural resource management. This is a much wider perspective, that sets much higher demands. The level of difficulty has increased seriously.

Stockholm Water is a typical example of an environmental engineering company. It is precisely in this type of company that the notion of a long horizon, of sustainable development, is most central. I would say that the company has been long aware of this, but that now it is easier to join forces with the inhabitants, because the public discourse is all about sustainability. There is a holistic view of things. We see water in Stockholm as a natural resource that is on

> loan to us. We take it to fulfill the city's needs, but then we must see
> to it that the water is purified in such a way that it can be given
> back, can enter the natural circulation without any damage. And
> this is what we work with: to improve, to optimize this system.
> (Stockholm, Observation 5/1)

This is the story of continuous modernization: if there is any break, any rupture, it dates back to the 'Dark Ages', two centuries ago. After that, whenever the state of affairs was reframed as unsatisfactory due to new knowledge, an appropriate action followed. The train of modernity proceeds without interruption, and there is no reason to assume that it will ever stop. Modernization has become an institution.

The plot of the story is somewhat hidden. It does not describe actions that produce the next state of affairs to be acted upon, as in fairy tales; it is the progress of science, invisible in the story, but taken for granted by the narrator; and its consequence is the growing sophistication of knowledge. This ultra-modern tale, however, serves, like the tales of old, as a means of demonstrating continuity rather than rupture. It has been centuries since Sweden has experienced dramatic events. Such a situation is rarely considered by the analysts of modernity who frame their analyses as a dichotomy: continuation (tradition) versus rupture (modernity). The reason may be that the majority of these analysts have dramatic ruptures in mind, such as the two World Wars, the French or Soviet revolutions. More recently, however, we experienced ruptures that mobilize continuity: the fall of the Berlin Wall in 1989, the terrorist attack in New York in 2001.

Also, as Giddens has noted, the idea of tradition is itself a creation of modernity.[23] And although he continues to contrast modernity and tradition, he also points to changes in what is believed to be a tradition. As time passes, it becomes clear that it is possible to speak of a *tradition of modernity* without creating an oxymoron.

SOCIAL MEMORY

Has the past been invented? Paul Connerton, in *How Societies Remember*,[24] introduces an important distinction between *social memory* and *historical reconstruction*. Social memory, he claims, resides in rituals and in bodily practices – not in individual heads or collective minds. Therefore, all successful attempts to drastically change the past must pass through the changes of ritual and bodily practice. Historical reconstruction, on the other hand, proceeds inferentially and consists of the intellectual activity of following the traces of past activities.

I would classify the invention of tradition as historiogesis (the reading of history) rather than historical reconstruction, the latter being another name for

---

[23] Giddens, 1999: 39–41.   [24] Connerton, 1989.

historiography (the writing of history). This historiogesis is grounded in what Connerton calls a communal (collective) memory. In this section, however, it is what he calls *bodily social memory* that is of interest. It is the type of memory most often neglected by theoreticians and reflective practitioners. One can draw many examples from studies of organizational change where the phenomenon was noticed but filed away as a 'resistance to change', and, in Carthesian spirit, deemed to be an 'emotional problem' to be solved by 'cognitive means'.

Connerton shows how numerous scholars attempted to reinterpret as cognitive action or rule-following that which Michael Oakeshott has dubbed 'habits of affection and conduct'.[25] An example from organization theory is March and Olsen's 'logic of appropriateness', which describes action grounded in such habits, but re-classifies it as a cognitive operation by the use of the term 'logic', however ironically.[26] I believe that 'habits of affection and conduct', crucial elements of social memory, are also of crucial importance in organizing. It should also be noted that such habits are acquired mimetically and through contact.

Although Connerton primarily used examples of revolutions (e.g. the French Revolution) and the recurrence of their rituals and bodily practices, the present context deals with events that are more evolutionary. I see evolution, however, as a process without destination, and not necessarily denoting progress or betterment. Also, Connerton equated rituals with commemorative ceremonies, and therefore continued to see rituals as 'compensatory devices' of modernization rather than as its tools, which is my claim. But the non-revolutionary type of change also means that the necessity of reframing rituals and bodily practices often goes unnoticed, and that the social memory thus preserved haunts any attempt at change, and it is often at odds with the communal memory. I could observe such examples by watching city council meetings and experiencing the ways in which the three city administrations treated external petitioners.

Budget Meetings: Conspiracy, Absenteeism, Confrontation

I observed the budget sessions of the three city councils. It lasted for one full day in Warsaw, and was considered extremely inefficient, another sediment of the old regime. An analogous session in Stockholm took three days, in Rome a week. 'Efficiency' was not a criterion applied to this type of proceeding in Stockholm or Rome. Sessions had a symbolic and ritual character, and were expressions of democracy rather than efficiency.

There was a certain peculiarity to the session in Warsaw. Its most striking characteristic was that a myriad of other meetings, proceedings, and discussions took

---

[25] Oakeshott, 1948/1991: 467–72.   [26] March and Olsen, 1989.

place parallel to the budget proceedings; they were held primarily in the same conference room, but also in corridors. The session's participants used these discussions as an opportunity to exchange information, carry out lobbying activities, and make deals with people with whom it was difficult to make daily contact. Although people usually chat and wander during budget sessions until it is their turn to speak, this was much more dramatic. Word would be passed around through a messenger, and all of a sudden a group of people would rise from their seats and hurry to the 'source'. Visually and acoustically, the whispers and constant changes in the group arrangement that characterized this activity inevitably suggested an overt conspiracy. It was difficult not to think of the diaries from the Warsaw Insurrection of January 1944, which mention groups of young people in trench coats whose 'conspiring mode' could be detected from a distance.

Of course, this is not how a true conspiracy looks; neither do I intend to suggest that a literal conspiracy took place – rather, a certain style of organizing that was visible at, but not limited to, council sessions. During daily observations in the offices, I witnessed the constant and spontaneous convocations of various groups discussing matters that had just come up on the agenda. These meetings were necessary because of the inefficient communication network, and they were possible because the planning of work was not fashionable. It was difficult to pinpoint the cause and effect.

Conspiracy in Poland has usually been associated with the fight against invaders. In many places, people told me that conspiracy as an organizing style was an anachronistic sediment of the past. I formed the impression, however, that the state of emergency *was* a normal state of affairs for top officials in Warsaw as well as for its councilors, a habitual frame from which their philosophy of action was derived. The historical legacy was strong, and it was difficult to deem it groundless. During my study, the city lived under the threat of 'commando rule', which, in the organizational sphere, can be compared to a state of emergency in the political sphere. The state-of-emergency mentality was not a state of group paranoia, but the result of an effective learning process. But, most of all, conspiracy was a physical practice.

In Rome, my colleague and I were surprised to see the city council meeting in a near-empty hall. As far as we could make out, only the Chair, the current speaker and the speaker to follow were present. The speeches seemed to last forever. As I later learned, they were officially limited to 15 min, but the limit was regularly violated, and admonitions from the Chair were constant. When my colleague and I moved to an adjacent bar for coffee, we met several of the councilors. Suddenly, the voice of the Chair came straight at our ears from a speaker above our heads. She was asking the councilors to return to the hall so a vote could take place. I have seen a similar procedure in Warsaw, but there the appeal was made by messengers rather than loudspeakers. As we learned from the barman, there were several bars and canteens in the building, all equipped with loudspeakers. An additional complication of this otherwise common procedure of absenteeism was the gender of the Chair:

A woman who is a President of a city council is forced to find herself in all those political rites, which are mostly male, but also must try to change certain ways of behaving, slowly but with an eye to the consequences. [*The present Chair*] had to experience forceful opposition, some of it public, when making decisions that appeared to her to be coherent and sensible. In June 1997 Council was debating a new version of the city plan, a strongly contested proposal, with all the usual fights among the political parties, where the Chair often took heat from the contestants. Proceeding slowly and patiently, she thought the end was in sight.

Now, I do not know how it works in other countries, but in Rome each councilor has the floor for 15 minutes, and after all the speeches that follow they have 5 minutes to say why they decided to vote for or against. At the end of the debate, however, there were no speakers registered. The Chair asked twice whether anybody wished to speak, but nobody came forward. Most of them talked into their mobile phones or were in some other room, not realizing that the final stage had been reached. The Chair put the bill to the vote nevertheless, earning many insults and protests from both the majority and the opposition. In her opinion, she had the right to cut through the irrelevant rituals and proceed according to common sense. Council could not be kept waiting for the missing councilors forever. At this moment, however, she felt her alienation strongly, as the protesting men indicated more or less openly that she was acting like a woman, that is, like somebody who does not understand the politics. (Rome, Interview 13: 7–8)

The Stockholm budget session took me by surprise. I expected all the councilors to be present, the speeches to be short and effective, and attention to be complete and polite. That was not what I witnessed. True, there were many more councilors present than in Rome (in Warsaw they were present but otherwise occupied), the speeches were not overly long, and the procedure was duly recorded both manually and on tape. It should also be added that the meetings were public and that the printed proceedings were available for observers. I saw a school excursion in an area open to the public. But politeness and attention were clearly lacking. One councilor was knitting during the entire session I attended (because she was using red wool she was photographed often by the reporters); the majority leader was wearing headphones during the opposition speeches (apparently he was learning a foreign language), and it seemed to be in good taste to leave the hall as soon as a political opponent started talking. People were openly engaging in private conversations and wandering among the benches. I was enlightened during the interviews:

> Swedish politics is incredibly confrontational, perhaps among the most confrontational in Europe. We always talk about consensus. Consensus my foot; here we are enemies. We fight. If a Moderate says something the Social Democrats assume it is nonsense and the other way around.
>
> The picture of consensus politics was invented by the Social Democrats. They could do it because they stayed in power for almost 40 years. There were conflicts even then, but they were repressed. And as foreign journalists interviewed only the Social Democrats, the idea was that everybody in Sweden thinks alike, that is, like Social Democrats. But it was never so.
>
> Since 1976, when they first lost power, and especially now, the picture has become more like the 'normal European way'. We now fight an enormous battle over the basic ideology, the view of the people. We are inside an enormous economic, mental, and political shift of the regime. . . (Stockholm, Interview 13: 7)

The next utterance comes from the same party and confirms the facts but not the interpretation. The speaker is a woman:

> There was no confrontational politics when I came to the Council in 1973. But when I listen to the debates now, I see how these new people seem keen to attack one another. Nothing constructive, no admission that the opposition has done something good or that we could do something together. I think it is very sad. It was much more interesting before. It was a different style. Everything was different.
>
> All councilors came to the meeting decently dressed: not necessarily in Saville Row suits, but properly. Now it seems obligatory to dress casually. It may be unimportant, but it marks lack of respect for the activity. And it earns no respect. Citizens watching men in shirts with tails hanging out of their trousers can be hardly expected to trust their councilors. There were also different rules of behavior before. Now one can take liberties that were not allowed before.
>
> Also, each small issue is discussed forever. The council never accomplishes anything. The meetings become unbearable, and the council manages to go through only two or three motions in an evening. Interpellations never end, because nobody ever gives up, and everybody repeats the same thing again and again. Sad, isn't it? Much of this has to do with their will to be seen, but it becomes boring for the media as well; they can hardly get any publicity this way. (Stockholm, Interview 14: 21)

If I were to judge from the three meetings, Stockholm has still a long way to go to reach the 'normal European way'. No doubt, however, it is on its way there. It is interesting to see that confrontational mores, that is, more aggressive ones, are also linked to male rituals; this is not to say that women do not follow such rituals, by choice or by necessity, as the example of the female Chair in Rome indicated. The councilors in Stockholm seem to be fully aware, however, that change happens through a change in rituals and bodily practices, where dressing styles are of utmost importance. But bodily practices are contained not only in clothing. The patterns of speech, and the ways of using technologies, also bear strong traces of social memory.

Budget sessions are powerful rituals; the actual organizing of resources takes place before and after the session.[27] But, as Connerton points out, they are not merely expressive or formal, nor are they limited in their effect to the ritual occasion. 'Rites have the capacity to give value and meaning to the life of those who perform them'.[28] Thus, the introduction of new rituals, as in the case of public tenders, or the change or subversion of existing rituals, as in the case of Stockholm's budget sessions, seem to be powerful reframing devices. And although I speak separatedly of rituals and bodily practices in my text, Stockholm's examples show that they are inseparable in a ritual context. Rituals differ from other symbolic expressions in that they are bodily practices. Reading a text that presents a new ideology is not the same as performing it, which is what happens in a ritual. It is easy to read a text and wholly disagree with it; it is painful, or at least embarrassing, to perform an unfamiliar ritual. Bodily practices are infinitely more resistant to globalization than abstract texts.

Bodies at Court and on the Telephone

Conspiracy in Warsaw can be traced to yet another context: that of a royal court. This metaphoric context is at home in Poland, a country with a court tradition, but out-of-place in Sweden, which defines itself as a peasant country without a court tradition. It is not, after all, only a metaphor. In the Austro-Hungarian Empire – the least hated invader of Poland – the court and public administration were one and the same. Many Poles made their administrative careers at the court of Franz Joseph, and many procedures were assimilated by the Polish administration. Two such procedures seemed to me to be characteristic of the organizing process that I observed: defense from 'petitioners' and 'antechambering' (the gathering of petitioners and employees in antechambers, or, in the context of contemporary life, in the secretaries' room). I had the bad luck of experiencing it myself:

> I had an appointment with a councilor. I entered City Hall and asked security guards where room number 19 was. Then I went in the direction indicated, only to find that the corridor ended and

[27] See Chapter 6 in Czarniawska, 1997.   [28] Connerton, 1989: 45.

there was no such room. I decided to enter Room 21, where I had been before and where, as it seemed to me, the Council Secretariat worked. The door was closed, and there was a note on the door: 'Information in Room 17'. Working through the doors with numbers and those without numbers, I concluded that the room I was looking for must be behind a door without a number. It was closed, too, so I went to Room 17. I knocked (which I was told later is not done and was probably why nobody would ever answer) and entered. There were three young women in the room. I inquired about seeing the councilor.

— Mr. Councilor is at a Council meeting.
— But I have an appointment!
— Maybe he will come down to meet you.
— He will come down where?
— To the hall.
— But where in the hall? [*It was enormous*]
— And where did you have your appointment?
— In Room 19, but it is closed.
— So it's probably here.
— Here in this room?
— Well no, here on the ground floor.
— But I don't know him, and he doesn't know me. How will he recognize me?
— He will go to Room 21.
— But Room 21 is closed.
— I can't do anything about that. We can't open it.

Stalemate. I keep thinking frenetically, but nothing comes to my mind.

— So what should I do?
— He will come to this room to pick up the keys.
— You will tell him that I am waiting for him, won't you?
— Yes, of course.
— But where can I wait?
— Here on the ground floor.
— But where? [*There were no chairs in the corridor*]
— There are chairs next to the reception desk.
— Thank you very much.

I settled next to the reception desk, next to the main entrance where the security guards were, and waited for an hour. In the meantime many people went in the direction of Room 17. One of them could very well have been the Councilor. I went back to the known corridor where Room 21 was now open.

— I had an appointment with the Councilor. Did he come back from the Council meeting?
— The Councilor isn't right here, but he is in the City Office. Pointing to the door of the Room Without a Number: You can go in and wait there if you want.

— But I had an appointment with him at noon. It is now 1:30 PM,
and I have another appointment at 2.
— He might be in Room 4. I will call there.

She calls, talks for a while, and puts the receiver down. – No, he is
not there any longer, but you can wait here. He was there but left.

— But I left a message in Room 17 that I was waiting for him.
— Mr. Councilor wasn't in Room 17 at all. He came here right away.
— But I couldn't wait here because the room was closed, and I went
to Room 17 because there was a note on the door.
— Of course it was closed; we were at the meeting. At any rate,
Room 17 didn't give us any information. (Field Diary)

The interview was rescheduled for another date. The councilor was very apologetic. He arrived late to Room 21, assumed that I had already left, and rushed to the room of the person who had arranged the appointment to apologize and fix another date.

Situations like this were common and sometimes without such a happy ending; for example, after daily telephone calls, I was finally able to make an appointment a few hours before my departure from Poland. When I arrived, it turned out that I was third in line to see the Important Official and that I could expect no more than a 20-minute interview. (It was a person with whom I had previously had a two-hour interview.) I left without an interview.

It would be utterly wrong to conclude that the secretarial service was poor. I have seen a whole range of service, and there were many who were competent, warm, and helpful. But the work time was unplanned, and seemed to be flexible – but flexible solely in terms of its extendibility, for everybody worked long hours and not always for pay. In my opinion, the clue to understanding the situation was precisely the defense from 'petitioners' and 'antechambering'.

The tradition of many years, perpetuated in different contexts, taught people that the only effective way of obtaining help was through intervention from above. Both the employees inside and the petitioners outside show little respect for the universally accepted procedure of registering complaints: begin with the employee who takes the information and, if necessary, work up the hierarchy to the direct supervisor and even beyond. Instead, they begin directly at the top.

If senior staff members were to meet everybody who wanted to see them, they would not be able to do anything else. The institution of a deputy whose job it was to meet the public did not stand the test of time, for everyone demanded 'to see the boss'. Therefore, a complex system of defense procedures was necessary, and secretarial offices specialized in these skills. In addition, both the petitioners and the 'courtiers' tended to gather in the secretaries' room because one never knew when the boss might appear, perhaps on the way to the toilet. Thus, there were many devices in place, intended to discourage the practice of passing time in front of the boss's door.

In the offices of one of the district mayors, I was surprised to see that the secretary's room had only chair – that of the secretary, who was a young and very attractive young woman. When, after a few visits, I realized that some young men were able to stand for hours in her room nevertheless, I understood that the lack of chairs was an indispensable self-defense, as well as the usual boss-defense. Of course, offices that served petitioners had waiting rooms and chairs.

Besides the official petitioners there were all sorts of people whom a director did not want to see. There was no barrier other than a secretary's office, so they entered directly. Here are observations from visits to two different offices:

> I am sitting in the Director's room and I can hear when a visitor enters. He learns that the Director is not in. The visitor says that he would like to invite the Director to visit him one day. The secretary says in a small voice, 'It is possible'. The visitor leaves. From the secretary's office I can hear a sigh and an exclamation 'Horrible indeed!' I cough with understanding and compassion. The secretary joins me.
>
> Secretary: It's terrible to be a secretary.
> BC: But you did very well. He left without protest.
> Secretary: Because I confused him. I told him he was late. Madam Director was in a hurry, so she had to go. But how unpleasant it is. Nothing but lies, lies, and lies. Besides, they mustn't see that I am lying.
>
> She returns to her room. I hear a voice from behind the door:
> — 'Is the Director in?'
> Secretary: She is in, but not here. (The phone rings.) Yes Madam, she is in, but not here. In this place everybody is in but just not here.
> (Warsaw, Observation 3: 6)

Later, I also fell victim to this secretary's special skills, but I could not blame her. This was really an organizationally impossible situation. Some of the encounters with unwanted petitioners were actually frightening:

> Secretary: This haunted guy is here again. One day he will strangle me, and then he will kill you. He invented something and it's on this squared piece of paper you have here somewhere.
>
> Director: He either has to be treated properly or not allowed to enter.
>
> Secretary: You mean that we ought to give his picture to six guards at the gates and tell them not to let him in? But even this wouldn't work. He is so polite, so very polite, but when he looks at me – when he merely looks at me – I know he is going to kill me one day.
>
> Director: Hopefully not today. Tell him that I am busy.
>
> Secretary: I will tell him that you are busy; but he wants so much to talk to you because what he invented is a work of genius.
> (Warsaw, Observation 6: 1)

It was difficult to decipher the line between a joke and the truth, because attempts at hot-headed entries also happened. It seemed that every office had at least one 'lunatic' for whom waiting rooms were the only place of interaction with other people. Here again, tradition created a problem, for any attempt to introduce guards or gates was associated with police methods and security services. Openness was a political requirement and an organizational problem.

I do not want to make literal claims about court tradition in Rome, although the Habsburg influence certainly reached the north and the south of Rome. At any rate, the habit of 'getting to the boss' was very strong even there. At the same time, the Roman administration fought to introduce openness and a client-oriented attitude. However, as I was to learn, bodily social memory was hard to erase. We were not allowed to shadow Rome's councilors and managers; thus all observations came from public events and from interview situations (which gave ample room for observation as they rarely took place as scheduled). The repetitive procedure connected with securing interviews illustrates the problem well, as shown in this half-fictitious composite:

Day 1

— Hallo?

— Good morning. My name is BC, and I am Professor of Management at Göteborg University. I have sent the Commissioner a description of my research project and asked her/him for an interview . . .

— Please wait. I will put you through to her/his secretary. . .

Loud music in the receiver.

— Hallo?

— Good morning. My name is . . ., I am . . . I have sent . . .

— Wait until I find my colleague who takes care of such matters.

Music.

— The Secretariat of the Commissioner, good morning!

— My name . . . I am . . .

— And?

— I have sent a letter to the Commissioner . . .

— I do not see anything like that. When did you do that?

— On . . . [date]

— It does not appear in our diary. If you could fax us the text of the letter on the headed paper . . .

— What is a headed paper?

— [*Explanation follows. The conversation is taking place in Italian, and BC is used to Swedish practices, i.e. sending official letters directly from her computer, using the University logo.*]

— I understand. What is your fax number?

— 6000 . . .

— Excellent. I will do it immediately. Thank you.

The fax does not connect, as the line seems to be permanently busy. It goes through during the night.

Day 2

— Hallo? Good morning. I would like to talk to the Commissioner's Secretary.
— Who are you?
— My name is . . . I am . . .
— Please wait for the connection.

Music.

— Good morning. I am . . . I have called yesterday and also sent a fax.
— Sorry but you talked to my colleague who is not here at the moment. Could you please call again [in 10 minutes, in an hour, after lunch, tomorrow]?
— Certainly. What is your colleague's name? [*BC is learning!*]
— [Surname].
— Thank you.

Day 3

— Hallo?
— Good morning, I am . . ., I would like to talk to madam/doctor Surname please.
— Here you are.

Music.

— Good morning, I am . . ., I called you two days ago . . .
— Yes, yes. Unfortunately I did not have an opportunity to show your fax to the Commissioner. If you leave me your telephone number, I will call you as soon as I reach him.
— Unfortunately I am moving constantly, as I am interviewing other people. May I call again?
— Certainly, call tonight, or even better tomorrow. (Field Diary)

Although this dialogue has been composed by me, it is a composite of a great many attempts to access commissioners (it was much easier to reach managers, with the exception of the city manager, who was living the life of a commissioner). On one extreme was a written answer to my letter from a commissioner who suggested the date and time for our interview; on the other was a commissioner who was never interviewed in spite of 50 (Yes! 50!) calls, one letter, and three faxes. Sometimes I was given a mobile number,[29] which would mean another 'hunting expedition' and a thorough familiarity with TIM's recorded messages.

There is a striking similarity between the Warsaw and Rome offices in terms of space management. Much as it was unpleasant to be their target, it was not difficult to understand the reasons for their persistence. The lack of confidence in the

---

[29] Italy and Finland are leading in the use of mobile telephones in Europe.

officials was still widespread (the petitioners have social memories, too), and the conviction that the higher one reaches, the better the chances of one's wishes being granted was unshakeable. The result was that 'the bosses' were virtually besieged by supplicants, and the commissioners rarely ended their working day before midnight. The complicated system of 'the secretariat' and 'the press office', which were, in theory, created to facilitate public contacts, were doing their best to filter and minimize them. Technology – from absent chairs to telephones and faxes – was used to create a barrier, which was especially paradoxical when 'communication technology' was put to such use.

What about Stockholm, then? I sent letters followed by a call, as in all three cities. The call would be answered by the secretary who would connect me to the councilor or the official; otherwise there would be voice mail. After having registered my request with a living or automatic secretary, my call would invariably be returned, with several suggestions for dates and times. The rule of public openness – transparency of public administration – is both a legal requirement and a bodily practice in Sweden.

HISTORIOGESIS AND BODILY RECALL

Does the history of city management determine its present? Or can people invent any tradition they please? Neither statement describes the situation I observed in the three cities. Even though some historians and readers continue to be annoyed by Hayden White's claim that there is no history, only historiographies, and that historical texts are literary artifacts, it is difficult not to agree with him.[30] The study of the three cities reveals a variation on the historian's work, which can be called historiogesis, that is, a reading of history as written or told by others. Historians, says White, plot their stories to arrive at a moral point; I would claim that managers plot their stories to arrive at a pragmatic point. Traditions are compiled from selectively combined elements of an existing repertoire, into a coherent version that serves a pragmatic purpose: organizing, legitimizing, reframing. The limits of this creative process are the limits of the accessible and legitimate repertoire. As I said before, the past 50 years in Warsaw and the past 20 or so in Italy did not provide a repertoire that could be used for inventing traditions. It is also generally postulated that creative operations on historical material are always more successful when there is an appropriate gap between the present and the elaborated past.[31] It is easier to invent tradition from times that cannot be recalled in living human memory.

At the same time, the immediate past is well entrenched in rituals and bodily practices, in what Connerton called the social memory, but what could also be

---

[30] See, e.g., *Tropics of Discourse* (White, 1978), or *The Content of the Form* (White, 1987).
[31] See, e.g., Taussig, 1993, who again traces it back to Benjamin.

called the *social recall*, to match the active character of historiogesis. Male rituals in political contexts, defense of the bosses, politeness or rudeness of public behavior, continue to be present in spite of ambitions to reframe. It takes a revolutionary awareness to interfere with rituals and bodily practices, whereas most of the public sector reforms are conducted in a rational, modernist spirit.

Past management, invented or preserved in embodied practices, is not the only material for organizing. There are also laws and regulations, philosophies and ideologies that are both local and translocal. I will therefore turn, in Chapter 6, to the 'cultural contexts of organizing', using this term cautiously, to denote the various elements of the contexts that were brought to my attention by my interlocutors and other commentators on city management, in explanation of their practices.

6

City Management in Its Cultural Context

. . . in different societies discord between fresh desires and old, between a new scientific idea and existing religious dogmas, is not always immediately perceived nor perceived within the same period of time. Besides, when the discord is perceived, the desire to put an end to it is not always equally strong.[1]

In this chapter, I try to interpret the local translations of translocal ideas described previously in terms of the cultural context of city management or local mimesis. Although I and not my interlocutors do this contextualization, it does not mean that I switch perspectives from local (or translocal) and concrete to speculative and abstract. In this chapter, I follow the clues given to me by the people I met in the field, clues that lead to more distant action nets – distant in time, more than 50 years, and distant in the type of activity. Management, almost by definition, is always connected to many non-managerial actions (the management of what?). Additionally, as Tarde noted, 'the social forces of any real importance at any period are not composed of the necessarily feeble imitations that have radiated from recent inventions, but of the imitations of ancient inventions, radiations which are alike more intense and more widespread because they have had the necessary time in which to spread out and become established as habits, customs . . .'[2]

Such excursions to distant action nets is the basis of my claim that the three cities we studied were exposed to two contrasting tendencies: that of rational idealism and that of pragmatism. The need to reconcile contradictory tendencies resulted in locally institutionalized thought structures of a hybrid character that I call 'isolationist automorphism' (Warsaw), 'relentless isomorphism' (Stockholm), and 'merciless idealism' (Rome).

CULTURAL CONTEXTS OF ORGANIZING AND OF THEORIZING

As mentioned earlier, the studies of the three cities were comparative in the sense popularized by Barney Glaser and Anselm Strauss, who spoke of a

---

[1] Tarde, 1888/1969: 179.   [2] Tarde, 1890/1962: 19.

'constant comparative analysis'.[3] To describe anything, it is necessary to compare it with something different. In that sense, all social studies are or should be comparative; the comparison should lead the researcher's shift between time and place.

When geographical distance crosses national frontiers, more complications than usual are expected. There is, however, no obvious argument that it must be so. Culture is what people at a given place and time take for granted, however, the limits of a place and a time are forever shifting. 'The Italian culture', if such an entity exists, does not begin in Bolzano, and 'the Austrian culture' does not end in Innsbruck. In fact, Bolzano and Innsbruck are much more alike than Bolzano and Palermo. Thus, on the one hand, researchers would do well to avoid stereotyping and creating 'total cultures'; on the other hand, they would do equally well by abandoning the notion of 'universals', both in the practice under study and in the study itself. To move across time and place is as problematic as it is necessary and informative.

One of the most important elements of time/space is the language used to describe the events and formulate the interpretations. In a research project with a trans-cultural dimension, linguistic differences play a fundamental role. My ambition was, therefore, to find expressions that were not mechanical translations from one language to another, but that occupied a similar semantic space in different language communities – expressions that were used in similar contexts with similar significance attributed to them. This task proved quite difficult, however.

In the field of city management, for example, there were two central groups of actors in Stockholm, as in other Swedish municipalities: politicians (*politiker*) and civil servants (*tjänstemän*). This terminology was misleading in Warsaw. For many years the word 'politician' had the negative meaning of 'careerist'. The word has now begun to recover, but not without difficulty. Most interlocutors prefer to use the word 'politician' to mean 'big politics' or 'capital-P politics'. City politicians are called *radni* (a word approximating the English term *councilors*) because their functions are perceived as societal rather than political. Thus, the political parties and the ruling government are exercising capital-P politics as well as small-p politics, or personal aspirations to power, and 'the societal function', which consists of representing the city inhabitants. There is no morally neutral expression for pursuing politics inside an organization. Actions that cannot be classified as 'officially political' are tinted gray by a suspicion of the personal motives and benefits involved.

The word *urzednik* refers to non-managerial positions (*clerk* in English) or to 'government employees'. The managerial positions in the city government (*officials* in British English, *officers* in American English) are called *menadzerskie* (a neologism), thus avoiding the unpleasant hint of bureaucracy hidden in words like *administrator* (administrator) or *zarzadca* (a dated, Slavic expression for administrator).

---

[3] In *The Discovery of Grounded Theory*, 1967.

In Rome, the problem consisted of the fact that there were not two but three groups, the third, hybrid group, being the most important. This group was formed first by *assessori* or commissioners, and also by presidents of some municipal companies, who were either employed as politicians or administrators with political functions.[4] Although this type of position also exists in Stockholm and in Warsaw, the incumbents in those two cities are not perceived as forming a group, and especially not as a group of central importance. They identify more with their party or with their committee than with one another. In Rome, a group of lesser importance but of the same 'hybrid' provenance consititued the members of the commissioners' staff, who could be either 'broiler politicians' or rising administrators; their future allegiance was uncertain even to them.

Thus, although it is possible to find appropriate terms in all three languages and to translate them into English, they do not necessarily denote the same or even similar positions. Still, it is quite usual to note linguistic differences in vocabularies of practice, especially in transcultural studies. It is somewhat less usual to speak of differences in vocabularies of theory: and although I believe they are as frequent, they remain unacknowledged. It took me some time to discover that my interlocutors (the practitioners) and I (the theorist) differed in our understanding of terms denoting the objects of my study. This was nowhere as clear as in the case of the concept crucial to both of us: the concept of *organizing*.

Organizing can be defined as an ordering activity: assuring that appropriate people and objects arrive at an appropriate place at an appropriate time.[5] My interlocutors and I agreed on that simple definition without difficulty: the problems began when we had to describe what must be done to bring people and objects to the right place at the right time. It was easy to find negative examples: a King Kong dummy was to climb the Culture Palace in Warsaw, but as a result of 'bad organization', did not do so until 22.00, when all the young potential spectators had gone to bed sorely disappointed. The Warsaw newspapers frequently reported various 'organizational troubles'. The 'Supertram' joining Casaletto with Largo Argentina was put into operation too soon, according to the Roman journalists. There were many examples of 'bad organization'. But how does one organize well?

Both theory and the field reflection about organizational practice do not devote much attention to the complexity of organizing, giving priority instead to 'organizations'. And yet organizations can be seen as nothing more or less than societal fictions,[6] legal persons called to life in order to facilitate the foundation of modern society: accountability.[7] The fiction of organization requires supporting fictions: norms and rules – legal, economic, and technical. 'Organizational structure' is one such fiction of a lesser caliber, one that helps in introducing

---

[4] The closeness of these two positions can be illustrated by the fact that in January, 2002, the CEO of ATAC was nominated the Commissioner for Traffic Issues.
[5] Latour, 1997.   [6] Knorr Cetina, 1994.   [7] Douglas, 1986.

accountability into society and that supports the organizing process without replacing it. Perfecting organizational structure may, but need not, influence the outcome of organizing. Structures (forms) and practices are, it has been said, *loosely coupled.*[8] The principle of loose coupling is considered functional, so far as it prevents the transfer of perturbations from one part of the net to another.

The organizational structures can only help or hamper the process, but they can be easily changed, redesigned, and constructed anew. Therefore, endless energy is devoted to their design and redesign in organizational practice. It is firmly believed that a change in structure is a way to change the processes or practices. But if processes are loosely coupled to structures, it is highly unlikely that they will change simultaneously. Why, then, should we not redesign the processes? Of course it is sometimes attempted, but never with ease. For processes are dynamic, complex, and often partially invisible entities – not because they are deliberately hidden, but because they are taken for granted.

Thus, the definition of organizing that I have adopted emphasizes aspects other than well-known planning, decision-making, and control. This perspective does not render planning, decision-making, and control any less important – it is merely another viewpoint that deserves the same attention as these concepts have already received. Moreover, the pragmatist perspective on organizing that I espouse sees them as rationality rituals rather than the central focus of organizing.

This perspective did not tally with my interlocutors' understanding of organizing, organization, and management. To take an extreme example, in Polish 'to organize' is also a slang expression meaning 'to provide something by any means', which usually denotes an illegal activity. In Swedish and Italian the use of the word is closer to that of organization theory, but more limited. My interlocutors saw organizing primarily as the imposition of structures (forms), and management as decision-making.

This does not mean that my interlocutors possessed clear and firm definitions that could be analyzed and compared to mine; neither is the correctness of any of these definitions at issue here. It is important to keep in mind that definitions have, in the practice of management, a *performative* character – they are constructed for practical purposes. Thus, definitions may vary from context to context or they may change in time.

One could say that my definitions gained an upper hand – but only in this text. They have but one advantage: they are more fixed than others, at least for the duration of this text, and thus, can be used as a basis for comparing other, more mobile and transformative definitions. My definitions are also performative, but they perform another function – that of structuring a text rather than a living experience. The field definitions continue to be constructed and reconstructed as the practice unfolds. Successful redefining is a key to successful reframing. And reframing is, actually, one concept on which we could all agree.

---

[8] Weick, 1976.

PURPOSEFUL REFRAMING

One of the routes to successful reframing is through an extirpation of collective memory and its props: networks, associations, and information channels. But such an operation which, one could claim, was successfully performed in post-socialist regimes, leaves the organization field empty. It is therefore easy to produce new solutions, but it is difficult to circulate and institutionalize them.

For example, Warsaw's city treasurer was developing an innovative procedure for preparing budgets that would be easily comprehended by the councilors. Such an attempt had been made in Stockholm several years earlier, but the pressure of professional norms rendered it unsuccessful. Because no such pressure existed in Warsaw, the treasurer easily solved the problem with which other city treasurers had struggled with little success.[9] An *undeveloped* organization field, however, meant that this innovative practice would most likely remain a local discovery and might vanish when the incumbent left her position. Indeed, the presentation of the budget went well during the tenure of one council, but the next council severely criticized the budget.[10]

In a *well-developed* organization field, the network of professional organizations would intervene either at an early stage, preventing the treasurer from deviating from what is considered a good practice, or at a later stage, defending the treasurer from attacks by arguing that a new 'good practice' is being developed. At first, the established newspapers fought fiercely against the new and successful daily *Metro*. Then came a frenetic imitation in the form of a spate of new dailies of the same kind. This newspaper example is the most salient contrast to organizing practices in Warsaw. In Stockholm, the well-developed field at first attacked the deviant; when the deviant persisted and achieved success, the same field quickly imitated its success. In Warsaw, the loosening of an institutional order created room for maneuver, experimentation, and creativity; but the same loose institutional order could not save and propagate the results of such creativity.

In Rome, as in other Italian cities, an attempt was made to introduce the practice of 'management accounting'.[11] As its procedural aspects were open and left to local interpretation, the old institutional order defended itself by translating the innovation into a set of practices that were not distinguishable from those it was meant to replace.

Also, it is easier to extirpate a network of interactions (as in post-1989 Poland or in Italy after the 'Clean Hands' campaign) than to eradicate the social memory of actions that took place in such a network. The old frame still interferes, although it is more visible to the observers than to the actors, who unconsciously reproduce old patterns of action. A vicious circle is established. Where the organization field is undeveloped, as in Poland, there is no organized debate on the processes of transformation, and there are no forms of organized reflection, such

[9] Czarniawska, 1997.   [10] Czarniawska, 2000.
[11] *Controllo di gestione*, see Gherardi and Lippi, 2000.

as development courses focused on analyzing everyday experience rather than abstract models. Where the organization field is *overdeveloped*, as in Italy, the old connections between actions persist even when the actors are replaced.

'An undeveloped organization field' is a notion that can be compared to a *regulatory vacuum*[12] – a concept used by Polish analysts themselves. In a report on the privatization of municipal services, the authors claimed that one of the difficulties of privatization lay in the lack of proper laws and regulations that would aid this process. A year later, however, the same team came to the opposite conclusion, saying that 'the excessive regulation of the process, especially in the form of impractical and unenforceable rules, turns out to be much less advantageous than giving the municipality autonomy'.[13] Warsaw found itself in a situation similar to that of Rome, which can be called a *regulatory jungle* or an overdeveloped organization field.

One may postulate that a well-developed organization field is not the one filled with regulations and rules; rather it features the standards and norms adopted at will, and not from a fear of formal sanctions. Stockholm has a similar problem, which is its propensity for eagerly following all managerial trends, which spread quickly in a well-developed organization field.

Although reframing was a conscious goal in both Warsaw and in Rome, the old frame continued to reappear in both cases. Extensive experimentation was conducted in Warsaw, but the new solutions were not properly anchored and they easily vanished into oblivion. The assumed necessity of a total rupture between 'the old frame' and 'the new frame' made comparisons, and therefore constructive reflection, difficult. The old frame became taboo, and by the same token it was more difficult to remove than if it were a topic of open discussion. The undeveloped organization field favored individual learning over collective learning. The 'metatranslation' – the translation of the institutional order – was hampered by all of this, which, in turn, hampered local translations and in particular the reframing of action nets.

It is likely that my interlocutors in Warsaw would easily agree with such a summary. What would become a contested point, however, is the 'old frame'. There has been an unquestioned agreement over the fact that the 'old frame' consisted of a so-called Communist order – an order that was no doubt obnoxious, but it was after all never legitimate and only 50 years old. Although such sediments were undeniably in play, the frame I saw underneath was much older and therefore more solid.

FRAMES: OLD AND NEW

As I claimed at the outset of this book, all the complex and contradictory processes that we sweepingly denote as globalization – whether they lead to

---

[12] Aziewicz, 1993.   [13] Aziewicz, 1994: 166.

isomorphism, allomorphism, or automorphism – are invariably based on translation. The transfer of ideas and practices from one context to another requires transportation, which always ends in transformation: this is what translation is all about. It comprises that which exists and that which is created – the relation between humans and ideas, ideas and objects, and humans and objects; all are necessary in order to reframe a city.

What exactly was being translated in Warsaw and Rome? I claim that, strangely enough, it was the same things that were translated in Stockholm, a city that makes a habit of constant reframing: the 'global', or translocal ideas of self-government, the modern city budget, effective management, and privatization. Each time in each city, the translation from the translocal into the local repertoire encountered difficulties that can be metaphorically depicted as resulting from the lack of a dictionary. As every translator knows, translation is a destabilizing operation. It destabilizes the text under translation, which is taken from its proper cultural context, and fits it onto another. And the language into which the translation is made is destabilized a little with every translation made. Thus, there is a need for the stabilizing role of dictionaries; if translators were left to decide, we would soon end up with another Tower of Babel. In Warsaw, but partly also in Rome, even the main dictionary – the institutional order – was under revision in order to embrace new and different translation possibilities. The dictionary itself was being translated.

In Poland, the model for the new dictionary was an institutional order known as a western-type democracy accompanied by a capitalist economy. As to the character of the old dictionary, it is difficult to label. I would agree with those who claim that, in 1989, it was a patchwork of incoherent influences rather than a planned economy in a socialist country. But as to the model, it is easy to agree that we are speaking of a post-Second World War model, best known in its Anglo-American version. If so, it is important to point out that this model is grounded in pragmatist philosophy (especially its US version) and in the common law (as different from the codex law). Does it fit the local tradition in Warsaw? Has it been assimilated in Stockholm and Rome?

What I saw in Warsaw was an attempt to translate a philosophy of management originating in a blend of liberal–pragmatist philosophy and the Anglo-American legal tradition. This attempt was met with an inadvertent but strong resistance from the local, rational–legalist, anti-pragmatist tradition (influenced by French rationalism, German idealism, and continental law). The anti-pragmatist tradition is accentuated to an even greater degree in Italy, a country characterized, as I see it, by a *merciless idealism* in its view of public administration and in its ways of reforming the latter. As for Poland, anti-pragmatism was practically invented there, but because it was defined as the only tradition worthy of emulation (thus my term *isolationist automorphism*), it could be simulaneously perceived as an obstacle to transformation. Officially, it was the 'Communist' frame that hindered the desired changes.

In Rome, the 'old frame' was that of corruption and bureaucratic inefficiency. The 'new frame' was to be one of transparency and managerial efficiency.

The ways of reframing were, however, found within the existing institutional order, which had a tendency to reproduce itself. The city managers in Warsaw and Rome seem to share the same frame of meaning, so they will be discussed together here, in contrast to Stockholm. Stockholm, it seems, experienced no conflict between an 'old' and a 'new' frame: it has been constantly adjusting its frame according to the newest fashion – therefore there is *relentless isomorphism*. The continuous reframing took place within a hybrid space created by a combination of pragmatic and rational–idealistic elements.

A short excursion into the differences between the pragmatist and the idealist frames might be in order at this point. The *Pears Cyclopaedia* is particularly useful for this purpose, because of its popular and therefore unabashedly ideological type of definitions. In the 1959 edition, *common law*, along with *equity* and *statute* law, which is the cornerstone of the law of England, is presented as follows:

The English Legal System is a *living organism*, not a dead, static code. The system as we know it began to develop in the thirteenth century, when Henry II extended the practice of sending the royal judges about the country 'on circuit', to deal with crimes and disputes, and to adapt and give official authority to the best of the local customs. . . . The judges did it by *empirical methods* – that is, by practical, commonsense decisions on actual cases. . . . Simple records of the most important decisions were kept from the earliest times; as the centuries passed, the gradual elaboration of a system of *law-reporting* ensured that the *facts* of significant cases, the *reasoned judgments* delivered on those facts, and the *principles* those judgments enshrined, should be recorded and preserved; at the same time the doctrine of *precedent* . . . ensured consistency throughout the country. Thus there was gradually developed a body of principles – living, growing, and adaptable to new sets of facts as they arose; principles, moreover, which rose above local differences of custom and became *common* to the whole Realm.[14]

The 'dead static code', the main rival of common law, is the continental or the Roman-Germanic code, called the code or civil law. The last label developed as a result of the legal reform in Prussia in 1896, where civil law, as regulating the private sphere (including enterprises) was strongly differentiated from the public sphere. However, in its original meaning, as introduced by Justinian in the Code of the Roman Empire, *jus civile* meant the 'law as applied to the citizens of Rome', as opposed to *jus gentium* or the 'law common to all the nations of the empire'.

The best-known codes in contemporary times are embodied in the Napoleonic Code, reformed in 1875, and *Juristenrecht* in its 1896 version. This information comes from *Encyclopaedia Britannica*, which, although scientific in intention and austere in tone, nevertheless adds:

The French Revolution established the idea that the basis of law is statute, not custom. Customs were to be tolerated as the basis of laws only until they were replaced by statutes. The civil code that Napoleon enacted sought to express all laws in written language comprehensible to the average citizen. It also sought to avoid ruptures with tradition when possible. The code is expressed in short articles arranged in comprehensive and logical manner . . .

The German system attempts to be more precise than the French and to be detailed in areas in which the French code is cursory. Its wording is more subdued and its tone less

---

[14]   *Pears Cyclopaedia*, 1959: D4.

didactic. As modified for conditions in West Germany today, the code is aimed at preserving social democracy.[15]

The differences diminished in contemporary practice. In the USA one finds codes regulating certain matters in a far-reaching and detailed way (e.g., the Uniform Commercial Code), and the situation differs from one state to another. In the UK there are voices claiming that a constitution should be written. Various European countries apply variations of the Napoleonic Code (Italy, but also Holland, Belgium, Luxembourg, and Spain) or *Juristenrecht* (Sweden, but also Austria, Switzerland, Norway, Denmark, and Japan). Poland, as far as I understand, combines the essence of the Napoleonic Code with the Swiss commercial law. Specialists in comparative law claim that the current Dutch law best meets the requirements of modernity.[16]

It is obvious that different frames express different assumptions concerning human nature. The common law is pragmatic and optimistic about human nature; left to themselves, people will construct what they need. The civil law is idealistic and therefore severe toward the human nature, which must be improved by sanctions and prescriptions. My interlocutors in Warsaw and Rome shared this pessimism toward their fellow human beings, assuming, to put it succinctly, that people direct themselves only by short-term self-interest, and are unable to demonstrate solidarity with one another. If unhindered by structures, they will therefore engage in incessant conflicts, which not only threaten the interests of the collective, but also, in the long run, their own self-interest. Consequently, the two frames dictate two different action programs.

THE TWO ACTION PROGRAMS AND THEIR MIXED RESULTS

There were highly diverse opinions on the issues of how to manage the city and how to introduce changes. Sometimes these opinions constituted a controversy, but more frequently they oscillated or mixed preferences between the two ways of changing and managing: one that recommends constant experimentation and the memorizing of successful solutions and one that recommends the creation of a vision of a desired future and a program for reaching that decision. I have summarized the two action programs in the table that follows.

Another way of contrasting the 'rational–legalist' and 'pragmatist' philosophies of management, would be to recall Oakeshott's two forms of moral life: that based on the *reflective application of a moral criterion*, and that based on the *habit of affection and conduct*.[17] The two are always mixed, says Oakeshott, but the mixture can give priority to one or to the other. Although habits of affection and conduct benefit from reflection, the dominance of ideals over habit results in a

[15] *Encyclopaedia Britannica*, 1990, *Micropaedia* vol. 3: 338–9.
[16] Michael Stolleis, personal communication, June 1995.
[17] Oakeshott, 1948/1991: 472, 461.

Method of introducing changes	Revolutionary	Evolutionary
Results	Visible in direct effects of the change	Long-term – resulting from necessary adaptations of the program of change and the learning process
Management understood as	Creation of structures, rules of conduct, and regulations	Conscious development of practices, utilization of emerging opportunities, and establishment of new ones
Decisive success factor	Charismatic leadership and integration of conflicting interests imposed from above	Goodwill of a group of people who negotiate an integrated line of action
Philosophy of management	Rational and legalistic	Pragmatist

permanent tension. This is the situation in Warsaw and Rome, as I see it. The two attitudes are not even mixed, but they exist side by side; the adoption of one or the other depends on whether one is the reformer or the reformed. In Stockholm, the inherited mixture gave precedence to the habit, but the emerging mixture tends to give precedence to rationalist reflection.

In other words, at any given time and place there is something like an 'institutionalized thought structure',[18] or a 'normal way of reasoning':[19] a set, rather than a system, of taken-for-granted assumptions that are not necessarily coherent. With a certain amount of simplification, one could thus claim that the rational–legalist management philosophy is a 'normal' way of reasoning in the context of formal organizing. Its contradictory character – the fact that it clashes with both the democracy and liberal economy – is usually overlooked. This is achieved through many a deceiving metaphor and many an imperfect memory. The Anglo-American practice of management applies the pragmatist line of action; whereas, the mainstream management theory in the USA propagates the rationalist line of reasoning. The combination may result in what Nils Brunsson called the *necessary organizational hypocrisy*:[20] the action follows the pragmatic program, whereas the decision takes on the rationalist façade, covering the unappealing muddling through, reframing, anchoring, and such other maneuvers that are typical in practice but shameful in theory. Such 'necessary hypocrisy' can be seen as typical of Stockholm's city management.

In Warsaw, the preference for a 'pure' rational–legalist philosophy was often expressed via the metaphor of a good master. As we have seen in Chapter 5, the

[18] Warren et al., 1974.   [19] Rorty, 1980.   [20] Brunsson, 1989.

metaphor was incorporated in the last pre-war mayor, Starzynski. As shown by Jacek Szymanderski, however, this patriarchal management model is, in fact, a direct heritage of the Polish People's Republic. Translated into the realities of a free market, it suggests that the 'invisible hand' is actually the hand of the master who 'gives everyone a clear task, as he knows his estate well and is thus able to reward and punish people fairly, according to their work and honesty. But cheaters and speculators, that is, all those who listened to the voice of the Satan of risk and chance, should count on no mercy from the good master's hand'.[21] The market is thus the central planner hidden in a computer.

Szymanderski convincingly demonstrates that there is little difference between socialism and capitalism if they are seen as Utopia. Most Utopian thinking excludes the role of chance, ambiguity, and relationships. And yet, the tolerance of these phenomena is common to all the so-called modern societies that can be deemed successful, in the sense that the majority of their citizens perceive them to be. This is why I do not intend to call for a 'correcting of mistakes', a 'clearing of misunderstandings', or a 'formulating of a consistent management philosophy' and 'following it rigorously'. On the contrary, I claim that all such purifying operations unnecessarily constrain organization and management, limit the adaptability of action, and lead to stagnation and paralysis.

The Roman and, more generally, the Italian public administration reforms could be advanced as another example of purism. The institutional thought structure prevailing in Italian public administration is very close to the one in Poland, and can be summarized by the conviction that it can only be reformed through legislation. The Italian idealism is merciless, however, in the sense that it establishes an exaggerated expectation of results from such reforms and does not permit itself to be softened by the modest effects of 'muddling through'. As a result, the reforms, quickly and superficially evaluated, seem to produce no effect'[22] or the effects are opposite to those intended.[23] In time this situation produces an attitude that Hirschman called fracasomania, a failure complex that he observed in Latin American countries attempting to undergo reform. Hirschman remarked that many a defamed law had in fact 'a variety of useful accomplishments to its credit'.[24]

My Italian interlocutors launched the perversity thesis quite often – when discussing the new institution of public tenders, for instance (see Chapter 4). The perversity thesis is only an ironic variation of the futility thesis where, says Hirschman, '[t]he contribution of Italian social science ... is preeminent'.[25] He mentions Michel's approving quote of the Italian proverb: '*Si cambia il maestro di capella/Ma la musica è sempre quella*'. Hirschman considers this proverb to be an equivalent of the famous French formulation of the perversity thesis: *Plus ça change, plus c'est la même chose* (1991: 59). Note, however, that the sayings are not identical. The French proverb suggests that the more things change, the more they remain the same. The Italian proverb says that replacing the actors does not

---

[21] Szymanderski, 1994: 79.   [22] The so-called futility thesis, Hirschman, 1991.
[23] The perversity thesis, ibid.   [24] Ibid: 33n.   [25] Ibid: 59.

necessarily change the pattern of action – the very point I have been trying to make about city management in Warsaw and Rome.

In Rome as in Warsaw, the attitudes about successful management and successful reform that our study discerned were mixed. There were at least two views – one is typical of the legislators and reformers that represented the rational–idealist stance in the extreme, in a way that I called a merciless idealism; the other is typical of people practicing management, that proffered pragmatism and obstinacy in muddling through. Perhaps, in time, they will merge into a 'merciful idealism' or some other benevolent mixture.

There may be many similarities between the city management of Rome and of Warsaw, but there are also many differences, resulting from different histories and the differing historical attitudes. Poland's history is marked by repeated ruptures: it starts with three partitions by neighboring powers (1772, 1793, and 1795), and continues into modernity with two contemporary occupations: by the Germans during 1939–45 and by the Soviet Union in 1945–89. As a result the Poles have a great respect for the achievements of their administrators during those short periods, like 1919–39, when Poland was independent. Left to themselves, it is felt the Poles would achieve wonders of efficient administration and modern management. This belief results in a refusal to imitate other countries or, in this case, the management of other cities, giving preference to an imitation of their own past, and to automorphism rather than isomorphism, as we have seen in Chapter 5.

The managers of Stockholm thoroughly approved of the pragmatist philosophy of management, but they often ended up in rational–idealist quandaries due to their tendency to follow and sometimes even to lead managerial fashions. Such trends are at the outset nothing more than fashionable ideas, which are disembedded in order to travel better. They are, therefore, prone to encounter implementation problems that are similar to those produced by a legalist way of reforming, but with none of its sanctions. I speak, however, of problems that are relative: Sweden's peaceful history, the success of the welfare state, and the pragmatist attitude, all cushioned Stockholm's ambitions to follow the current trends.

CONSTRUCTING HYBRIDS: SWEDEN

When two conflicting traditions, like the rationalist–legalist and the pragmatist tradition, meet by design, the contradictory elements of both can function side by side in an illogical but functioning myth; otherwise, the contradictions can be removed by means of local adaptations, as seems to have happened in Sweden. The country had confronted the necessity of incorporating pragmatic action models into the sediments of various other institutional orders, creating a new landscape of organization and management.

Sweden's legal system has the same roots as Italy's and Poland's. For many decades the country was also strongly influenced by the German idealist philosophy, and the first initiation into the capitalist order took place with Germany as its model. As Sweden has only 8.9 million inhabitants, one can actually speak of a high level of societal consensus, which gives the legal system a less central place than it requires in countries with a heterogeneous population and multiple conflicts. A typical welfare state, Sweden has developed a sophisticated public administration that intervenes deeply in the life of its citizens, especially in matters of social welfare, based on a loose legal framework that allows a high degree of interpretive freedom.[26]

To illustrate this aspect of the managerial philosophy, which is common in Sweden, one might take the following excerpt from *Goda utsikter* ('Good Perspectives') by Sten Jönsson, in which the author presents the Swedish institutional order and, more specifically, the role of the legal system:

Some of our institutions are laid down in laws that are expressions of society's collective experience of what is considered exemplary behavior (and what behavior is to be condemned). The law, however, cannot prescribe in detail how things are to be done, for society is in constant change, and new situations arise.

Legislation often trails behind and legitimizes what has already become 'good practice'. Acknowledging this, the so-called framework laws purposely let practice develop its own norms. This is the case, for example, in the area of accounting, where the legislator explicitly recommends that good accounting practices be established and maintained by interested parties.

Then there may be professional groups, such as the auditors, who elaborate recommendations and directives and see to it that unsatisfactory practice is eliminated. An erring member of the profession may, for instance, have his license to practice withdrawn, a powerful sanction that requires the authorization of the state. Correspondingly, the norms for what is considered 'reckless driving' are shaped by traffic regulations and schools of motoring, so that we can dare hit the road confident of right-hand traffic. Established practice provides the basis for accurate expectations, so we can drive at a higher speed than we otherwise would consider. Institutional relations in the economy function in the same way. Legislation and codified practice are, of course, fundamental, but of real interest are patterns of behavior resulting from what is expected of others and what they expect in turn.[27]

It is interesting that Jönsson uses traffic as an example in the present context, where traffic has been given so much attention. As my Italian coworkers and contemporaries have explained to me, they see traffic as a stage built by 'them' (the authorities) and afflicted by the Others (people different from themselves). The transgressions are seen as heroic;[28] further, following the rules and regulations is not a proof of reliability and responsibility, but of rigidity or gullibility. One dares to drive on the road, not because others are reliable, but because one is a good

---

[26] Nils Brunsson, personal communication, June 1995. It is worth noticing that in Sweden, a 'framework law' is a generally formulated law to be interpreted in practice; the same expression in Italy denotes a general law that is to be filled with more detailed laws.

[27] Jönsson, 1995: 118–19, my translation.

[28] The slogan of the 1960s was: *È proibito proibire* (It is forbidden to forbid).

driver and an astute non-conformist. The rules and sanctions are required for those who are neither.

It is difficult to imagine a stronger contrast between such a stance and Jönsson's pragmatist way of seeing the world. According to the latter, instead of a priori prescribing proper actions and proscribing improper ones, the law system describes what practice was selected as advantageous. The 'proper' actions are taken not to avoid sanctions, they are the result of the trust that other members of the same interpretive community will act in a similar way. Where did such a pragmatic attitude originate?

Sten O. Karlsson claims in his analysis of the roots of Swedish social democracy that they are not to be found in Marxism, as is often assumed. Social democracy's visions of society dating from the 1880s were to be found in at least three alternative socialist movements: 'chair socialism' (a German movement so denoted because its main ideologues were university professors), the Fabians, and the US pragmatists William James and John Dewey.[29] Michele Micheletti performed a historical analysis of Swedish political relations, and concluded that there were clear traces of pragmatism in the first program of the Social Democratic Party of the 1930s. It was expressed, above all, in the way that the party chose to tackle the class conflict of the time. Disappointed with what they observed in other European countries, especially in Germany, which served as a role model for Sweden early in the era of industrialization, the Social Democrats chose 'cooperation, pragmatism and compromise rather than conflict with and impertinence towards the capitalist class'.[30] After the Second World War, Sweden cut its ties with Germany almost completely and turned to the United States as the symbol of modernity, informality, and efficiency.[31] The success in building a welfare state attracted the most talented and best-educated young people to seek employment in the public sector; this also symbolized progress and the ideals of modernity. In a short time graduates with degrees in business administration, a discipline that also shed the German influence in favor of the US line of thought, filled many executive positions in a sector that was previously filled by lawyers.

In the meantime, however, 'social engineering', which was a positive term when coined by Gunnar Myrdal, had become an insult,[32] and the traditional social democratic program began to be equated with the near-caricature of the 'Rationalist' as depicted by Oakeshott, the famous British conservative philosopher:

The conduct of affairs, for the Rationalist, is a matter of solving problems . . . In this activity the character which the Rationalist claims for himself is the character of the engineer, whose mind (it is supposed) is controlled throughout by the appropriate technique and whose first step is to dismiss from his attention everything not directly related to his

---

[29] *Det intelligenta samhället. En omtolkning av socialdemokratins idéhistoria,* 2001.

[30] Micheletti, 1995: 61. This program shows the beginnings of a rhetorical tradition that differs drastically from that which is observed at present in Rome (Chapter 3).

[31] Löfgren, 1993.   [32] Hirdman, 1989.

specific intentions. This assimilation of politics to engineering is, indeed, what may be called the myth of rationalist politics. . . .

Two other general characteristics of rationalist politics may be observed. They are the politics of perfection, and they are the politics of uniformity. . . . The essence of rationalism is their combination. The evanescence of imperfection may be said to be the first item of the creed of the Rationalist. . . . what he cannot imagine is politics, which do not consist in solving problems, or a political problem of which there is no 'rational' solution at all. Such a problem must be counterfeit. And the 'rational' solution of any problem is, in its nature, a perfect solution. . . . And from this politics of perfection springs the philosophy of uniformity: a scheme which does not recognize circumstance can have no place for variety.[33]

Although Oakeshott had British politicians in mind, many critics, such as his colleague from the London School of Economics, Karl Popper, considered Swedish social democracy to be the perfect incorporation of such rationalism. It is difficult to imagine that any ruling elite could have espoused both these management philosophies simultaneously, and yet this is how the historians portray the situation. As Yvonne Hirdman said with some irony, the Swedish reformists from the 1930s believed that the common sense of the people should play the leading role in determining the future of the country; at the same time, the people are backward and do not always know what is best for them, so the role of the state is to show them the way.[34]

From the point of view of formal logic, this paradox is amusing, but not from the point of view of practical consequences. One could hazard an opinion that the early successes of Sweden's Social Democratic Party were due to the wisdom of its paradoxical thinking, whereas its present problems are due to the dogmatism and purism that it developed during many years of success. Similarly, the rationalist management theory focused on problem-solving and decision-making, which easily survives in parallel with the practice of management focused on muddling through. The problems begin when the theory is allowed to purify practice.

The ways of coping with paradoxes vary across time and place. The blending of rationalism and pragmatism in Sweden looked different in 1938 during the historical agreement in Saltsjöbaden, than it did in 1998 at the time of this study. In the 1930s, rationality concerned the people's way of life; now it concerns the country's economy. 'The Swedish way' is unique in that it is an adapted, local blend of traditions, aspirations, opportunities, and constraints, but it is typical in that many countries in western Europe made such a concoction for themselves and continue doing so.[35] Common to them are the influence of the liberal tradition, the US life style as the symbol of modernity, the influence of continental rationalist philosophy, and the continental legal system. The rest of the ingredients, however, are local, as is the final blend.

---

[33] Oakeshott, 1947/1991: 9–10.   [34] Hirdman, 1989.
[35] More on that theme is to be found in Chandler (1990) and Jönsson (1995).

AWAY FROM PURIST EXTREMES: BLENDING RATIONALISM AND PRAGMATISM, THE GLOBAL AND THE LOCAL

Michel Crozier and Erhard Friedberg compared the US (Californian) and French hospital system reforms, and noticed that although the reforms were practically identical, the Californians seem to have achieved more. Their explanation was as follows:

... because the French group adopted a strategy of rupture, it underestimated the difficult-ies of implementing the reform and forgot that it was attacking a very complex system of action. What is more, it erroneously believed that it could impose a new structure simply because in theory it ought to have been more effective.[36]

This comparison is close to my description of Warsaw and Stockholm's reforms of their respective administration systems. Warsaw city managers, like the French group and in sharp contrast to the Stockholm reformers, showed a remarkable lack of interest in the difficulties of implementation. They refused to circulate information to the interested parties, thus failing to anchor the reform.[37]

Crozier and Friedberg emphasized the ultimate paradox of the situation: the French, in selecting a strategy for the rupture with tradition, actually followed a rooted, stereotyped pattern according to which 'Americans are supposed to be a pragmatic people given to negotiation, while Frenchmen are held to be dogmatic and given to dramatic breaks with the past'.[38]

One could say the same about the city management in Warsaw and in Rome. Attempts to break with the past usually, though unintentionally, take a tradi-tional form: 'This is how we used to break with tradition here'. The observance of tradition, however, acquires new forms in each period.[39] In order to better under-stand this paradox, it could be useful to quote another French author, Philippe d'Iribarne, who compared the '*gestion à la française*' with US and Dutch man-agement styles. The latter is described as being ruled by the logic of consensus and thus closely associated with what is perceived as the Swedish style.[40]

In order to understand the contemporary dilemmas of managerial practice, says d'Iribarne, one must relate them to the Great Modern Dream – that of break-ing with tradition once and for all, of purifying human life from prejudice and religion, of liberating future generations from the suffocating trap of the past and the local community, and of placing hope in Nature and Reason, both accessible through Science. Grounded in rational knowledge and technology produced by science, and facilitating a continuous process of innovation where there is no room for tradition, the 'business enterprise' was one of the typical means for actualizing that dream. Thus, it was necessary to create universal methods, procedures, and structures that were supposed to bring about the same results regardless of context.

---

[36] Crozier and Friedberg, 1980: 199.   [37] Czarniawska, 1998.
[38] Crozier and Friedberg, 1980: 199.   [39] Löfgren, 1993.   [40] d'Iribarne, 1989.

The last decades of the twentieth century have been dedicated to a critical reflection about that dream. This reflection sometimes ends in a modernist lament: either 'not enough effort was put into fulfilling the modernist dream' or 'so much effort was put into it that it nearly destroyed the planet'. A different conclusion is that of a postmodern celebration, which claims that, having awoken from the dream, the people might now do something sensible. The most convincing is the stance that incorporates all these reflections. After all, as d'Iribarne has suggested, the contemporary enterprises are *simultaneously* traditional and rational, and, I might add, the contemporary public administration organizations are simultaneously conservative and reformist.

This observation can be applied not only to various hybrids like those discussed here, but also to the very models themselves, such as the UK or the USA, which represent pure models on paper only. Is not the 'logic of the fair deal' a US tradition, and the pragmatist philosophy its modernist philosophy? The uniqueness of the USA lies in the fact that it has one tradition only – that of modernity (it has, therefore, been called the oldest country in the modern world). In Sweden, modernity is not the only tradition, but it is one enhanced by 60 years of a successful welfare state: to be Swedish is to be modern.[41] It needs to be remembered that Sweden is one of two European countries that did not experience the ruptures caused by two World Wars; there is a continuity in Sweden that only Switzerland shares in Europe.

Albert Hirschman is exceptionally skillful at exposing the faults of purist attitudes, of both reactionary and progressive types. He rescues from oblivion or ideological attack another element, which is conservative, by suggesting that

An essential component of [Edmund] Burke's thought was his assertion, based primarily on the English historical experience, that existing institutions incorporated a great deal of collective evolutionary wisdom and that they were, moreover, quite capable of evolving gradually.[42]

Surely this can be said about any country's historical experience? Nevertheless, it does not exclude the possibility that a country's own institutional order can be usefully enriched by the experiences of other countries, resulting in innovative hybrids. Acknowledging the role of direct and vicarious experience might help to avoid the extremes of isolationist automorphism, relentless isomorphism, and merciless idealism.

Paradoxically, the isolationist automorphism in Warsaw and the merciless idealism in Rome are defended on the grounds of rational idealism or, as Oakeshott would call it, a reflective application of a moral criterion; but it presents itself to an observer as a habit of affection and conduct. Like the French reformers in Crozier and Friedberg's study who broke with tradition out of tradition, the Romans and the Varsovians are rational by habit. Their attitudes toward management are mixed, but it is a mixture that suffers, according to Oakeshott, from continuous tension. It is not the action-producing tension of a paradox, however, or that grain of sand that will produce a pearl. Rather, it is an upside-down world, where '[s]elf-consciousness is asked to be creative, and habit is given the role of critic'.[43]

But, with years, even the Swedish hybrid begins to show the strain, as suggested by the adjective 'relentless' accompanying the isomorphism, or the tendency to imitate. Tarde set custom against fashion, but the Swedish public administration discovered the possibility of a customary following of fashions.[44] In such a case reflection becomes habitual, and no longer plays the role of a critic.

The exchange of experiences is a usual remedy against the habituation of reflection. Perhaps the constant encounters between folk wisdoms on such an arena as the EU can attain importance, although there are few signs of it as yet. The not-so-successful meeting of EU-countries in Nice in December 2000, produced at least one memorable symbolic encounter: that between the President of the European Commission Romano Prodi, and the next Country-President of the Council, Göran Persson. Commenting on Swedish demands and postulates, Prodi has been repeatedly quoted as citing a Tuscany proverb, *Non si puo avere la botte piena e la moglie ubbriaca* (You cannot have a drunken wife and a full bottle at home.) Any Swede, however, would be able to explain to him that the feat could, in fact, be easily performed, depending on how rich you are. Prodi has unerringly located the core of wisdom in the Swedish welfare state – and found it ridiculous. Let us hope that his purist conclusion was too hasty, and that time will increase curiosity and diminish xenophobia among the EU members. To begin with, Stockholm and Rome could swap their city managers for a while . . .

Another interesting contrast is that between an isolationist automorphism and a relentless isomorphism. The first revolves around the construction of alterity ('we are unique'), the second around the construction of identity ('we are like you' or 'you should become like us'). Although the present times favor identity over alterity construction, even here a mixture seems to be most appealing. Fashion leaders tend to start from the alterity dimension, but resign themselves to the identity dimension when they fail to become fashion leaders. 'A city unlike any other' is a city that makes no sense; 'a city like any other' is a city that lacks attraction. It must be added, however, that city managers hardly need my encouragement in the art of creating hybrids: this is what they do all the time.

It would be good to remember the conclusion formulated by Philippe d'Iribarne as the result of his comparison of three countries. If there is any managerial skill that is universal, he says, it is the skill of combining the modern with the traditional, the rational with the pragmatic. But the character of this combination is specific to each place and time. There are no universal principles, there are only local practices.

---

[43] Oakeshott, 1948/1991: 482.

[44] Tarde, 1890/1962. Nils Brunsson called this phenomenon 'reforms as routine' (Brunsson and Olsen, 1993).

7

The Fashionable City

. . . why, given one hundred different innovations conceived of at the same time . . . ten will spread abroad, while ninety will be forgotten?[1]

Tarde's question should be preceded by another: Why do cities build and maintain connections with other cities and with other types of action nets? The city officials and managers want to know what others do, and want others to know what they are doing. They do not want to be left behind. Besides, 'everybody globalizes'. They want to become models for others, to emulate or to go their own, original way: they want to be in the market, and they want the market to come to them. The current rhetoric of motives focuses primarily on economic arguments, but the non-modern motives are also present: the pride in one's city, a 'metropotism'.

Although my interlocutors would probably all agree that they want their city to be fashionable, or in fashion, they would have problems accepting the possibility that they follow fashion. Fashion remains a phenomenon fit only for women and frivolous men; management will have nothing to do with it. And yet I shall claim, in the manner of some sociologists, that fashion is a crucial societal phenomenon without which the understanding of the contemporary world can never be complete.

GLOBALIZATION AS EVERYDAY WORK

Let me recapitulate the phenomena of globalization and localization as illustrated throughout this book. In the context of city management, globalization means a growing number and speed of connections among collective actions that can be gathered under the label of city management. Action nets grow and multiply. This means that a great number of ideas, objects, technologies, and

---

[1] Tarde, 1888/1969: 177.

practices circulate among places and times. Homogenization in space is accompanied by heterogenization in time. The shop windows in Stockholm, Rome, and Warsaw might look alike, but they will look different in a month. Although, in everyday language, such translocalization is often traced along connections between units (cities, organizations), it should be noted that such units are outcomes rather than originating forces. And although it makes analytic sense to delineate an action net called 'city management', in practice the actions of city management are connected to many other collective actions: financing, mass media, education, and so on.

What are the carriers – processes or mechanisms, depending on one's perception – of globalization? There are several carriers, which are usually at play simultaneously. There is *coercion*, usually, but not always, of a legal nature; we have seen an example of it in Chapter 4. There is *ethos*, binding the members of a group and serving to guide, control, or regulate the proper and acceptable ways of acting; such groups are usually professions but also trade unions, bound by their ethos to 'fight battles', as we have seen in Chapter 3. There is *mimesis*, an unreflected imitation prompted by vicinity (the local versions of public tenders described in Chapter 4 can be seen as examples of it), and also *emulation*, a purposeful striving to equal or excel some model, which could be derived from a historical source, as in Chapter 5.

As these factors are simultaneously present in organizational practice, they are also present in every chapter. The combinations can be very interesting. The case of public tenders is a perfect illustration of legal coercion aimed at isopraxism, or identical practices, but as local mimesis sets to work, it ends with an isomorphism only. The professional ethos can be seen as partly coercive; after all, breaking professional rules is punished with exclusion from a profession. Although many professions are involved in city management, it can be suggested that city management is itself becoming a profession, or at least an occupational group.[2] Will it have the same ethos in different cities? Emulation differs from mimesis only in its purpose, but its very purposefulness sets it closer to coercion and ethos: following the example of 'Warsaw-between-the wars' was not a joking matter in Warsaw. In all these cities, with their variety of positive models, there were also negative models that were sometimes simply silenced: the bureaucracy, socialist centralism, and the various cities that stood for the Opposite and even the Other in varying contexts.

My hesitation as to whether I should call these 'mechanisms' or 'processes' comes from a conviction that neither grasps the character of these carriers nor the connections that result from their travels. Globalization happens neither automatically nor organically; it happens as the result of translation. Acts of translation make globalization possible. What can be seen as the micro-character of the material used in this book is meant to illustrate how globalization is carried out by all of us in our everyday lives – in this case, our everyday working lives.

[2] See Panozzo, 2001.

This book is meant to complement the abstract and sweeping macro-descriptions of globalization, which perhaps permit the readers to get a whole picture, but leaves them bewildered as to its construction. This bewilderment is shared by city workers, who often perceive globalization as something happening above their heads (presumably ordered by the politicians), thus failing to notice their own (positive or negative) contribution to it. Not even when I moved to the cultural context in Chapter 6, did I abandon the idea of imitation through translation; I only extended it in time and space.

Such a detailed, down-to-earth picture justifies the separation I introduced in such established terms as 'coercive isomorphism'. Isomorphism might be the purpose of coercion (although it is more likely to be isopraxism), but not necessarily its result. My examples were intended to illustrate how the various kinds of globalization work might lead, separately, in conjunction, or in opposition, to a variety of results. And although isopraxism is likely to be an outcome of mimesis and isomorphism of coercion, it can also be the other way around. Even as most purposeful attempts aim at achieving similarity, they are apt to increase allomorphism as well, through errors in the reproduction of forms and practices.

It is, therefore, important to stress the multiplicity of the results of globalization or translocalization. A suggestion made by Jan Nederveen Pieterse is to denote them, jointly, as hybridization, as a separation of forms from practices and a recombination with new forms in new practices.[3] From such a perspective, he says, the histories of the hybridization of metropolitan cultures should be particularly revealing, as counter-narratives to national histories.

Pieterse makes two caveats to his suggestion, both of which are worth quoting. Hybridization as a concept, he says, makes sense only as long as essentialism remains a strategic mobilization device – in theory and practice. Indeed, if or when purism and the search for 'the true identity' ever abate, the postulating of hybridization would become trivial. It is an important point, as it clarifies that the usefulness of a concept is not measured by its correspondence to a given phenomenon, but by its relation to other concepts. Hybridization is not how things *are*; it is a concept that makes sense in the present time and place.

Second, he says that it is important not to see globalization as modernization (and westernization) only. While this caveat makes sense historically and globally, in the case of the three cities discussed here, modernization was undoubtedly the main motor of translation and imitation.

Thus, all the three cities wanted to be modern, but what did they mean by the term? The word 'modern' carries in most languages, although not in English, a double meaning: espousing the ideals of modernity, and following the fashion of the moment. It so happens that modernity is not particularly in fashion now. How did that influence the representation work in the city?

The image of the European capital produced in Warsaw was that of modernity incarnate – an ideal that is more suited to the turn of the previous century.

---

[3] Pieterse, 1995: 45–68.

The image was thus coherent, in accordance with the ideals of purity.[4] The hybrid-like character of actual practice was held under a constant critique. Stockholm's idea of the European big city at the turn of the century was fashion-sensitive and therefore truly *past*-modern: hybrid organization forms, IT-programs, and the postmodern kaleidoscope-like spectacle went hand-in-hand during the Cultural Capital of Europe program in 1998.[5] Rome combined all these elements: the modernist dream of an ordered city (that is, one with a traffic system), the premodern cultural tradition, and the postmodern idea of hybrid organizational forms.

MODERNIZATION AND REFRAMING

Authors who, like myself, allude to *A Tale of Two Cities*, tend to quote the first paragraph: 'It was the best of times, it was the worst of times. . . .'[6] in order to claim a similarity between the times described in the book: Dickens' times and the present. Had they quoted the second paragraph, this similarity would become problematic. It goes: 'In both countries [*England and France*] it was clearer than crystal to the lords of the State preserves of loaves and fishes, that things in general were settled for ever'.

Today, even if the lords of the State preserves might wish for things in general to be settled forever, they would not dare to express their wishes publicly. And although my description of translocalization, presented above, could be, presumably, applied to Dickens' description of London and Paris before and during the French Revolution (the two cities were very well connected indeed), it was only afterwards that modernization left its clear stamp on globalization. This stamp can be described in my terms as a duty of constant reframing. While drastic reframing, like that in Warsaw or in Rome, is usually forced by a historical contingency, the city managers in all three cities considered reframing to be their professional duty. It has been coerced by legislation, normalized by occupational customs, set as a model to emulate, and by its very omnipresence has become an object of mimesis. Although the old frames stubbornly surfaced, the general belief – shared by many students of institutionalization processes – was that two years should be just about long enough to institutionalize anything one could wish for. The debate between Gellner and Oakeshott – if 70 years were enough time to institutionalize the London School of Economics – would be met with incredulity by a contemporary organizer.[7] 'Institute' and 'institutionalize' are taken to be synonyms.

---

[4] Sennett, 1970; Bauman, 1991; Latour, 1993; Zaborowska, 2001.
[5] Pipan and Porsander, 2000.   [6] *A Tale of Two Cities*, 1859/1994: 13.
[7] Gellner, 1995.

This paradoxical belief in the stability of ephemeral forms, and the question of whether reframing can take any shape and direction, might find a common answer if the notion of fashion is explored more thoroughly.

The English language, choosing 'fashion' instead of 'mode' to denote a prevailing custom, usage, or style, has lost an insight preserved in many other languages, including Swedish and Italian. Especially in Swedish, it is impossible to say whether 'modern' is intended to mean 'modern' or 'fashionable'; indeed, the two are assumed to be one and the same.[8] Although fashion was no doubt an important phenomenon in ancient Egypt and Rome, globalization paid fashion a service by helping it to spread; fashion reciprocated by helping globalization to choose what to globalize.

FASHION

Fashion plays the same role in translation/imitation theory as did concentration (saturation) in the diffusion theory: it provides the direction. The analogy might be even closer, in that concentration has been paid little attention in the diffusion theory, too. The diffusion theory contented itself with an assumption that ideas flow from places with a high concentration of ideas to those of low concentration.

My understanding of the role that fashion plays in translocalization follows that of Tarde's: an invention is imitated, but because of 'the necessary weakening of that which is imitated . . . new inventions or entirely fresh sources for imitation are therefore necessary for the timely re-animation of expiring social energy'.[9] The ideas, practices, or objects that are widely spread are not fashionable anymore; an established fashion becomes its opposite – an institution or a custom. When all or almost all city services are privatized, it becomes impossible to privatize anymore. The next step is municipalization or nationalization, unless a completely fresh invention has arrived in the field. Fashion constantly renews itself, but it chooses among the many inventions that are present at a certain time and place.

As to the place, Tarde was also of the opinion that big cities, and especially capitals, were places where inventions were first demonstrated, if not always produced, and where imitation happened rapidly, if only because of the density of population. But back to the question that opened this chapter: Which inventions are imitated?

Those that are imitated are allegedly superior, on the grounds of their qualities (Tarde calls these 'logical reasons'; I would call them pragmatic) or on the grounds of their provenance in time and place (Tarde's extra-logical reasons;

---

[8] In Polish, 'fashion' is called 'moda', but 'modern' is called 'nowoczesny' (newfangled), so the two meanings are also separated.   [9] Tarde, 1890/1962: 210.

I would call them power-symbolic). It is impossible to tell the difference between the two at any given time, as the power-symbolic superiority tends to masquerade as a superiority of quality. Are the present fashion leaders – Berlin, London, Paris and Barcelona – 'better managed' cities? Time will provide the perspective and a more thorough test of pragmatic utility. The third type of superiority characterizes ideas that have many allies in other ideas – ideas that are well anchored or that do not threaten the institutionalized thought structure.

Tarde has already noted the special role that journalists play in establishing fashion: they act as fashion's masters of ceremony, propagating what is in and what is out; and also as the distributors of fashion.[10] I can add that they also act as the providers of vicarious contact, where only copying is possible. This does not make them outsiders to fashion – they are subject to fashion like every other profession – but additionally, they propagate fashions in other fields (such as city management).

Thus, an invention (including an invention of tradition) in city management, but also in general management, happens at some place, becomes known, and is marketed by the inventors themselves and by consultants, journalists, and researchers. Some of them are imitated: privatization, the rapid tram, centralization or decentralization, electronic networks. Although, in principle, an invention can crop up anywhere, in practice, the cities are watching those who are considered to be the fashion leaders: certain big cities but also, at present, the big corporations. The translation that necessarily occurs when a displacement takes place, makes that which was imitated into something else: same form, different content; same content, different form. All this renews, and sometimes even reframes the city management; it also produces additional outcomes such as the city's identity and alterity.

IDENTITY–ALTERITY INTERPLAY

Fashion is the imitation of a given example and satisfies the demand for social adaptation. . . . At the same time, it satisfies in no less degree the need of differentiation, the tendency for dissimilarity, the desire for change and contrast. . . .[11]

Fashion is that which both regulates and enables the identity–alterity interplay. How does this happen? In a classic article, Herbert Blumer postulated that fashion is a competition mechanism that influences the market and distorts the demand and supply curves, both using and serving the economic competition.[12] Its important element is a *collective choice* among tastes, things, and ideas; it is oriented toward finding but also toward creating what is typical of a given time. One could add that fashion operates at the institutional fringes. On the one hand, its variety is limited by the 'iron cage' of existing institutions, which fashion

---

[10] Tarde, 1890/1962: 182, 226.   [11] Simmel, 1904/1971: 296.   [12] Blumer, 1969.

actually reproduces; on the other hand, fashion is engaged in a constant subversion of the existing institutional order, gnawing at its bars. This is the first paradox connected to fashion: its simultaneous unimportance and saliency.

The notion of translation helps us to understand the second paradox: fashion is created even as it is followed. It is the subsequent translations that simultaneously produce and reproduce variations in fashion. Hence, the third paradox: fashion followers act differently as a result of their attempt to follow the fashion: fashion encompasses and feeds on the identity–alterity interplay. Tarde has pointed out that this concept need not be treated as a contradiction, merely as a difficulty: a difficulty consisting of discovering an original idea within an already dominating style.[13] This statement can be directly applied to managers, and not only city managers. Fashion is for them an expression of what is modern, of what the community to which they belong – that is, an organization field – recently chose as the most valuable or exciting. For people in high organizational positions who perceive their mission to be that of bringing progress to organizations, to follow what is modern often feels like a duty.[14] However, this obligation is only part of their mission. Their duty is, equally, to protect organizations from what might be a passing fad. Reframing, yes, but not every time and not in any haphazard way. One of their tasks is to keep a distance from 'mere' fashion, or to detect fads.

Fashion stands for change, and thus for reframing. But as fashion is also repetitive, in a long-range perspective it stands for tradition, as well; it revokes the old frames.[15] It is enough to remember an acid remark concerning city traffic by Jane Jacobs, which, although made in 1961, is worthy of repetition today:

... it is understandable that men who were young in the 1920's were captivated by the vision of the freeway Radiant City, with the specious promise that it would be appropriate to an automobile age. At least it was then a new idea; to men of the generation of New York's Robert Moses, for example, it was radical and exciting in the days when their minds were growing and their ideas forming. Some men tend to cling to old intellectual excitements, just as some belles, when they are old ladies, still cling to the fashions and coiffures of their exciting youth. ... It is disturbing to think that men who are young today, men who are being trained now for their careers, should accept *on the grounds that they must be 'modern' in their thinking*, conceptions about cities and traffic which are not only unworkable, but also to which nothing of significance has been added since their fathers were children.[16]

Indeed, an interesting observation made in one of the early fashion studies was that fashion is not related to progress (although it stands for modernity):

In a real sense, fashion is evolution without destination. The world generally considers that progress in material things consists in changes that make them more useful, or better looking,

---

[13] Tarde, 1902/1969: 157. This is why Lyotard (1979/1987) insisted on differentiating between an invention and an innovation (Tarde, or at least his translators – treat them as synonymous): while an innovation remains within the already prevailing style, an invention changes the style.

[14] Forssell, 1989.

[15] For a description of repetitive organizational fashions, see Røvik, 1996.

[16] Jacobs, 1961: 371.

or less expensive. In the long run fashion never attains these objectives. Its idea is slow, continuous change, unhampered by the restrictions of either aesthetics or practicality.[17]

The concept of fashion, thus, illuminates ways of changing that are not related to the usual notion of progress, and is descriptive rather than normative in character. Agnes Brook Young's observation, quoted above, makes the paradoxical character of change more obvious: fashion operates through dramatized 'revolutions', but '. . . in a real sense, fashion is evolution . . .'.[18] Tarde would agree: in his view, fashion at first opposes custom, and then, if successful, becomes a custom itself, only to be opposed by the next fashion.

Fashion, then, transpires to be a highly paradoxical process. Its constitutive paradoxes: invention *and* imitation, variation *and* uniformity, distance *and* interest, novelty *and* conservatism, unity *and* segregation, conformity *and* deviation, change *and* status quo, revolution *and* evolution, are only variations on the basic duality of communal life, which are the collective and the personal construction of alterity *and* identity. Separately, the two processes are often tackled, even within organization theory. But as a whole, understanding the details of social construction – such as city management – remains largely a theoretical claim. And yet, it lies at the very heart of organizational life and action.

To understand the role of fashion in city management, the most important point is that fashion (together with other processes like control or negotiation) introduces order and uniformity into what might seem an overwhelming variety of possibilities. In this sense fashion helps us to come to grips with the present. At the same time, it 'serves to detach the grip of the past in the moving world. By placing a premium on being in the mode and derogating what developments have been left behind, it frees actions for new movement.'[19] It also introduces some appearance of order and predictability into preparations for what is necessarily disorderly and uncertain: the future. Fashion, in its gradual emergence, attenuates the surprises of the next fashion, and tunes into the collective by making it known to itself, as reflected in the present fashion and in the rejection of past fashions.

The importance of relating city management to fashion and vice versa translates, therefore, into an imperative to study the process of fashion and not, as is more common, its results. Fashion also plays its tricks on fashion research: focusing on its products, scholars reach the conclusion that fashion is fickle and ephemeral. But in reaching this conclusion, they miss the stable character of the production process itself. Indeed, by the time my report of the Stockholm study was published, many of the catchwords had been exchanged for new more fashionable ones. The central projects of the city were no longer that of fiber optic network, but of the broadband; not that of the Cultural Capital but the Police World Championship.[20] But as my collaborators who stayed longer in the field could witness, the process by which these new projects were introduced was the

---

[17] Young, 1937/1973: 109.   [18] Ibid.   [19] Blumer, 1969: 279.   [20] Dobers, 2002*a*.

same. Also, there were issues like the 'third track' in Stockholm, which remained for many years, renewing only their form.[21]

The notion of a 'fashionable city' is not a new one, although undoubtedly it is a modern one. Tarde quotes an author who studied the cities of the old regime in France and who noted that it was fashionable in the eighteenth century to use secret ballots in municipal elections. Moreover, Angers adopted this mode of voting as early as the sixteenth century, justifying it by the example of Venice, Genoa, Milan, and Rome.[22]

The authors who suggest that modernization is the contemporary face of globalization[23] would probably agree with these conclusions. Unlike Hobsbawm, they would not be surprised to see that fashion in the city chooses strange forms to reproduce, including some very old forms. After all, loose coupling or decoupling permits practices to develop as a weak connection to the form, which is more easily circulated. This final chapter, thus, reinstates John Meyer's observation that modernization was never a process limited to non-modern countries, but a process that continues and involves everyone in the contemporary world, although in different forms and with varying results. Bruno Latour's postulate of a symmetrical anthropology is, therefore, of great importance, particularly in the field of management, which has traditionally been excluded from anthropological scrutiny.[24] Symmetrical anthropology involves the equal treatment of all forms and practices under study, with an equal sense of wonder. It has already been adopted by such prominent anthropologists as Marshall Sahlins and Ulf Hannerz.[25] Although the wave of organizational culture studies made the first encroachment into this tradition, it is now time to go further, to collapse such dichotomies as 'technical–ideological' or 'symbolic–practical' and to shift attention to the rituals of modernity and to the role of fashion, emulation, and mimesis in the global economy.

A NEED FOR A SYMMETRICAL ETHNOLOGY IN MANAGEMENT STUDIES

The moderns confused products with processes. They believed that the production of bureaucratic rationalization presupposed rational bureaucrats; that the production of

---

[21] Corvellec, 2001a,b.   [22] Tarde, 1890/1962: 293.s

[23] Meyer and Rowan, 1977; Meyer, 1986; Robertson, 1992, 1995; and Meyer, 1999.

[24] This way of doing research is at home in cultural geography: beginning with David Harvey's (1985) detailed description of Paris 1850–70, it continues with such studies as Allan Pred's (1995) marvelous collage-portrait of Stockholm, Linda McDowell's *Capital Culture* (1997), and Kris Olds's *Globalization and Urban Change* (2001). For an amazing example of a micro-study of a city, see Bruno Latour's and Emilie Hermant's *Paris ville invisible* (1998).

[25] Sahlins, 1996, 2001. It might be suggested that Hannerz's (1980) suggestion of replacing 'tribes' with 'networks' and, generally of introducing more sociological notions into urban anthropology counters my postulate, but I do not read it this way. I do not propose a mechanical

universal science depended on universalist scientists; that the production of effective technologies led to the effectiveness of engineers; that the production of abstraction was itself
abstract; that the production of formalism was itself formal . . . Science does not produce
itself scientifically any more than technology produces itself technologically or economy
economically.[26]

One could continue this list by pointing out that organizing is rarely an organized
process, and that management consultants do not manage their companies in
the way they advise others to do. What, then, can a 'past-modern' researcher try
to achieve?

My tentative answer is: to engage in a symmetrical ethnology. Although I am
obviously using Latour's idea of a symmetrical anthropology and although I
depend on anthropological research myself, this colonial term makes me somewhat unhappy. Management studies are not about 'the man' (economic or not,
female or not) or about human nature; they are about certain ways of life, and,
more specifically, about certain ways of work. Although it is perhaps unnecessary
to grapple with such neologisms as 'ergonographies',[27] I find strange comfort in
using terms that etymologically mean what I wish to express, rather than using
inherited labels that drag along a plethora of obscure associations. The approach
itself, however, follows Latour's precepts:[28]

- using the same terms to explain truths and lies, failures and successes, trials
  and errors; in other words, rendering the method judgment-free;
- simultaneously studying the production of, and by, humans and non-human
  actants (this approach requires that greater attention be directed toward
  things and machines – a perspective sorely missing in management studies –
  but also toward varying degrees of existence and actorhood);
- avoiding any a priori declarations concerning the differences between westerners and non-westerners, primitive and modern societies, rationality and
  irrationality; construction of alterity should be a study object on a par with
  identity construction.

The first precept is easy to understand and embrace by anyone who has conducted
field research: it becomes abundantly clear that what is a failure and what is a success depends on who is doing the evaluation and when they are doing it. There is
nothing to prevent the researcher from forming an independent judgment,[29] but it
is difficult to arrive at a clear-cut judgment with so many voices pleading their

transfer of anthropological concepts to management studies, but a selective one, where the
application of such selected concepts would be literal rather than metaphorical.

[26] Latour, 1993: 115–6.
[27] Ethnographies of work, a term I coined in *Narrating the Organization* (1997).
[28] Latour, 1993: 103.
[29] Weber never said that researchers must be dispassionate, only that university lectures were
not the proper place for Nazi propaganda ('Science as Vocation', 1922/1974). Although it is taken
for granted that party meetings are forbidden on university grounds, the hasty conclusion of the
need for an 'uninvolved stance' remains unchallenged.

rights. Even if such a judgment is reached, it is of importance only to the researcher and possibly to her readers in terms of creating an Author's character. It has a wider, practical consequence only when it is co-opted by a political stance, and this often happens against the author's explicit wishes. My colleagues and I frequently met with co-optation proposals during this study, and we were criticized for our stance by two opposing coalitions. The city managers in Rome believed that we were overly critical of their work, and the political opposition believed that we had written a panegyric to the governing group. In the view of a symmetric management ethnologist, a clear stance is needed for action. A reflection representing a clear stance is proof that the plurivocality of the field has not been acknowledged.

As to the second precept, it relates to a particular historical development of management studies that began, in part, as a branch of engineering,[30] and therefore in close proximity to machines; it proceeded to metaphorize machines, and then dropped the machine to move to other metaphors.[31] The symbolic turn in organization theory enriched it immensely, but excluded some things from view. 'Nature' returned partly through an interest in the environment, and artifacts through a theoretical interest in the studies of science and technology. It is now perfectly clear both in managerial and non-managerial action, that the practical, economical, and political aspects of every kind of activity are intermingling.

There is, however, a good explanation for this lack of interest in artifacts: as Jan Mouritsen and I argue, managers expend a great deal of effort in insulating themselves from the world of artifacts.[32] Having achieved that goal, they indulge in the creation of peculiar objects, such as 'managerial technologies' or 'objects of investment' (the process clearly visible in Roman privatization). Similarly, they work on turning people into objects of management, as in Human Resource Management. Inventing traditions is also an interesting aspect of these variable ontologies, as Latour calls them: the observation that things and facts (such as a subway train or profit) that seem stable and obvious today did not exist yesterday and might not exist tomorrow.

Burkhart Holzner wrote nearly 30 years ago about the 'degrees to which something or somebody can be an object or subject'.[33] However, he continued, 'we are accustomed to dealing with objects as things and subjects as consciousness, neither of which seems to be matters of more or less'. And yet, he pointed out, a focused reflection makes it obvious that there are 'degrees of objectness' and 'degrees of subjectness'. Holzner anticipated the interest in semiotics that arose later, by defining the concept of an actor in exactly the way that Greimas, and after him, Latour, spoke of 'actants': 'some entity which is the source of a pattern of action'.[34] Thus, quicksand became a historical enemy of the subway construction in Warsaw, and Tram No. 8 acquired a demonical persona in Rome, while the mass media, quite unintentionally, turned the politicians and city managers of both cities into hackneyed characters in their own soap operas.

[30] Shenhav, 2000.   [31] Morgan, 1986.   [32] Czarniawska and Mouritsen, forthcoming.
[33] Holzner, 1973/1978: 298.   [34] Ibid: 294.

The third precept is an obvious invitation to doing anthropology *à rebour*, or applying the same methods to study various societies and collectives. While ethnology in most countries was seemingly doing just that, in its traditional version it actually traced the primitive society within the modern society: folklore, vanishing customs and the like. Ethnology is taking rapid steps on the way to symmetry, which is especially visible in its interest in marketing.[35] Treating public tenders as rituals was not the way to demonstrate that premodern sediments must be expurgated from modern management; I agree both with Latour's dictum that we have never been modern, and with John Meyer's observation that modernity proceeds by non-modern means. Similarly, although I used the notion of cultural contexts of organizing, these were not a priori entities that I put into the practices I studied; rather, I relied upon my re-construction of the clues that the actors had given me. Therefore, I tried to avoid the concept of 'cultures' and the sweeping descriptions of 'Italian' or 'Swedish' ways of doing things (with no doubt an occasional relapse into everyday stereotyping, or 'a commonplace grammar of representation', as Joep Leerssen so aptly put it).[36]

It is correct to say that a symmetrical ethnology has the aim of making management more exotic, but only in a certain sense of the word. 'Ethnologizing management' does not mean that it needs to be (further) mystified or demonized. The city managers are hard-working people who deserve respect. The fact that they engage in rituals must not diminish this respect, it must only change the understanding of modernity. In this sense, I aim at the de-exoticization of city management, although it needs to be rendered more exotic in the sense of interesting, fascinating, and little known. 'For what is exoticism? A fascination with what is different, a desire to get in touch with otherness; and that desire is ultimately impossible.'[37]

Although it is impossible, it makes for an interesting pursuit. At this juncture, it is possible to contrast the two meanings of alterity mentioned at the outset. The city managers are interested in creating their own difference, but have little interest in knowing the Other. This attitude is by no means limited to city managers. People rarely have a clue about what other people do at work, yet, they have a plethora of ready-made images at their disposal. The public tend to assume that it knows what the city managers do (either make decisions or implement the decisions made by the city politicians), and that, when no scandals or dramas are involved, their work is immensely boring. My claim is that public opinion is best versed in the abstract representations of managerial work, made for apologetic or critical purposes. In a fascinating autobiography of a finance salesman, Michael Lewis tells the story of how a trainee program for future traders and salespersons focused on emptying them of the knowledge of financial markets that they had acquired at university.[38] While such autobiographical accounts

---

[35] See e.g. Löfgren, 1990.
[36] Leerssen (1991) offers, among other things, a thoughtful and original reading of Hofstede's famous culture studies, which should be of interest to organization scholars.
[37] Leerssen, 1991: 136.   [38] *Liar's Poker*, 1989.

written by people with a flair for reflection will always be invaluable in the debunking of stereotypes, the more mundane social science studies can make a solid contribution toward spreading the knowledge of actual developments in working places. At the very least, such studies should comfort people by showing them that their own workplace is not a crazy anomaly.

City management in the times of intense globalization can be thus portrayed as a quest for an – unholy – grail: not a story of pursuits by male heroes, but of the everyday drudgery of an occupational group that desires something impossible, but which in its futile search of a truly modern management makes our cities run. The present attempt at compiling such a story witnesses the traces of many strains of thoughts, many different times and places: the US pragmatism and its continuation in Italian semiotics; the German phenomenology, continued and developed in the USA and France; the east European linguistic and literary tradition continued and developed in France; the anthropology and urban studies conducted in a culturalist vein; the Scandinavian management studies anchored in the US institutionalist tradition; the studies of science and technology developing rapidly in France, Germany, and the UK – the list is far from complete.

Why is there such an inveterate poaching across disciplines? Why the constant hybridization of vocabularies? Surely each of those fields provides a rich and complete vocabulary of its own? While I must confess that sirens of purism sang sweetly sometimes,[39] the list of credits I began to unroll above contains part of the answer. None of the schools of thought at which I studied are pure; all are hybrids. Big city management must be conceptualized in a hybrid way as well; a complexity of practice demands a complexity (not a complication!) of theory.

The other part of the answer lies in my topic of interest. Apart from my own discipline, none of the others disclose an interest in the object of my study, the study of management. Although Deirdre McCloskey argued repeatedly and continuously that the economy is too important to be left to economists, management is being left to managers and consultants. When attention from outside management studies turns to such issues, it usually comes in the form of a judgment made on a pre-existing image of what management is: public and scholarly opinions coincide. Management might be worth condemning, but not worth studying. This assumption neglects the fact that, as Alfred Chandler demonstrated in his studies long ago, control moved centuries ago from the hands of the owners to those of the managers.[40] This insight has been incorporated in popular discourse, but is interpreted in traditional terms: it is assumed that managers *have* power, and therefore there is no need to know more about them, as a knowledge of the nuances might hamper their demonization or hagiography, depending on the ideological preferences of the writer. In my reading, these are two meanings of alterity that separate on the way to identity. In the global landscape, the Manager is the Other worth knowing, but 'we' are not different: managers are us.

---

[39] I am not quite sure what is an equivalent of sirens for a female traveler.

[40] Chandler, 1977. See also O'Barr and Conley, 1992; and McCloskey, 1985.

REFERENCES

ACKER, JOAN (1994), 'The Gender Regime of Swedish Banks', *Scandinavian Journal of Management*, 10/2: 117–30.

ADOLFSSON, PETRA (1999), 'An Object of Many Qualities', presented at the conference *Managing Big Cities*, Gothenburg, August.

—— (2002), *Miljömätningars många ansikten i staden* (Göteborg: BAS).

AZIEWICZ, TADEUSZ (ed.) (1993), *Przeksztalcenia w sektorze uslug komunalnych* (Warszawa: Instytut Badan nad Gospodarka Rynkowa).

—— (ed.) (1994), *Prywatyzacja uslug komunalnych w Polsce* (Gdansk-Lublin: Instytut Badan nad Gospodarka Rynkowa).

BATESON, GREGORY (1959/1972), *Steps to an Ecology of Mind* (New York: Chandler).

BAUMAN, ZYGMUNT (1991), *Modernity and Ambivalence* (Cambridge: Polity Press).

—— (1998), *Globalization: The Human Consequences* (Cambridge: Polity Press).

BEKSIAK, JANUSZ (1994), 'O restauracji kapitalizmu w Polsce', in *Piec lat po czerwcu* (Warszawa: Centrum im. Adama Smitha), 11–32.

BENEVOLO, LEONARDO (1993), *The European City* (Oxford: Blackwell).

BLUMER, HERBERT G. (1969), 'Fashion: From Class Differentiation to Collective Selection', *Sociological Quarterly*, 10: 275–91.

BORJA, JORDI and CASTELLS, MANUEL (1997), *Local and Global Management of Cities in the Information Age* (London: Earthscan).

BOYM, SVETLANA (2001), 'Nostalgia, Moscow Style', *Harvard Design Magazine*, 13: 4–12.

BRAUNFELS, WOLFGANG (1988), *Urban Design in Western Europe, Regime and Architecture 900–1900* (Chicago: The University of Chicago Press).

BRUNSSON, KARIN (1998), 'Non-learning Organization', *Scandinavian Journal of Management*, 14(4): 421–32.

BRUNSSON, NILS (1989), *The Organization of Hypocrisy* (Chichester: Wiley).

—— and HÄGG, INGEMUND (eds.) (1993), *Marknadens makt* (Stockholm: Carlssons).

—— and JACOBSSON, BENGT (eds.) (2000), *A World of Standards* (Oxford: Oxford University Press).

—— and OLSEN, JOHAN P. (1993), *The Reforming Organization* (London: Routledge).

CASTELLS, MANUEL (1989), *The Information City* (Oxford: Blackwell).

—— (1997), *The Power of Identity* (Oxford: Blackwell).

DE CERTEAU, MICHEL (1975/1988), *The Writing of History* (New York: Columbia University Press).

—— (1984), *The Practice of Everyday Life* (Berkeley, CA: University of California Press).

CHANDLER, ALFRED D., JR. (1977), *The Visible Hand: The Managerial Revolution in American Business* (Cambridge, MA: Harvard University Press).

—— (1990), *Scale and Scope. The Dynamics of Industrial Capitalism* (Cambridge, MA: Harvard University Press).

CHAPIN, STUART (1928), *Cultural Change* (Dubuque, IA: W.C. Brown).

CLARK, TERRY N. (1969), 'Introduction', in Terry N. Clark (ed.), *Gabriel Tarde on Communication and Social Influence* (Chicago: The University of Chicago Press), 1–69.

COHEN, MICHAEL D., MARCH, JAMES G., and OLSEN, JOHAN P. (1972), 'A Garbage Can Model of Organizational Choice', *Administrative Science Quarterly*, 17/1; repr. in James G. March (1988), *Decisions and Organizations* (Oxford: Blackwell), 294–334.

CONNERTON, PAUL (1989), *How Societies Remember* (Cambridge: Cambridge University Press).

CORBEY, RAYMOND and LEERSSEN, JOEP (1991), 'Studying Alterity: Backgrounds and Perspectives', in Raymond Corbey and Joep Leerssen (eds.), *Alterity, Identity, Image. Selves and Others in Society and Scholarship* (Amsterdam: Rodopi), vi–xviii.

CORVELLEC, HERVÉ (2001*a*), 'The New Rhetoric of Infrastructure Projects', in Barbara Czarniawska and Rolf Solli (eds.), *Organizing Metropolitan Space and Discourse* (Malmö: Liber), 192–209.

—— (2001*b*), 'Talks on Tracks – Debating Urban Infrastructure Projects', *Studies in Cultures, Organizations and Societies*, 7/1: 25–53.

CROZIER, MICHEL and FRIEDBERG, ERHARD (1980), *Actors and Systems: The Politics of Collective Action* (Chicago: The University of Chicago Press).

CZARNIAWSKA, BARBARA (1997), *Narrating the Organization. Dramas of Institutional Identity* (Chicago: The University of Chicago Press).

—— (1998), 'Changing Organizations in a Changing Institutional Order: The Reform of Warsaw's Governance System', *Studies in Cultures, Organizations and Societies*, 4/1: 1–27.

—— (1999), *Det var en gång en stad på vatten. Berättelser om organisering och organisering av berättelser i Stockholm* (Stockholm: SNS).

—— (2000), *A City Reframed. Managing Warsaw in the 1990s* (Reading, UK: Harwood Academic Publishers).

—— (2001), 'Is It Possible to Be a Constructionist Consultant?', *Management Learning*, 32/2: 253–72.

—— (2002), 'Remembering While Forgetting: The Role of Automorphism in City Management in Warsaw', *Public Administration Review*, 62/2: 165–74.

—— (2003), 'The Role of Metaphors in Organizing', *International Journal of Sociology and Literature*, forthcoming.

—— and JOERGES, BERNWARD (1996), 'Travels of Ideas', in Barbara Czarniawska and Guje Sevón (eds.), *Translating Organizational Change* (Berlin: de Gruyter), 13–48.

—— MAZZA, CARMELO, and PIPAN, TATIANA (2001), *Gestire grandi città* (Milan: FrancoAngeli).

—— and MOURITSEN, JAN (forthcoming) 'What Is the Object of Management?'.

—— and SEVÓN, GUJE (1996), 'Introduction', in Barbara Czarniawska and Guje Sevón (eds.), *Translating Organizational Change* (Berlin: de Gruyter), 1–12.

DARNTON, ROBERT (2000), 'Paris: The Early Internet', *New York Review of Books*, June 29: 42–7.

DELEBARRE, MICHEL (1992), 'Information Technologies: An Opportunity for the Cities', in *Cities and New Technologies* (Paris: OECD).

DELEUZE, GILLES (1968/1997), *Difference & Repetition* (London: Athlone).

DICKENS, CHARLES (1859/1994), *A Tale of Two Cities* (London: Penguin).

DIMAGGIO, PAUL J. (1983), 'State Expansion in Organizational Fields', in Richard H. Hall and Robert E. Quinn (eds.), *Organizational Theory and Public Policy* (Beverly Hills, CA: SAGE), 147–61.

DiMaggio, Paul J. and Powell, Walter W. (1984/1991), 'The Iron Cage Revisited: Institutional Isomorphism and Collective Rationality', in Walter W. Powell and Paul J. DiMaggio (eds.), *The New Institutionalism in Organizational Analysis* (Chicago: The University of Chicago Press), 63–82.

Dobers, Peter (2001), 'Netting the Information Infrasystem of Stockholm. An Idea Spreads Throughout the World', in Hans Glimell and Oskar Juhlin (eds.), *The Social Production of Technology. On the Everyday Life with Things* (Göteborg: BAS), 189–206.

—— (2002), 'Broadband – Boom and Bust in the New Economy', in Ingalill Holmberg, Miriam Salzer-Mörling, and Lars Strannegård (eds.), *Stuck in the Future. Tracing the 'New Economy'* (Stockholm: Bookhouse), 79–104.

—— (2003), 'Image of Stockholm as an IT City: Emerging Urban Entrepreneurship', in Björn Bjerke, Frédéric Delmar, Daniel Hjorth, and Chris Steyaert (eds.), *Entrepreneur-ship: New Movements* (Aldershot: Edward Elgar Publishing), forthcoming.

—— and Strannegård, Lars (2001), 'Loveable Networks. A Story of Affection, Attraction and Treachery', *Journal of Organizational Change Management*, 14/1: 28–49.

Douglas, Mary (1986), *How Institutions Think* (London: Routledge and Kegan Paul).

Drozdowski, Marian Marek (1990), *Warszawa w latach 1914–1939* (Warszawa: PWN).

Eco, Umberto (1994), *The Six Walks in the Fictional Woods* (Cambridge, MA: Harvard University Press).

—— (1995), *The Search for the Perfect Language* (Oxford: Blackwell).

Edelman, Murray (1988), *Constructing the Political Spectacle* (Chicago: The University of Chicago Press).

Encyclopaedia Britannica, The New (1990), Micropaedia 3 (Chicago: The University of Chicago Press), 338–9.

Erlingsdottir, Gudbjörg (1999), *Förförande ideer i sjukvården* (Lund: Lund University Press).

Featherstone, Mike and Lash, Scott (1995), 'Globalization, Modernity and the Spacialization of Social Theory: An Introduction', in Mike Featherstone, Scott Lash, and Roland Robertson (eds.), *Global Modernities* (London: Sage), 1–24.

Ferrarotti, Franco (1995), 'Civil Society as a Polyarchic Form: The City', in Philip Kasinitz (ed.), *Metropolis. Centre and Symbol of Our Times* (London: Macmillan), 450–68.

Foa, Vittorio (1989), 'Introduction' to Tatiana Pipan, *Sciopero contro l'utente* (Turin: Bollati Boringheri).

Forssell, Anders (1989), 'How to Become Modern and Businesslike: An Attempt to Understand the Modernization of Swedish Savings Banks', *International Studies of Management & Organization*, 19/3: 32–46.

Gellner, Ernest (1995), 'No School for Scandal', *Times Literary Supplement*, May 26: 3–4.

Gergen, Kenneth J. (1994), *Realities and Relationships. Soundings in Social Construction* (Cambridge, MA: Harvard University Press).

Gherardi, Silvia and Lippi, Andrea (eds.) (2000), *Tradurre le riforme in pratica. Il ruolo della conoscenza nel cambiamento amministrativo* (Milano: Raffaelle Cortina).

Giddens, Anthony (1991), *Modernity and Self-identity: Self and Society in the Late Modern Age* (Cambridge: Polity Press).

—— (1999), *The Runaway World. How Globalization Is Reshaping Our Lives* (London: Profile Books).

Glaser, Barney and Strauss, Anselm (1967), *A Discovery of Grounded Theory* (Chicago: Aldine).

Goffman, Erving (1974), *Frame Analysis* (New York: Harper and Row).

Graham, Stephen and Aurigi, Alessandro (1997), 'Urbanizing Cyberspace?', *City*, 7: 18–39.

GREIMAS, ALGIRDAS JULIEN, and COURTÉS, JOSEPH (1982), *Semiotics and Language. An Analytical Dictionary* (Bloomington, IN: Indiana University Press).

GROYS, BORIS (2001), 'Uniform Pluralism', *Harvard Design Magazine*, 13: 13–9.

HANNERZ, ULF (1980), *Exploring the City. Inquiries Toward a Urban Anthropology* (New York: Columbia University Press).

—— (1992), *Cultural Complexity: Studies in the Social Organization of Meaning* (New York: Columbia University Press).

—— (1996), *Transnational Connections* (London: Routledge).

HARVEY, DAVID (1985), *Consciousness and the Urban Experience* (Oxford: Blackwell).

HEPWORTH, MARK E. (1990), 'Planning for the Information City. The Challenge and the Response', *Urban Studies*, 27/1: 537–58.

HIRDMAN, YVONNE (1989), *Att lägga livet till rätta* (Stockholm: Carlssons).

HIRSCHMAN, ALBERT O. (1991), *The Rhetoric of Reaction. Perversity, Futility, Jeopardy* (Cambridge, MA: Belknap Harvard).

HOBSBAWM, ERIC (1983), 'Introduction: Inventing Tradition', in Eric Hobsbawm and Terence Ranger (eds.), *The Invention of Tradition* (Cambridge, UK: Cambridge University Press), 1–14.

HOCHSCHILD, ARLIE RUSSELL (1997), *The Time Bind. When Work Becomes Home and Home Becomes Work* (New York: Metropolitan Books).

HOLZNER, BURKHART (1973/1978), 'The Construction of Social Actors: An Essay on Social Identities', in Thomas Luckmann (ed.), *Phenomenology and Sociology* (Harmondsworth, UK: Penguin), 291–310.

D'IRIBARNE, PHILIPPE (1989), *La logique de l'honneur. Gestion des enterprises et traditions nationales* (Paris: Seuil).

JACOBS, JANE (1961), *The Death and Life of the Great American City* (New York: Random House).

JACOBSSON, BENGT (1997), *Europa och staten* (Stockholm: Fritzes).

JOERGES, BERNWARD and CZARNIAWSKA, BARBARA (1998), 'The Question of Technology or, How Organizations Inscribe the World', *Organization Studies*, 19/3: 363–85.

JÖNSSON, STEN (1995), *Goda utsikter* (Stockholm: Nerenius & Santérus).

KADEFORS, ANNA (1999), 'The Power of Moral Indignation – Fairness Norms as Source of Distrust in Client–Contractor Relations', presented at the conference *Managing Big Cities*, Gothenburg, August.

KANTER, ROSABETH MOSS (1977), *Men and Women of the Corporation* (New York: Basic Books).

KARLSSON, STEN O. (2001), *Det intelligenta samhället. En omtolkning av socialdemokratins idéhistoria* (Stockholm: Carlssons).

KNORR CETINA, KARIN (1994), 'Primitive Classification and Postmodernity: Towards a Sociological Notion of Fiction', *Theory, Culture & Society*, 11: 1–22.

—— (1999), *Epistemic Cultures. How the Sciences Make Knowledge* (Cambridge, MA: Harvard University Press).

KOCIATKIEWICZ, JERZY and KOSTERA, MONIKA (2001), 'The Pope as Organizing Principle', in Barbara Czarniawska and Rolf Solli (eds.), *Organizing Metropolitan Space and Discourse* (Malmö: Liber), 154–74.

KULSKI, JULIAN (1990), *Stefan Starzynski w mojej pamieci* (Warszawa: PWN).

LATOUR, BRUNO (1986), 'The Powers of Association', in John Law (ed.), *Power, Action and Belief* (London: Routledge and Kegan Paul), 261–77.

—— (1993), *We Have Never Been Modern* (Cambridge, MA: Harvard University Press).

—— (1996), *Petite réflexion sur le culte moderne des dieux faitiches* (Le Plessis-Robinson: Synthélabo).

LATOUR, BRUNO (1997), *Artefaktens återkomst* (Stockholm: Nerenius & Santérus).

—— (1999*a*) *Pandora's Hope* (Cambridge, MA: Harvard University Press).

—— (1999*b*), 'Les monolithes de Stockholm', *La Recherche*, December: 326.

—— (2001), 'Gabriel Tarde and the End of the Social', in Patrick Joyce (ed.), *The Social in Question* (London: Routledge).

—— and HERMANT, EMILIE (1998), *Paris ville invisible* (Paris: Les Empêcheurs de penser en rond/La Découverte).

LAW, JOHN (1994), *Organizing Modernity* (Oxford: Blackwell).

LEACH, EDMUND R. (1968), 'Ritual', *The International Encyclopedia of the Social Sciences* (New York: Free Press), 520–6.

LEERSSEN, JOEP (1991), 'Reflections upon Foreign Space', in Raymond Corbey and Joep Leerssen (eds.), *Alterity, Identity, Image. Selves and Others in Society and Scholarship* (Amsterdam: Rodopi), 123–38.

LEFEBVRE, HENRI (1996), *Writings on Cities* (Oxford: Blackwell).

LEWIS, MICHAEL (1989), *Liar's Poker* (London: Hodder and Stoughton).

LINDBLOM, CHARLES (1979), 'Still Muddling, not yet Through', *Public Administration Review*, November/December: 517–26.

LÖFGREN, ORVAR (1990), 'Consuming Interests', *Culture & History*, 7: 7–36.

—— (1993), 'Materializing the Nation in Sweden and America', *Ethnos*, 3–4: 161–96.

LUCKMANN, BENITA (1978), 'The Small Life-Worlds of Modern Man', in Thomas Luckmann (ed.), *Phenomenology and Sociology* (Harmondsworth, UK: Penguin), 275–90.

LUKES, STEVEN (1975), 'Political Ritual and Social Integration', *Sociology*, 9: 289–308.

LYOTARD, JEAN-FRANÇOIS (1979/1987), *The Postmodern Condition. A Report on Knowledge* (Manchester: Manchester University Press).

MARCH, JAMES G. and OLSEN, JOHAN P. (1989), *Rediscovering Institutions: The Organizational Basis of Politics* (New York: Free Press).

MARCH, JAMES G. and SIMON, HERBERT A. (1958/1993), *Organizations* (Oxford: Blackwell).

MAZZA, CARMELO (1999), 'Azioni, parole ed attori istituzionali nella privatizzazione della Centrale del latte di Roma', *Rivista trimestrale di scienza dell'amministrazione*, 3: 119–49.

—— (2001), 'En milk-shake av ord och handlingar', in Rolf Solli and Barbara Czarniawska (eds.), *Modernisering av storstaden – marknad och management i stora städer vid sekel-skiftet* (Malmö: Liber), 128–58.

MCCLOSKEY, D.N. (1985), *The rhetoric of economics* (Wisconsin, MD: The University of Wisconsin Press).

MCDOWELL, LINDA (1997), *Capital Culture. Gender at Work in the City* (Oxford: Blackwell).

MERTON, ROBERT (1985), *On the Shoulders of Giants. A Shandean Postscript* (New York: Harcourt and Jovanovich).

MEYER, JOHN W. (1986), 'Myths of Socialization and of Personality', in T.C. Heller, Maurice Sosna, and David E. Wellbery (eds.), *Reconstructing Individualism: Autonomy, Individuality and the Self in Western Thought* (Stanford, CA: Stanford University Press), 208–21.

—— (1999), *Globalization: Sources, and Effects on National States and Societies*, paper presented at the conference 'Globalizations: Dimensions, Trajectories, Prospects', Stockholm, 1998.

—— and ROWAN, BRIAN (1977/1991), 'Institutionalized Organizations: Formal Structure as Myth and Ceremony', *American Journal of Sociology*, 83: 340–63; repr. in Walter W. Powell and Paul J. DiMaggio (eds.), *The New Institutionalism in Organizational Analysis* (Chicago: The University of Chicago Press), 41–62.

MICHELETTI, MICHELE (1995), *Civil Society and State Relations in Sweden* (Aldershot: Avebury).

MORGAN, GARETH (1986), *Images of Organization*, (London: Sage).

MUMFORD, LEWIS (1938/1995), 'The Culture of Cities', in Philip Kasinitz (ed.), *Metropolis. Centre and Symbol of Our Times* (London: Macmillan), 21–9.

NIEDERHAUSER, EMIL (1982), *The Rise of Nationality in Eastern Europe* (Budapest: Corvina Kiadó).

OAKESHOTT, MICHAEL (1947/1991), 'Rationalism in Politics', in *Rationalism in Politics and Other Essays* (Indianapolis: Liberty Press), 5–42.

——(1948/1991), 'The Tower of Babel', in *Rationalism in Politics and Other Essays* (Indianapolis: Liberty Press), 465–87.

O'BARR, WILLIAM M. and CONLEY, JOHN M. (1992), *Fortune and Folly: The Wealth and Power of Institutional Investing* (Homewood, IL: Business One Irwin).

OLDS, KRIS (2001), *Globalization and Urban Change. Capital, Culture, and Pacific Rim Mega-Projects* (Oxford: Oxford University Press).

OLSON, OLOV, GUTHRIE, JAMES, and HUMPHREY, CHRISTOPHER (eds.) (1998), *Global Warning. Debating International Developments in New Public Financial Management* (Oslo: Capelen Akademisk Forlag).

OTNES, PER (1997), 'La loi du plus gros – By Superior Bulk', in Ove Källtrop, Ingmar Elander, Ove Ericsson, and Mats Franzén (eds.), *Cities in Transformation – Transformation in Cities. Social and Symbolic Change of Urban Space* (Aldershot: Avebury), 360–76.

Oxford English Dictionary (The New Shorter) (1993), (Oxford: Oxford University Press).

PANOZZO, FABRIZIO (2001), 'Den överbefolkade ledningen', in Rolf Solli and Barbara Czarniawska (eds.), *Modernisering av storstaden – marknad och management i stora städer vid sekelskiftet* (Malmö: Liber), 74–83.

Pears Cyclopaedia (1959–1960), (Bungay, Suffolk: Richard Clay and Co).

PIETERSE, JAN NEDERVEEN (1995), 'Globalization as Hybridization', in Mike Featherstone, Scott Lash, and Roland Robertson (eds.), *Global Modernities* (London: Sage), 45–68.

PIPAN, TATIANA (1989), *Sciopero contro l'utente* (Turin: Bollati Boringheri).

——(2001), 'Jubileum som nödläge', in Rolf Solli and Barbara Czarniawska (eds.), *Modernisering av storstaden* (Malmö: Liber), 159–79.

—— and PORSANDER, LENA (2000), 'Imitating Uniqueness: How Big Cities Organise Big Events', *Organization Studies*, 1–27.

PORSANDER, LENA (2000), 'Translating a Dream of Immortality in a (Con)temporary Order', *Journal of Organizational Change Management*, 13: 14–29.

PORTER, MICHAEL E. (1985), *Competitive Advantage* (New York: Free Press).

POWELL, WALTER W. and DiMAGGIO, PAUL J. (eds.) (1991), *The New Institutionalism in Organizational Analysis* (Chicago: The University of Chicago Press).

POWER, MICHAEL (1997), *The Audit Society. Rituals of Verification* (Oxford: Oxford University Press).

PRED, ALLAN (1995), *Recognizing European Modernities. A Montage of the Present* (New York: Routledge).

PUTNAM, ROBERT D. (1993), *Making Democracy Work. Civic Traditions in Modern Italy* (Princeton, NJ: Princeton University Press).

RABINOW, PAUL (1989), *French Modern: Norms and Forms of the Social Environment* (Cambridge, MA: The MIT Press).

RICOEUR, PAUL (1981), 'The Model of the Text: Meaningful Action Considered as Text', in John B. Thompson (ed. and trans.), *Hermeneutics and the Human Sciences* (Cambridge, UK: Cambridge University Press), 197–221.

ROBERTSON, ROLAND (1992), *Globalization. Social Theory and Global Culture* (London: Sage).

—— (1995), Glocalization: Time–space and Homogeneity–heterogeneity', in Mike Featherstone, Scott Lash, and Roland Robertson (eds.), *Global Modernities* (London: Sage), 25–44.

RORTY, RICHARD (1980), *Philosophy and the Mirror of Nature* (Oxford: Basil Blackwell).

—— (1991), 'Inquiry as Recontextualization: An Anti-dualist Account of Interpretation', in *Objectivity, Relativism and Truth. Philosophical Papers Vol. 1* (New York: Cambridge University Press), 93–110.

RØVIK, KJELL-ARNE (1996), 'Deinstitutionalization and the Logic of Fashion', in Barbara Czarniawska and Guje Sevón (eds.), *Translating Organizational Change* (Berlin: de Gruyter), 139–72.

SAHLIN-ANDERSSON, KERSTIN (1996), 'Imitating by Editing Success. The Construction of Organization Fields', in Barbara Czarniawska and Guje Sevón (eds.), *Translating Organizational Change* (Berlin: de Gruyter), 69–92.

SAHLINS, MARSHALL (1996), 'The Sadness of Sweetness: The Native Anthropology of Western Cosmology', *Current Anthropology*, 37: 395–415.

—— (2001), '"Sentimental Pessimism" and Ethnographic Experience or, Why Culture Is Not an Disappearing "Object" ', in Lorraine Daston (ed.), *Biographies of Scientific Objects* (Chicago: The University of Chicago Press), 178–202.

SASSEN, SASKIA (2001), *The Global City. New York, London, Tokyo* (Princeton, NJ: Princeton University Press).

SCHULTZ, MAJKEN, HATCH, MARY JO, and LARSEN, MOGENS HOLTEN (eds.) (2000), *The Expressive Organization. Linking Identity, Reputation and the Corporate Brand* (Oxford: Oxford University Press).

SCHWARTZ, BIRGITTA (1997), *Det miljömedvetna företaget* (Stockholm: Nerenius & Santérus).

SENNETT, RICHARD (1970), *The Uses of Disorder. Personal Identity and City Life* (New York: Norton).

SEVÓN, GUJE (1996), 'Organizational Imitation in Identity Transformation', in Barbara Czarniawska and Guje Sevón (eds.), *Translating Organizational Change* (Berlin: de Gruyter), 49–67.

SHENHAV, YEHOUDA (2000), *Manufacturing Rationality. The Engineering Foundations of the Managerial Revolution* (Oxford, UK: Oxford University Press).

SIMMEL, GEORG (1904/1971), 'Fashion', in Donald N. Levine (ed.), *Georg Simmel on Individuality and Social Forms* (Chicago: The University of Chicago Press)), 294–323.

SOJA, EDWARD W. (1995), ' Postmodern Urbanization: The Six Restructurings of Los Angeles', in Sophie Watson and Katherine Gibson (eds.), *Postmodern Cities & Spaces* (Oxford: Blackwell).

SOLLI, ROLF and CZARNIAWSKA, BARBARA (2001), 'Vad är på modet i storstaden?', in Rolf Solli and Barbara Czarniawska (eds.), *Modernisering av storstaden* (Malmö: Liber), 5–14.

STEINER, GEORGE (1992), *After Babel. Aspects of Language & Translation* (Oxford: Oxford University Press).

SZYMANDERSKI, JACEK (1994), 'Zalamanie rewolucyjnej utopii czyli Solidarnosc 1980–94', in *Piec lat po czerwcu* (Warszawa: Centrum im. Adama Smitha), 69–79.

TARDE, GABRIEL (1888/1969), 'Logical Laws of Imitation', in Terry N. Clark (ed.), *Gabriel Tarde on Communication and Social Influence* (Chicago: The University of Chicago Press), 177–84.

—— (1890/1962), *The Laws of Imitation* (Gloucester, MA: Peter Smith).

—— (1899/1974), *Social Laws. An Outline of Sociology* (New York: ARNO Press).

—— (1902/1969), 'Invention', in Terry N. Clark (ed.), *Gabriel Tarde on Communication and Social Influence* (Chicago: The University of Chicago Press), 149–64.

—— (1904/1969), 'A Debate with Emile Durkheim', in Terry N. Clark (ed.), *Gabriel Tarde on Communication and Social Influence* (Chicago: The University of Chicago Press), 136–40.

TAUSSIG, MICHAEL (1993), *Mimesis and Alterity. A Particular History of the Senses* (London: Routledge).

TORGOVNICK, MARIANNE (1990), *Gone Primitive. Savage Intellects, Modern Lives* (Chicago, IL: University of Chicago Press).

TOULMIN, STEPHEN (1990), *Cosmopolis. The Hidden Agenda of Modernity* (Chicago: University of Chicago Press).

TURNER, VICTOR (1982), *From Ritual to Theatre* (New York: Performing Arts Journal Publications).

VEBLEN, THORSTEN (1889/1994), *The Theory of the Leisure Class* (Mineola, NY: Dover Publications).

WARREN, ROLAND L., ROSE, STEPHEN M., and BERGUNDER, ANN F. (1974), *The Structure of Urban Reform. Community Decision Organizations in Stability and Change* (Lexington, MA: Lexington Books).

WEBER, MAX (1922/1974), 'Science as Vocation', in Hans H. Gerth and C. Wright Mills (ed. and trans.), *From Max Weber: Essays in Sociology* (London: Routledge & Kegan Paul), 129–55.

WEDEL, JANINE R. (2001), *Collision and Collusion* (New York: Palgrave).

WEICK, KARL E. (1976), 'Educational Organizations as Loosely Coupled Systems', *Administrative Science Quarterly*, 21: 1–19.

—— (1979), *The Social Psychology of Organizing* (Reading, MA: Addison-Wesley).

—— (1995), *Sensemaking in Organizations* (Thousand Oaks, CA: Sage).

WHETTEN, DAVID A and GODFREY, PAUL C. (1998), *Identity in Organizations. Building Theory Through Conversations* (Thousand Oaks, CA: Sage).

WHITE, HAYDEN (1978), *Tropics of Discourse* (Baltimore, MR: John Hopkins University Press).

—— (1987), *The Content of the Form* (Baltimore, MR: John Hopkins University Press).

WILLIAMS, ROSALIND (1990), *Notes on the Underground. An Essay on Technology, Society, and the Imagination* (Cambridge, MA: MIT Press).

WILSON, ELISABETH (1991), *The Sphinx in the City* (London: Virago Press).

YOUNG, AGNES BROOK (1937/1973), 'Recurring Cycles of Fashion', in Gordon Wills and David Midgley (eds.), *Fashion Marketing* (London: Allen & Unwin), 107–24.

ZABOROWSKA, MAGDALENA J. (2001), 'Three Passages Through (In)visible Warsaw', *Harvard Design Magazine*, 13: 52–9.

ZAHAVI, DAN (1999), *Self-Awareness and Identity: A Phenomenological Investigation* (Evanston, IL: Northwestern University Press).

ZEIDLER-JANISZEWSKA, ANNA (ed.) (1997), *Pisanie miasta, czytanie miasta* (Poznan: Humaniora).

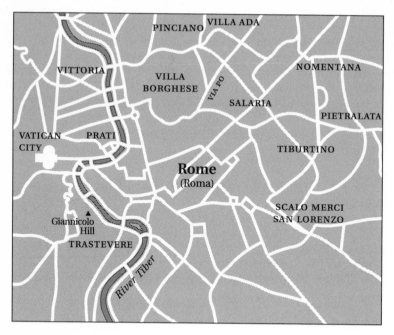

Map. 1. Rome

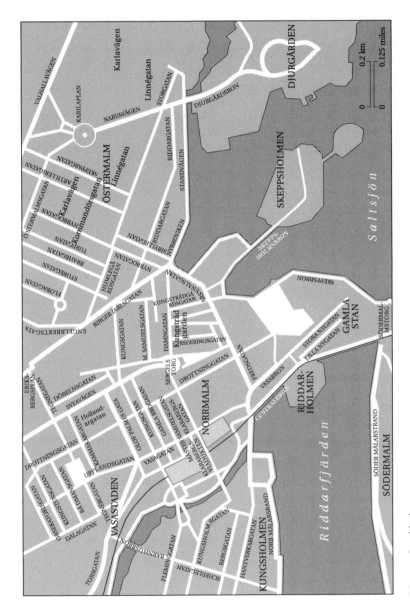

Map. 2. Stockholm

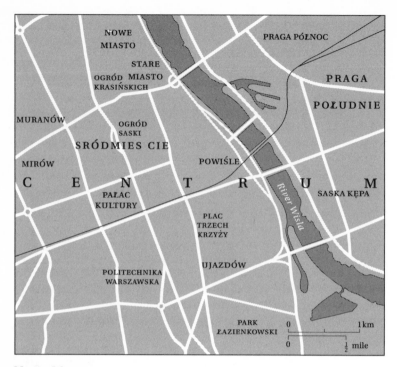

Map. 3. Warsaw

INDEX